# NATIONAL HOCKEY LEAGUE

# Official Rules
## 2016-2017

## National Hockey League Official Rules 2016-2017



Diagrams of equipment reproduced courtesy of USA Hockey, Inc.

Printed in Canada.

Design, production by:
Raster Graphics
931 Schaeffer Outlook
Newmarket, Ontario L3X 1V9   905-895-3546   Fax 905-895-5295

**The National Hockey League**

1185 Avenue of the Americas, New York, New York 10036
1800 McGill College Avenue, Suite 2600, Montreal, Quebec H3A 3J6
50 Bay Street, 11th Floor, Toronto, Ontario M5J 2X8

**www.NHL.com**

# 2016-2017 NHL OFFICIATING TEAM

| REFEREES | | LINESMEN | |
|---|---|---|---|
| Jersey No. | Name | Jersey No. | Name |
| 2 | McIsaac, Jon | 50 | Cherrey, Scott |
| 3 | Leggo, Mike | 52 | Alphonso, Shandor |
| 4 | McCauley, Wes | 54 | Devorski, Greg |
| 5 | Rooney, Chris | 55 | Heyer, Shane |
| 6 | Charron, Francis | 56 | Wheler, Mark |
| 7 | Rank, Garrett | 57 | Sharrers, Jay |
| 8 | Jackson, Dave | 58 | Gibbons, Ryan |
| 9 | O'Rourke, Dan | 59 | Barton, Steve |
| 10 | Rehman, Kyle | 63 | Knorr, Trent |
| 11 | Sutherland, Kelly | 64 | Gawryletz, Brandon |
| 12 | St. Pierre, Justin | 65 | Racicot, Pierre |
| 13 | O'Halloran, Dan | 66 | Gibbs, Darren |
| 15 | Hebert, Jean | 68 | Driscoll, Scott |
| 16 | Pochmara, Brian | 70 | Nansen, Derek |
| 17 | L'Ecuyer, Frederick | 71 | Kovachik, Brad |
| 19 | Dwyer, Gord | 73 | Rody, Vaughan |
| 20 | Peel, Tim | 74 | Cameron, Lonnie |
| 21 | Luxmore, Thomas John | 75 | Amell, Derek |
| 22 | Hebert, Ghislain | 76 | Cormier, Michel |
| 23 | Watson, Brad | 77 | Nowak, Tim |
| 24 | Skilliter, Graham | 78 | Mach, Brian |
| 25 | Joannette, Marc | 79 | Murchison, Kiel |
| 27 | Furlatt, Eric | 82 | Galloway, Ryan |
| 28 | Lee, Chris | 83 | MacPherson, Matt |
| 29 | Walsh, Ian | 84 | Sericolo, Anthony |
| 30 | Nicholson, Kendrick | 87 | Berg, Devin |
| 31 | Hanson, Trevor | 89 | Miller, Steve |
| 32 | Kowal, Tom | 91 | Henderson, Don |
| 33 | Pollock, Kevin | 92 | Shewchyk, Mark |
| 34 | Meier, Brad | 93 | Murphy, Brian |
| 36 | Morton, Dean | 94 | Pancich, Bryan |
| 38 | St-Laurent, Francois | 95 | Murray, Jonny |
| 40 | Kozari, Steve | 96 | Brisebois, David |

| Minor League Team Members | | Minor League Team Members | |
|---|---|---|---|
| 39 | Romasko, Evgeny | 81 | Daisy, Ryan |
| 41 | Voss, Cameron | 97 | Nagy, Kory |
| 42 | Brenk, Jacob | 98 | Grandt, John |
| 43 | Chmielewski, Tom | | |
| 44 | South, Furman | | |
| 45 | MacDougall, Peter | | |
| 46 | Lewis, Dave | | |
| 47 | Lambert, Pierre | | |
| 48 | Schlenker, Chris | | |

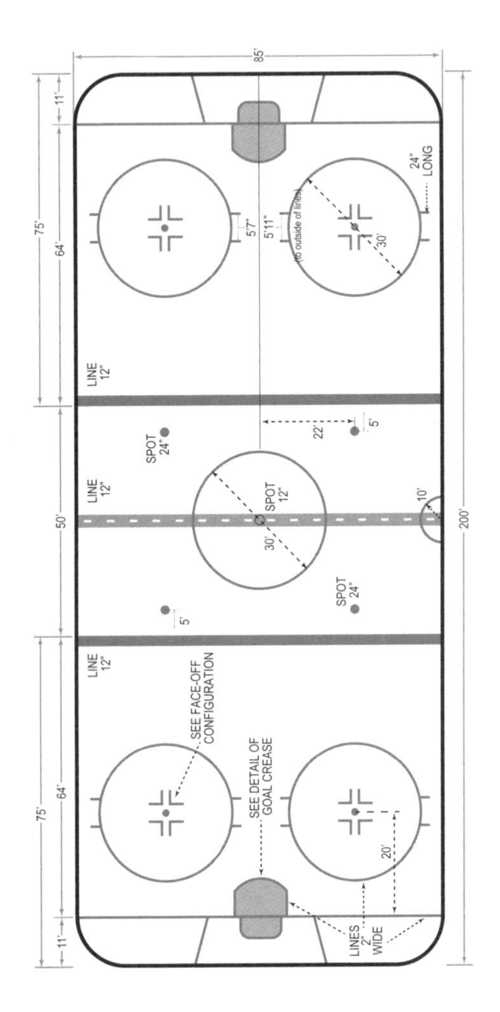


**OFFICAL DIMENSIONS OF RINK SURFACE**

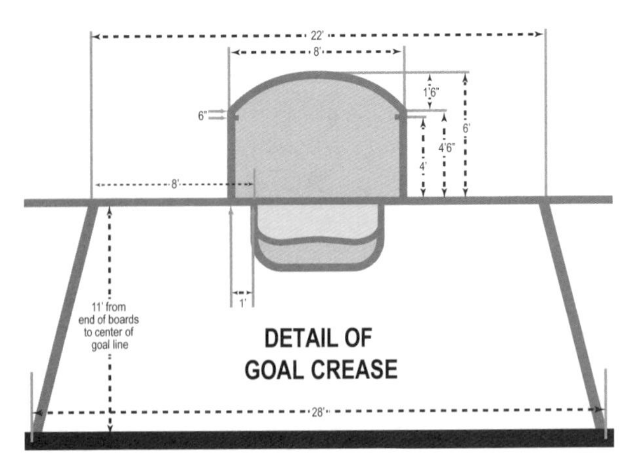


**DETAIL OF GOAL CREASE**

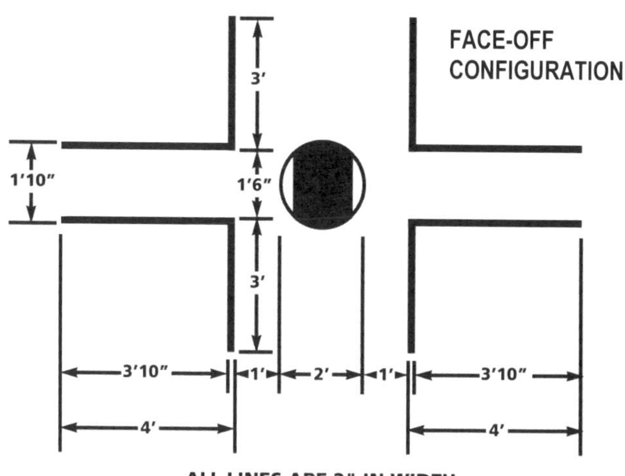


ALL LINES ARE 2" IN WIDTH

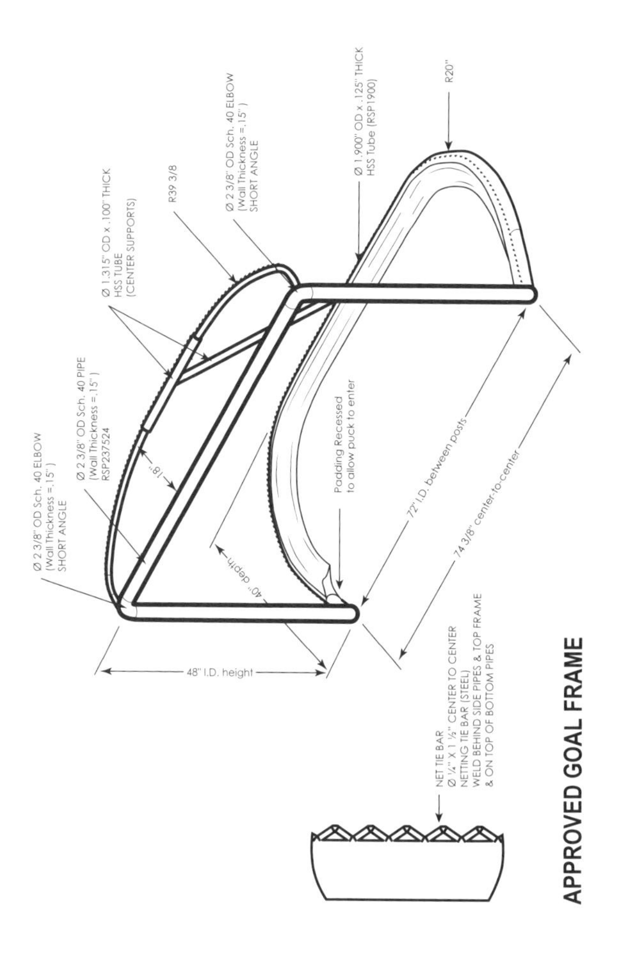

## Section 1 – Playing Area



## Section 2 – Teams



## Section 3 – Equipment



## Section 4 – Types of Penalties



## Section 5 – Officials

## Section 5 – Officials (continued)



## Section 6 – Physical Fouls



## Section 7 – Restraining Fouls



## Section 8 – Stick Fouls



## Section 9 – Other Fouls

## Section 9 – Other Fouls (continued)



## Section 10 – Game Flow



## Reference Tables

Reference Tables (continued)

# SECTION 1 – PLAYING AREA

## Rule 1 – Rink

1.1 **Rink** - National Hockey League games shall be played on an ice surface known as the "Rink" and must adhere to the dimensions and specifications prescribed by the League and these rules. No ice markings shall be permitted except those provided for under these rules unless express written permission has been obtained from the League. On-ice logos must not interfere with any official ice markings provided for the proper playing of the game.

In the interval between periods, the ice surface shall be flooded unless mutually agreed to the contrary.

1.2 **Dimensions** - The official size of the rink shall be two hundred feet (200') long and eighty-five feet (85') wide. The corners shall be rounded in the arc of a circle with a radius of twenty-eight feet (28'). See diagram on page iv preceding the table of contents.

1.3 **Boards and Glass** - The rink shall be surrounded by a wall known as the "boards" which shall extend not less than forty inches (40") and not more than forty-eight inches (48") above the level of the ice surface. The ideal height of the boards above the ice surface shall be forty-two inches (42"). Except for the official markings provided for in these rules, the entire playing surface and the boards shall be white in color except the kick plate at the bottom of the boards, which shall be light yellow in color.

Any variations from any of the foregoing dimensions shall require official authorization by the League.

The boards shall be constructed in such a manner that the surface facing the ice shall be smooth and free of any obstruction or any object that could cause injury to players.

Affixed to the boards and extending vertically shall be approved safety glass extending eight feet (8') above the boards at each end of the rink and not less than five feet (5') along both sides of the rink.

The glass and gear to hold them in position shall be properly padded or protected. Protective glass shall be required in front of the penalty benches to provide for the safety of the players on and off the ice. All equipment used to hold the glass or screens in position shall be mounted on the boards on the side away from the playing surface.

1.4 **Spectator Netting** – Spectator netting shall be hung in the ends of the arena, of a height, type, and in a manner approved by the League.

1.5 **Lines** - Eleven feet (11') from each end of the rink and in the center of a red line two inches (2") wide drawn completely across the width of the ice and continued vertically up the side of the boards, regulation goal posts and nets shall be set in such a manner as to remain stationary during the progress of a game.

The red line, two inches (2") wide, between the goal posts on the ice and extended completely across the rink, shall be known as the "GOAL LINE."

In front of each goal, a "GOAL CREASE" area shall be marked by a red line two inches (2") in width.

The ice area between the two goals shall be divided into three parts by lines, twelve inches (12") in width, and blue in color, drawn sixty-four feet (64') out from the goal lines, and extended completely across the rink, parallel with the goal lines, and continued vertically up the side of the boards. (Paint code PMS 286.)

There shall also be a line, twelve inches (12") in width and red in color, drawn completely across the rink in center ice, parallel with the goal lines and continued vertically up the side of the boards, known as the "CENTER LINE." This line shall contain regular interval markings of a uniform distinctive design, which will readily distinguish it from the two blue lines, the outer edges of which must be continuous. (Paint code PMS 186.)

1.6 **Division of Ice Surface** - That portion of the ice surface in which the goal is situated shall be called the "DEFENDING ZONE" of the Team defending that goal; the central portion shall be known as the "NEUTRAL ZONE," and the portion farthest from the defended goal as the "ATTACKING ZONE."

1.7 **Goal Crease / Referee Crease** - The goal crease shall be laid out as follows: One foot (1') outside of each goal post a two-inch (2") line shall be painted extending four feet, six inches (4'6") in length. These lines shall be at right angles to the goal line. A semi-circle line six feet (6') in radius and two inches (2") in width shall be drawn using the center of the goal line as the center point and connecting both ends of the side of the crease. On the side of the crease lines, four feet (4') from the goal line, extend a five-inch (5") line into the crease. (see diagram on page iv preceding the table of contents)

The goal crease area shall include all the space outlined by the crease lines and extending vertically four feet (4') to the level of the top of the goal frame. The area outlined by the crease line and the goal line shall be painted a light blue color. (Paint code PMS 298.)

The area inside the goal frame to the goal line shall be painted a gloss white color.

On the ice immediately in front of the Penalty Timekeeper's seat there shall be marked in red on the ice a semi-circle of ten foot (10') radius and two inches (2") in width which shall be known as the "REFEREE'S CREASE."

1.8 **Goalkeeper's Restricted Area** - A restricted trapezoid-shaped area behind the goal will be laid out as follows: Seven feet (7') outside of each goal crease (eight feet (8') from each goal post), a two-inch (2") red line shall be painted extending from the goal line to a point on the end of the rink ten feet (10') from the goal crease (eleven feet (11') from the goal post) and continuing vertically up the kick plate (see diagram on the page iv preceding the table of contents). (Paint code PMS 186).

1.9 **Face-off Spots and Circles** - A circular blue spot, twelve inches (12") in diameter, shall be marked exactly in the center of the rink; and with this spot as a center, a circle of fifteen feet (15') radius shall be marked with a blue line two inches (2") in width.

Two red spots two feet (2') in diameter shall be marked on the ice in the neutral zone five feet (5') from each blue line. Within the face-off spot, draw two parallel lines three inches (3") from the top and bottom of the spot. The area within the two lines shall be painted red, the remainder shall be painted white. The spots shall be forty-four feet (44') apart and each shall be a uniform distance from the adjacent boards.

In both end zones and on both sides of each goal, red face-off spots and circles shall be marked on the ice. The face-off spots shall be two feet (2') in diameter. Within the face-off spot, draw two parallel lines three inches (3") from the top and bottom of the spot. The area within the two lines shall be painted red, the remainder shall be painted white.

The circles shall be two inches (2") wide with a radius of fifteen feet (15') from the center of the face-off spots. At the outer edge of both sides of each face-off circle and parallel to the goal line shall be marked two red lines, two inches (2") wide and two feet (2') in length and five feet seven inches (5'7") apart.

One foot away from the outer edge of the face-off spot, two lines shall be drawn parallel with the side boards that shall be four feet (4')in length and eighteen inches (18") apart. Parallel to the end boards, commencing at the end of the line nearest to the face-off spot, a line shall extend two feet ten inches (2'10") in length. All lines shall be two inches (2") in width. See diagram on page v preceding the table of contents.

The location of the face-off spots shall be fixed in the following manner:

Along a line twenty feet (20') from each goal line and parallel to it, mark two points twenty-two feet (22') on both sides of the straight line joining the center of the two goals. Each such point shall be the center of a face-off spot and circle.

1.10 **Ice Cleaning** - Aside from the normal ice resurfacing that is performed during the intermissions between each period of play, the following snow removal activities shall be performed:

*(i) During each commercial time-out, the ice cleaning crew shall remove snow from the goal crease area, in front of the players' and penalty benches and from side to side from the top of the circles to the end boards (ideally, the entire end zone from the blue lines in).*

*(ii) During the regular season, at the end of the third period in a tied game and prior to the commencement of the five minute overtime period, the entire ice surface shall be shoveled by arena personnel utilizing the same procedures as are utilized during TV time-outs.*

*(iii) During the regular season, at the end of the five minute overtime period in a tied game and prior to the commencement of the shootout, the entire ice surface shall be shoveled by arena personnel utilizing the same procedures as are utilized during TV time-outs.*

*(iv) During overtime in the playoffs, the procedure outlined in (i) above will take place at the first stoppage of play following the 10:00 mark of the period. This will occur regardless as to whether or not an icing has occurred or a penalty for either team is in effect.*

Specific and technical guidelines for the above procedures are available from the NHL Hockey Operations Department and are distributed when updated to the arena managers as required.

## Rule 2 – Goal Posts and Nets

2.1 **Goal Posts** - The goal posts shall be kept in position by means of flexible pegs affixed in the ice or floor. The flexible pegs shall be ten inches (10") in length and yellow in color.

The goal posts shall be of approved design and material, extending vertically four feet (4') above the surface of the ice and set six feet (6') apart measured from the inside of the posts. A crossbar of the same material as the goal posts shall extend from the top of one post to the top of the other. See diagram on page v preceding table of contents.

The goal posts and crossbar shall be painted in red and all other exterior surfaces shall be painted in white.

2.2 **Nets** - There shall be attached to each goal frame a net of approved design made of white nylon cord which shall be draped in such a manner as to prevent the puck coming to rest on the outside of it, yet strung in a manner that will keep the puck in the net.

A skirt of heavy white nylon fabric or heavyweight white canvas shall be laced around the base plate of the goal frame in such a way as to protect the net from being cut or broken. This protective padding must be attached in a manner that will not restrict the puck from completely crossing the goal line. This padding must be set back six inches (6") from the inside of the goal post. This skirt shall not project more than one inch (1") above the base plate.

The frame of the goal shall be draped with a nylon mesh net so as to completely enclose the back of the frame. The knotless nylon netting shall be made of heat set, resin treatment twine (0.197 inch (5 mm) diameter) or equivalent braided twine of multifilament white nylon with an appropriate break strength of 550 to 600 pounds (250-275 kilograms). The size of the mesh shall be two and one-half inches (2½") (inside measurement) from each knot to each diagonal knot when fully stretched. The net shall be laced to the frame with medium white nylon cord no smaller in size than No. 21.

The thin nylon mesh netting on the top of the goal frame shall be white 12 ply, four braid construction and 62 mm inside to inside mesh. This netting will be attached with 2.2 mm clear coated white twine of Dynemma braided construction.

## Rule 3 – Benches

3.1 **Players' Benches** - Each rink shall be provided with seats or benches for the use of players of both teams. The accommodations provided, including benches and doors, MUST be uniform for both teams. Such seats or benches shall have accommodation for at least fourteen (14) persons of each team. The benches shall be placed immediately alongside the ice as near to the center of the rink as possible. Two doors for each bench must be uniform in location and size and as convenient to the dressing rooms as possible.

Each players' bench should be twenty-four feet (24') in length and when situated in the spectator area, shall be separated from the spectators by a protective glass of sufficient height so as to afford the necessary protection for the players. The players' benches shall be on the same side of the playing surface opposite the penalty bench and should be separated by a substantial distance, if possible.

Each players' bench shall have two doors which must be uniform in location and size. ("Mirrored image benches") All doors opening to the playing surface shall be constructed so that they swing inward.

3.2 **Penalty Bench** - Each rink must be provided with benches or seats to be known as the "PENALTY BENCH." These benches or seats must be capable of accommodating a total of ten persons including the Off-Ice Officials. Separate penalty benches shall be provided for each Team and they shall be situated on opposite sides of the Timekeeper's area, directly across the ice from the players' benches. The penalty bench(es) must be situated in the neutral zone.

Each Penalty Bench shall be protected from the spectator area by means of a glass partition which shall not be less than five feet (5') above the height of the boards.

## Rule 4 – Signal and Timing Devices

4.1 **Signal Devices** - Each rink must be provided with a siren, or other suitable sound device that will sound automatically at the conclusion of each period of play. Should the sound device fail to sound automatically when time expires, the determining factor as to whether or not the period has ended shall be the timing device.

Behind each goal, electrical lights shall be set up for the use of the Goal Judges. A red light will signify the scoring of a goal and a green light will signify the end of a period or a game.

A goal cannot be scored when a green light is showing.

A light, normally red in color, will be situated at or near the Timekeeper's Bench and will be illuminated when a commercial time-out is in progress. This light will be extinguished when the commercial time-out is complete to indicate to the teams and the officials that play may resume. This light is controlled by an authorized National Hockey League Commercial Coordinator.

4.2 **Timing Devices** - Each rink shall be provided with some form of electronic clock for the purpose of keeping the spectators, players and game officials accurately informed as to all time elements at all stages of the game including the time remaining to be played in any period and the time remaining to be served by at least five penalized players on each Team.

Time recording for both game time and penalty time shall show time remaining to be played or served.

The game time clock shall measure the time remaining in tenths of a second during the last minutes of each period.

# SECTION 2 - TEAMS

## Rule 5 – Team

5.1 **Eligible Players** - A team shall be composed of 20 players (18 skaters and two goalkeepers) who shall be under contract to the Club they represent. For the purposes of these playing rules, any reference to "player" shall refer to both skaters and goalkeepers. Any reference to "goalkeeper" shall mean that the section of the rule is specific to goalkeepers.

At the beginning of each game, the Manager or Coach of each team shall list the players who shall be eligible to play in the game. Not more than eighteen (18) skaters and two (2) goalkeepers, shall be permitted. One non-uniformed player shall be permitted on the players' bench in a coaching capacity. He must be indicated on the Roster Sheet submitted by the Coach to the Referee or Official Scorer prior to the start of the game.

A list of names and numbers of all eligible players must be handed to the Official Scorer before the game, and no change shall be permitted in the list or addition thereto shall be permitted after the commencement of the game.

Prior to the game, if an official (on-ice or off-ice) notices that a player is in uniform but has not been included on the Official Game Report, the Referee shall bring this to the attention of the offending team so that the necessary correction can be made to the Official Game Report (and no penalty is assessed).

5.2 **Ineligible Player** - Only players on the list submitted to the Official Scorer before the game may participate in the game. The determining factor when considering whether or not a player is eligible is that the player's name, and not necessarily the player's number, must be correctly listed by the Manager or Coach of that team.

Whenever an ineligible player is identified to the Referee, the ineligible player will be removed from the game and the Club shall not be able to substitute another player from its roster. No additional penalties are to be assessed but a report of the incident must be submitted to the Commissioner. For an ineligible goalkeeper, see **5.3**.

If a goal is scored when an ineligible player is on the ice (whether he was involved in the scoring or not), the goal will be disallowed. This only applies to the goal scored at the stoppage of play whereby the player was deemed to be ineligible. All other goals scored previously by the ineligible player's team (with him on the ice or not) shall be allowed. The ineligible player will be removed from the game and the Club shall not be able to substitute another player from its roster. No additional penalties are to be assessed but a report of the incident must be submitted to the Commissioner.

5.3 **Goalkeeper** - Each team shall be allowed one goalkeeper on the ice at one time. The goalkeeper may be removed and another skater substituted. Such substitute shall not be permitted the privileges of the goalkeeper.

Each team shall have on its bench, or on a chair immediately beside the bench, a substitute goalkeeper who shall, at all times, be fully dressed and equipped ready to play.

Except when both goalkeepers are incapacitated, no skater in the playing roster in that game shall be permitted to wear the equipment of the goalkeeper.

In regular League and Playoff games, if both listed goalkeepers are incapacitated, that team shall be entitled to dress and play any available goalkeeper who is eligible. This goalkeeper is eligible to sit on the player's bench, in uniform. In the event that the two regular goalkeepers are injured or incapacitated in quick succession, the third goalkeeper shall be provided with a reasonable amount of time to get dressed, in addition to a two-minute warm-up (except when he enters the game to defend against a penalty shot). If, however, the third goalkeeper is dressed and on the bench when the second goalkeeper becomes incapacitated, the third goalkeeper shall enter the game immediately and no warm-up is permitted.

The recalling of minor league goalkeepers (as a result of suspensions incurred to both goalkeepers under Rule **11** – Goalkeeper's Equipment) to ensure a complete lineup for subsequent games shall be deemed to be an emergency recall and subject to the twenty-three (23) man roster limitations.

5.4 **Coaches and Team Personnel** - No one but players in uniform, non-playing team personnel duly registered on the Roster Sheet as the Manager, Coach(es), Trainer, Equipment Manager, etc. shall be permitted to occupy the benches so provided.

One non-uniformed player shall be permitted on the players' bench in a coaching capacity. He must be indicated on the Roster Sheet submitted by the Coach to the Official Scorer prior to the start of the game.

## Rule 6 – Captain and Alternate Captains

6.1 **Captain** - One Captain shall be appointed by each team, and he alone shall have the privilege of discussing with the Referee any questions relating to interpretation of rules which may arise during the progress of a game. He shall wear the letter "C," approximately three inches (3") in height and in contrasting color, in a conspicuous position on the front of his sweater. No co-Captains are permitted. Either one Captain and no more than two Alternate Captains, or no Captain and no more than three Alternate Captains are permitted (see **6.2**).

Only the Captain, when invited to do so by the Referee, shall have the privilege of discussing any point relating to the interpretation of rules. Any Captain, Alternate Captain or any player who comes off the bench and makes any protest or intervention with the officials for any purpose shall be assessed a minor penalty for unsportsmanlike conduct under Rule **39** – Abuse of Officials. Should this protest continue, he may be assessed a misconduct penalty, and if it further continues, a game misconduct penalty shall be warranted.

A complaint about a penalty is NOT a matter "relating to the interpretation of the rules" and a minor penalty shall be imposed against any Captain, Alternate Captain or any other player making such a complaint.

The Referee and Official Scorer shall be advised, prior to the start of each game, the name of the Captain and the Alternate Captains of both teams.

No playing Coach or playing Manager or goalkeeper shall be permitted to act as Captain or Alternate Captain.

6.2 **Alternate Captains** – If the permanent Captain is not on the ice, Alternate Captains (not more than two) shall be accorded the privileges of the Captain. Alternate Captains shall wear the letter "A" approximately three inches (3") in height and in contrasting color, in a conspicuous position on the front of their sweaters.

Only when the Captain is not in uniform, the Coach shall have the right to designate three Alternate Captains. This must be done prior to the start of the game.

## Rule 7 – Starting Line-up

7.1 **Starting Line-up** - Prior to the start of the game, at the request of the Referee, the Manager or Coach of the visiting team is required to name the starting line-up to the Referee or Official Scorer.

Prior to the start of the game, the Manager or Coach of the home team, having been advised by the Official Scorer the names of the starting line-up of the visiting team, shall name the starting line-up of the home team. This information shall be conveyed by the Official Scorer to the Coach of the visiting team.

No change in the starting line-up of either team as given to the Official Scorer, or in the playing line-up on the ice, can be made unless reviewed and approved by the Referee prior to the start of the game.

7.2 **Violation** - For an infraction of this rule, a bench minor penalty shall be imposed upon the offending team, provided such infraction is called to the attention of the Referee before the second face-off in the first period takes place. This is an appeal play and must be brought to the Referee's attention prior to the second face-off in the game. There is no penalty to the requesting team if their appeal is unsustained. The determining factor when considering whether or not a player or goalkeeper is listed in the starting line-up is that the player or goalkeeper's name, and not necessarily the player or goalkeeper's number, must be correctly listed by the Manager or Coach of that team.

In the event a team scores on the first shift of the game, and it is brought to the attention of the Referee by the opposing team that the team that scored did not have the correct starting line-up on the ice, the goal shall be allowed and a bench minor penalty assessed to the offending team for having an improper starting line-up. If the team that scores the goal on the first shift of the game challenges the starting line-up of the opposing team and the opposing team did not have the correct starting line-up, the scoring of the goal would nullify the bench minor penalty and no further penalties would be assessed.

## Rule 8 – Injured Players

8.1 **Injured Player** - When a player is injured or compelled to leave the ice during a game, he may retire from the game and be replaced by a substitute, but play must continue without the teams leaving the ice.

During the play, if an injured player wishes to retire from the ice and be replaced by a substitute, he must do so at the players' bench and not through any other exit leading from the rink. This is not a legal player change and therefore when a violation occurs, a bench minor penalty shall be imposed.

If a penalized player has been injured, he may proceed to the dressing room without the necessity of taking a seat on the penalty bench. If the injured player receives a minor penalty, the penalized team shall immediately put a substitute player on the penalty bench, who shall serve the penalty until such time as the injured player is able to return to the game. He would replace his teammate on the penalty bench at the next stoppage of play. If the injured player receives a major penalty, the penalized team shall place a substitute player on the penalty bench before the penalty expires and no other replacement for the penalized player shall be permitted to enter the game except from the penalty bench. For violation of this rule, a bench minor penalty shall be imposed.

Should the injured penalized player who has been replaced on the penalty bench return to his players' bench prior to the expiration of his penalty, he shall not be eligible to play until his penalty has expired. This includes coincidental penalties when his substitute is still in the penalty box awaiting a stoppage in play. The injured player must wait until his substitute has been released from the penalty box before he is eligible to play. If, however, there is a stoppage of play prior to the expiration of his penalty, he must then replace his teammate on the penalty bench and return to play once his penalty has expired.

When a player is injured so that he cannot continue play or go to his bench, the play shall not be stopped until the injured player's team has secured control of the puck. If the player's team is in control of the puck at the time of injury, play shall be stopped immediately unless his team is in a scoring position.

In the case where it is obvious that a player has sustained a serious injury, the Referee and/or Linesman may stop the play immediately.

When play has been stopped by the Referee or Linesman due to an injured player, or whenever an injured player is attended to on the ice by the Trainer or medical personnel, such player must be substituted for immediately. This injured player cannot return to the ice until play has resumed.

When play is stopped for an injured player, the ensuing face-off shall be conducted at the face-off spot in the zone nearest the location of the puck when the play was stopped. When the injured player's team has control of the puck in the attacking zone, the face-off shall be conducted at one of the face-off spots outside the blue line in the neutral zone. When the injured player is in his defending zone and the attacking team is in possession of the puck in the attacking zone, the face-off shall be conducted at one of the defending team's end-zone face-off spots.

8.2 **Injured Goalkeeper** - If a goalkeeper sustains an injury or becomes ill, he must be ready to resume play immediately or be replaced by a substitute goalkeeper and no additional time shall be allowed by the Referee for the purpose of enabling the injured or ill goalkeeper to resume his position. The substitute goalkeeper shall be allowed a two (2) minute warm-up during all pre-season games. No warm-up shall be permitted for a substitute goalkeeper in all regular League or Playoff games.

The Referee shall report to the Commissioner for disciplinary action any delay in making a goalkeeper substitution.

The substitute goalkeeper shall be subject to the regular rules governing goalkeepers and shall be entitled to the same privileges.

When a substitution for the regular goalkeeper has been made, such regular goalkeeper shall not resume his position until the next stoppage of play. For a violation, a minor penalty for delay of game shall be assessed.

When play has been stopped by the Referee or Linesman due to an injured goalkeeper, such goalkeeper must be substituted for only if he has to proceed to the players' bench to receive medical attention. If the Trainer has come onto the ice to attend to the goalkeeper and there is no undue delay, the goalkeeper may remain in the game without substitute. However, no additional time shall be permitted by the Referee for the purpose of enabling the injured goalkeeper to resume his position (i.e. no warm-up).

8.3 **Blood** – A player who is bleeding or who has visible blood on his equipment or body shall be ruled off the ice at the next stoppage of play. Such player shall not be permitted to return to play until the bleeding has been stopped and the cut or abrasion covered (if necessary). It is required that any affected equipment and/or uniform be properly decontaminated or exchanged.

# SECTION 3 – EQUIPMENT

## Rule 9 – Uniforms

9.1 **Team Uniform** – All players of each team shall be dressed uniformly with approved design and color of their helmets, sweaters, short pants, stockings and skates.

Altered uniforms of any kind, i.e. Velcro inserts, over-sized jerseys, altered collars, etc., will not be permitted. Any player or goalkeeper not complying with this rule shall not be permitted to participate in the game. For violations, refer to **9.5**.

Each member Club shall design and wear distinctive and contrasting uniforms for their home and road games, no parts of which shall be interchangeable except the pants. Any concerns regarding a player's uniform (including the goalkeeper) shall be reported by the Referee to the NHL Hockey Operations Department.

9.2 **Numbers** - Each player listed in the line-up of each team shall wear an individual identifying number at least ten inches (10") high on the back of his sweater. Sweater numbers such as 00, ½ (fractions), .05 (decimals), 101 (three digit) are not permitted. In addition, each player shall wear his surname in full, in block letters three inches (3") high, across the back of his sweater at shoulder height.

9.3 **Player's Jersey** – (see **9.4** for goalkeeper) The maximum jersey size is (see diagram).

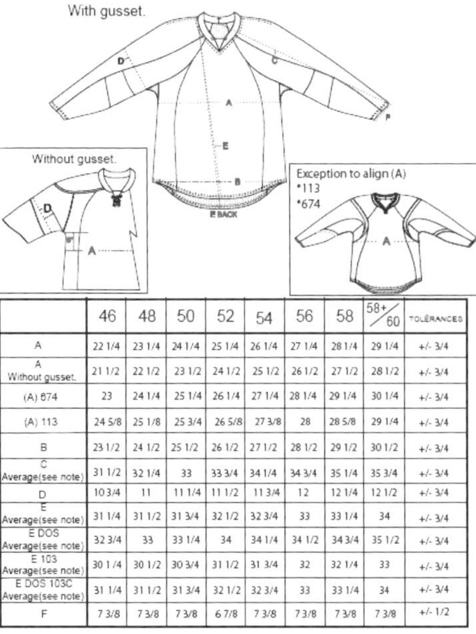


| | 46 | 48 | 50 | 52 | 54 | 56 | 58 | 58+/60 | TOLÉRANCES |
|---|---|---|---|---|---|---|---|---|---|
| A | 22 1/4 | 23 1/4 | 24 1/4 | 25 1/4 | 26 1/4 | 27 1/4 | 28 1/4 | 29 1/4 | +/- 3/4 |
| A Without gusset. | 21 1/2 | 22 1/2 | 23 1/2 | 24 1/2 | 25 1/2 | 26 1/2 | 27 1/2 | 28 1/2 | +/- 3/4 |
| (A) 674 | 23 | 24 1/4 | 25 1/4 | 26 1/4 | 27 1/4 | 28 1/4 | 29 1/4 | 30 1/4 | +/- 3/4 |
| (A) 113 | 24 5/8 | 25 1/8 | 25 3/4 | 26 5/8 | 27 3/8 | 28 | 28 5/8 | 29 1/4 | +/- 3/4 |
| B | 23 1/2 | 24 1/2 | 25 1/2 | 26 1/2 | 27 1/2 | 28 1/2 | 29 1/2 | 30 1/2 | +/- 3/4 |
| C Average(see note) | 31 1/2 | 32 1/4 | 33 | 33 3/4 | 34 1/4 | 34 3/4 | 35 1/4 | 35 3/4 | +/- 3/4 |
| D | 10 3/4 | 11 | 11 1/4 | 11 1/2 | 11 3/4 | 12 | 12 1/4 | 12 1/2 | +/- 3/4 |
| E Average(see note) | 31 1/4 | 31 1/2 | 31 3/4 | 32 1/2 | 32 3/4 | 33 | 33 1/4 | 34 | +/- 3/4 |
| E DOS Average(see note) | 32 3/4 | 33 | 33 1/4 | 34 | 34 1/4 | 34 1/2 | 34 3/4 | 35 1/2 | +/- 3/4 |
| E 103 Average(see note) | 30 1/4 | 30 1/2 | 30 3/4 | 31 1/2 | 31 3/4 | 32 | 32 1/4 | 33 | +/- 3/4 |
| E DOS 103C Average(see note) | 31 1/4 | 31 1/2 | 31 3/4 | 32 1/2 | 32 3/4 | 33 | 33 1/4 | 34 | +/- 3/4 |
| F | 7 3/8 | 7 3/8 | 7 3/8 | 6 7/8 | 7 3/8 | 7 3/8 | 7 3/8 | 7 3/8 | +/- 1/2 |

* C,E an D are average measurement from sampling. Use for reference only . There are not pattern measurement.

No inserts or additions are to be added to the standard players' jersey as produced by the manufacturer. (Modifications at the manufacturer are not allowed unless approved in advance by the League)

No alteration of the neck opening is permitted.

Sleeves must extend into the cuff of the glove.

Jerseys must be "tied down" properly at all times.

9.4 **Goalkeeper's Jersey** – The maximum jersey size is (see diagram).

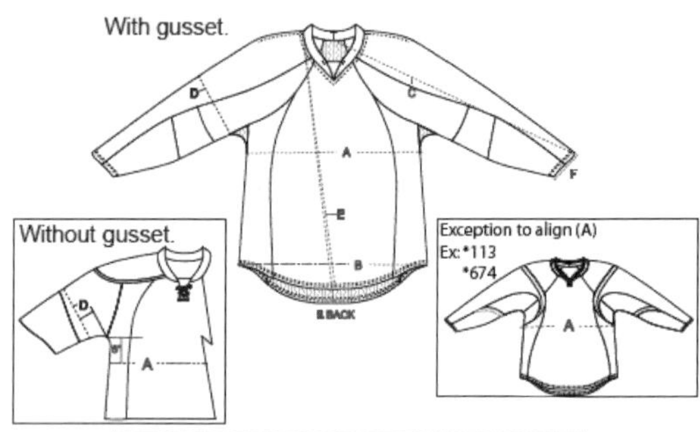


| | 54 | 56 | 58 | 58+/60 | TOLERANCES |
|---|---|---|---|---|---|
| A | 28 1/2 | 29 1/2 | 30 1/2 | 31 1/2 | +/- 3/4 |
| A without gusset | 28 7/8 | 29 7/8 | 30 7/8 | 31 7/8 | +/- 3/4 |
| (A) 113,674 | 29 1/4 | 30 1/4 | 31 1/4 | 32 1/4 | +/- 3/4 |
| B | 28 1/2 | 29 1/2 | 30 1/2 | 31 1/2 | +/- 3/4 |
| C Average(see note) | 34 | 34 1/2 | 35 | 35 1/2 | +/- 3/4 |
| D | 15 | 15 1/4 | 15 1/2 | 15 3/4 | +/- 3/4 |
| E Average(see note) | 31 3/4 | 32 | 32 1/4 | 33 | +/- 3/4 |
| E BACK Average(see note) | 35 3/4 | 36 | 36 1/4 | 37 | +/- 3/4 |
| E BACK 103C Average(see note) | 34 1/4 | 34 1/2 | 34 3/4 | 35 1/2 | +/- 3/4 |
| F | 8 3/4 | 8 3/4 | 8 3/4 | 8 3/4 | +/- 1/2 |

* C,E are average measurement from sampling. Use for reference only . There are not pattern measurement.

No inserts or additions are to be added to the standard goalkeeper-cut jersey as produced by the manufacturer. Modifications at the manufacturer are not allowed unless approved in advance by the League.

No "tying down" of the sweater is allowed at the wrists if it creates a tension across the jersey such that a "webbing effect" is created in the armpit area.

No other tie downs are allowed that create a "webbing effect."

The length of a jersey is illegal if it covers any area between the goalkeeper's legs.

9.5 **Protective Equipment** - All protective equipment, except gloves, headgear and goalkeepers' leg guards must be worn under the uniform. Should it be brought to the attention of the Referee that a player is wearing, for example, an elbow pad that is not covered by his jersey, he shall instruct the player to cover up the pad and a second violation by the same player would result in a minor penalty being assessed.

Whenever it is deemed by the Referee that a player is wearing protective equipment that does not meet with League regulations, he shall instruct the player to change or remove the piece of equipment. If the player refuses to make the necessary change he shall be assessed a minor penalty for delay of game and should he return to the ice without making the necessary change he shall be assessed a misconduct penalty. Should this happen a third time, the player shall be assessed a game misconduct penalty.

All player pants must be worn in a uniform fashion by all players. The pants must one consistent color around and throughout the leg of the pant. Pant legs are not to be ripped, cut, or torn in the leg/thigh area.

9.6 **Helmets** - All players of both teams shall wear a helmet of design, material and construction approved by the League at all times while participating in a game, either on the playing surface or the players' or penalty benches.

A player may continue to participate in the play without his helmet. However, if he goes to his players' bench to be substituted for, he may not return to the ice during play without a helmet (nor may a player exit the penalty bench during play without a helmet). Should he do so, the play shall be stopped once his team has gained control of the puck. If the play is stopped for such an infraction in the attacking zone, the ensuing face-off will take place at the nearest face-off spot in the neutral zone of the non-offending team. If the play is stopped for such an infraction in the defending or neutral zone, the ensuing face-off will take place at the nearest face-off spot to the location of the puck in that zone when the play was stopped.

When a goalkeeper has lost his helmet and/or face mask and his team has control of the puck, the play shall be stopped immediately to allow the goalkeeper the opportunity to regain his helmet and/or face mask. When the opposing team has control of the puck, play shall only be stopped if there is no immediate and impending scoring opportunity. This stoppage of play must be made by the Referee. When play is stopped because the goalkeeper has lost his helmet and/or face mask, the ensuing face-off shall take place at one of the defending team's end zone face-off spots.

When a goalkeeper deliberately removes his helmet and/or face mask in order to secure a stoppage of play, the Referee shall stop play as outlined above and in this case assess the goalkeeper a minor penalty for delaying the game. If the goalkeeper deliberately removes his helmet and/or face mask when the opposing team is on a breakaway, the Referee shall award a penalty shot to the non-offending team, which shot shall be taken by the player last in possession of the puck. If the goalkeeper deliberately removes his helmet and/or face mask during the course of a penalty shot or shootout attempt, the Referee shall award a goal to the non-offending team.

9.7 **Visors** - Beginning with the 2013-2014 season, all players who have fewer than 25 games of NHL experience must wear a visor properly affixed to their helmet. Visors are to be affixed to the helmets in such a fashion as to ensure adequate eye protection.

9.8 **Dangerous Equipment** - The use of pads or protectors made of metal, or of any other material likely to cause injury to an opposing player is prohibited. Referees have the authority to prohibit any equipment they feel may cause injury to any participants in the game. Failure to comply with the Referees' instructions shall result in the assessment of a minor penalty for delay of game.

A mask or protector of a design approved by the League may be worn by a player who has sustained a facial injury.

In the first instance, the injured player shall be entitled to wear any protective device prescribed by the Club doctor. If any opposing Club objects to the device, it may record its objection with the Commissioner.

In cases where a stick may have been modified and it is evident that the edges have not been beveled, the Referee shall deem the stick to be dangerous equipment and removed from the game until the edges can be beveled sufficiently. No penalty is to assessed initially unless the player returns to the ice with the unmodified stick, in which case he will be assessed a minor penalty for delay of game.

## Rule 10 – Sticks

10.1 **Player's Stick** – (see **10.2** for goalkeeper) The sticks shall be made of wood or other material approved by the League, and must not have any projections. Adhesive tape of any color may be wrapped around the stick at any place for the purpose of reinforcement or to improve control of the puck.

No stick shall exceed sixty-three inches (63") in length from the heel to the end of the shaft nor more than twelve and one-half inches (12½") from the heel to the end of the blade.

Requests for an exception to the length of the shaft (only) may be submitted in writing to and must be approved by the League's Hockey Operations Department prior to any such stick being approved for use. Only players 6'6" tall or more will be considered for exception. Maximum length of a stick granted an exception under this rule is sixty-five inches (65").

The blade of the stick shall not be more than three inches (3") in width at any point between the heel and ½" in from the mid-point of the tip of the blade, nor less than two inches (2"). All edges of the blade shall be beveled (see **9.8**). The curvature of the blade of the stick shall be restricted in such a way that the distance of a perpendicular line measured from a straight line drawn from any point at the heel to the end of the blade to the point of maximum curvature shall not exceed three-quarters of an inch (¾").

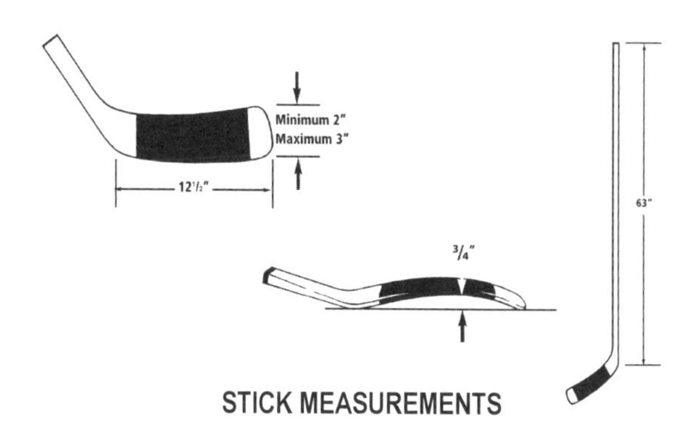


STICK MEASUREMENTS

10.2 **Goalkeeper's Stick** - In the case of a goalkeeper's stick, there shall be a knob of white tape or some other protective material approved by the League. This knob must not be less than one-half inch (1/2") thick at the top of the shaft.

Failure to comply with this provision of the rule will result in the goalkeeper's stick being deemed unfit for play. The goalkeeper's stick must be changed without the application of a minor penalty.

The blade of the goalkeeper's stick shall not exceed three and one-half inches (3 1/2") in width at any point except at the heel, where it must not exceed four and one-half inches (4 1/2") in width; nor shall the goalkeeper's stick exceed fifteen and one-half inches (15 1/2") in length from the heel to the end of the blade.

There is to be no measurement of any of the dimensions of the goalkeeper's stick during the course of the game. The League's Hockey Operations Department is specifically authorized to make a check of all goalkeepers' sticks to ensure the compliance with the rule. It shall report its findings to the Commissioner for his disciplinary action (see **11.9**).

The widened portion of the goalkeeper's stick extending up the shaft from the blade shall not extend more than twenty-six inches (26") from the heel and shall not exceed three and one-half inches (3 1/2") in width.

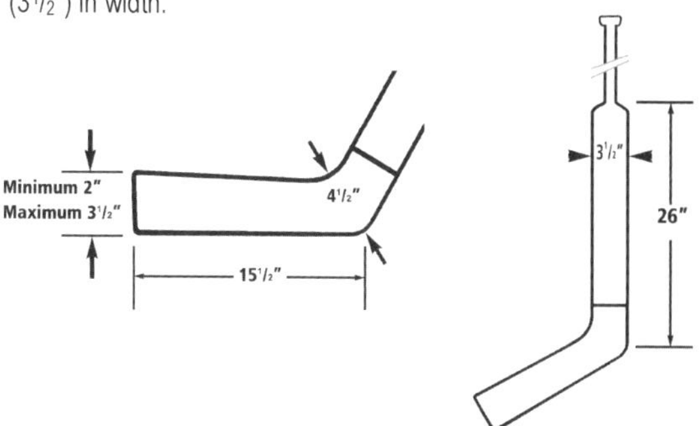


GOALKEEPERS' STICK MEASUREMENTS

10.3 **Broken Stick – Player** - A broken stick is one which, in the opinion of the Referee, is unfit for normal play.

A player without a stick may participate in the game. A player whose stick is broken may participate in the game provided he drops the broken stick. A minor penalty shall be imposed for an infraction of this rule.

A player who has lost or broken his stick may receive a replacement stick by having one handed to him from his own players' bench; by having one handed to him by a teammate on the ice; or, by picking up his own unbroken stick or that of a teammate's from the ice. A player will be penalized if he throws, tosses, slides or shoots a stick to a teammate on the ice, or if he picks up and plays with an opponent's stick. A player may not participate in the play using a goalkeeper's stick. A minor penalty shall be imposed for an infraction of this rule.

A player tendered a stick thrown on the ice from the players' or penalty bench will not receive a penalty. However, the person responsible for throwing the stick will receive a bench minor penalty.

10.4 **Broken Stick – Goalkeeper** - A goalkeeper may continue to play with a broken stick until a stoppage of play or until he has one legally handed to him by a teammate. The teammate must hand the stick to him. He cannot throw it or slide it to the goalkeeper (this includes situations where the goalkeeper has lost his stick and a teammate is trying to return it to him). For a violation of this rule, a minor penalty for throwing the stick shall be assessed to the offending player (no penalty to the goalkeeper for receiving the stick).

A goalkeeper whose stick is broken or illegal may not go to the players' bench for a replacement but must receive his stick from a teammate. A goalkeeper may participate in the play using a skater's stick until such time as he is legally provided with a replacement goalkeeper's stick.

For an infraction of this rule, a minor penalty shall be imposed on the goalkeeper.

10.5 **Stick Measurement** - A request for a stick measurement shall be limited to one request per team during the course of any stoppage in play.

When a formal complaint is made by the Captain or Alternate Captain of a team, against the dimensions of any stick of an opponent, that opponent must be on the ice at the time the request is made to the Referee. Once the request is made, and as long as the Officials maintain visual contact with the stick, it can be measured. This means that if the player whose stick is about to be measured steps off the ice onto his players' bench, his stick may still be measured provided the request was received prior to him leaving the ice surface and the stick remains in the view of at least one of the on-ice Officials.

The Referee shall take the stick to the penalty bench where the necessary measurement shall be made immediately. Players on both

teams shall retire to their respective benches. To measure the curvature of the blade of the stick, the Referee must draw an imaginary line along the outside of the shaft to the bottom of the blade and then along the bottom of the blade - this will determine the location of the heel. Using a League-approved measuring gauge, the Referee shall secure the gauge at the heel of the stick and measure the curvature of the blade from the heel to any point along the toe of the blade. To measure any other dimension of the stick, the Referee shall use a measuring tape.

The result shall be reported to the Penalty Timekeeper, who shall record it on the back of the Penalty Record form. The Referee will convey the result of the measurement to Captain or Alternate Captain of the player whose stick was measured. If the stick proves to be illegal, the stick shall remain at the penalty bench until the end of the game.

A player whose stick has been measured and it is found not to conform to the provisions of this rule shall be assessed a minor penalty and a fine of two hundred dollars ($200). For a second offense in the same season, the player shall (in addition to the minor penalty) be fined one thousand dollars ($1000). For a third offense in the same season, the player shall (in addition to the minor penalty) be assessed a game misconduct and an automatic one game suspension. For all additional violations in the same season, the automatic suspension to the player shall (in addition to the minor penalty and game misconduct assessed during the game) double for each subsequent violation of this rule (i.e. first suspension - one game, second suspension - two games, third suspension – four games etc.)

If the complaint is not sustained, a bench minor penalty shall be imposed against the complaining Club in addition to a fine of one hundred dollars ($100).

A player who participates in the play, who checks or who intentionally prevents the movement of an opponent, or who intentionally plays the puck while carrying two sticks (including while taking a replacement stick to his goalkeeper) shall incur a minor penalty under this rule but the automatic fine of two hundred dollars ($200) shall not be imposed. If his participation causes a foul resulting in a penalty, the Referee shall report the incident to the Commissioner for disciplinary action.

A request for a stick measurement in regular playing time is permitted, including after the scoring of a goal, however, a goal cannot be disallowed as a result of the measurement. A request for a stick measurement following a goal in overtime (including one scored on a penalty shot in overtime) is not permitted. Stick measurements prior to or during the shootout are permitted, subject to the guidelines outlined in **10.7**.

Any player who deliberately breaks his stick or who refuses to surrender his stick for measurement when requested to do so by the Referee shall be assessed a minor penalty plus a ten-minute (10) misconduct. In addition, this player or goalkeeper shall be subject to a two hundred dollar ($200) fine.

10.6 **Stick Measurement – Prior to Penalty Shot** – A stick measurement request may be made prior to a penalty shot following these guidelines:

First Stick

If the stick is "legal" the complaining Club is assessed a bench minor penalty, a player is placed in the penalty box immediately. Regardless as to the result of the penalty shot, the bench minor penalty is assessed and served.

If the stick is "illegal" the player will be assessed a minor penalty. He will be ordered to obtain a new (second) stick prior to the penalty shot. After he takes the shot he will be required to serve his penalty.

Second stick

The player will be told that the second stick will be measured prior to the penalty shot to verify the legality of the stick.

If the second stick is "legal", proceed with the penalty shot.

If second stick is "illegal", disallow the opportunity for the penalty shot and assess one minor penalty for the first illegal stick.

If the player refuses to surrender his stick for measurement prior to the penalty shot, the penalty shot shall not be permitted and the player shall be assessed a misconduct penalty.

10.7 **Stick Measurement – Prior to Shootout Attempt** – A stick measurement request must be made prior to the Referee blowing his whistle to begin the shootout attempt.

If the stick is "legal" the complaining Club forfeits their next shootout attempt. In addition, the complaining Club's Coach shall be fined one thousand dollars ($1000) and the Club shall be fined five thousand dollars ($5000). Their next shootout attempt would be recorded as "no goal".

If the stick is "illegal", the offending team forfeits that shootout attempt by that player, and the player becomes ineligible to participate in the shootout. In addition, the player is fined one thousand dollars ($1000) and his Club is fined five thousand dollars ($5000). This shootout attempt would be recorded as "no goal".

Stick measurement violations during the shootout shall not be subject to the fines and suspensions outlined in **10.5**.

## Rule 11 – Goalkeeper's Equipment

11.1 **Goalkeeper's Equipment** - With the exception of skates and stick, all the equipment worn by the goalkeeper must be constructed solely for the purpose of protecting the head or body, and he must not wear any garment or use any contrivance which would give him undue assistance in keeping goal.

The League's Hockey Operations Department is specifically authorized to make a check of each teams' equipment (including goalkeepers" sticks) to ensure the compliance with the rule. It shall report its findings to the Commissioner for his disciplinary action.

11.2 **Leg Guards** – The leg guards worn by goalkeepers shall not exceed eleven inches (11") in extreme width when on the leg of the player. Each goalkeeper must wear pads that are anatomically proportional and size specific based on the individual physical characteristics of that goalkeeper. The League's Hockey Operations Department will have the complete discretion to determine the maximum height of each goalkeeper's pads based on measurements obtained by the League's Hockey Operations Department, which will include the floor to center of knee and center of knee to pelvis measurements. Each goalkeeper will be given a Limiting Distance Size based on these measurements. The Limiting Distance Size will be the sum of the floor to knee and 45% of the knee to pelvis measurements plus a four inch (4") allowance for the height of the skate. The Limiting Distance Size is a vertical measurement from the playing surface and will be measured with the Limiting Distance Gauge when inspected at the clearing house phase and during post game spot checks to ensure compliance. Any pads deemed too large for a goalkeeper will be considered illegal equipment for that goalkeeper, regardless of whether or not they would have fallen within previous equipment maximums. The minimum length of the boot of the pad is to be no less than seven inches (7"). The goal pad must have a defined boot channel with no inserts. The channel must be big enough so that the skate slots into it and is not resting on the pad. No attachments such as plastic puck foils are permitted. Pads can only be ten and one-half inches ($10^1/_2$") deep. The measurement will be taken from the front face of the pad to the last edge of the inner knee protection.

Calf-wing protectors can no longer be attached to the five-hole or the five-hole seam. Calf-wings must be inset one-half inch ($^1/_2$") from the inside five-hole, creating a distinct edge, and attached to the back cover. Calf-wing protectors must be one piece and cannot include wedges (removable or non-removable). Calf-wing protectors may be flat for five and one-half inches ($5^1/_2$") before contouring to the shape of the leg. Calf-wing protectors must contour and cannot be visible to the shooter when strapped to the goalkeeper's leg. Calf-wing protectors may not exceed one inch (1") in thickness. Calf-wing protector straps must run through or wrap around so the calf protector follows the contour of the goalkeeper's leg even if the straps are worn loosely. No zippers, Velcro, or Velcro attachments are allowed.

The knee strap pad is not to exceed six inches (6") in length by five and one-half inches ($5^1/_2$") in width. The knee strap pad must be fastened to the inner risers/lifts The inner knee risers are not to exceed seven inches (7") in length by five and one-half inches ($5^1/_2$") in width. The length of seven inches (7") is measured from where the inner padding attaches to the leg pad and back to the end of the inner padding. The total measurement of the entire inner knee padding (pad risers) including the outer knee strap pad must not exceed two and one-half inches ($2^1/_2$") in thickness and will be measured when non-compressed. Knee strap pads and riser/lifts must have a one inch (1") radius (rounded) on the top edge. Knee straps must wrap around the knee build-ups and cannot come out behind or through knee build-ups. Medial rolls (raised seam ridges) will not be permitted. All knee protection attached to the leg pad must be worn under the thigh guard of the pant.

11.3 **Chest and Arm Pads** – No raised ridges are allowed on the front edges or sides of the chest pad, the inside or outside of the arms, or across the shoulders.

Layering at the elbow is permitted to add protection but not to add stopping area. This layering, both across the front and down the sides, to protect the point of the elbow shall not exceed seven inches (7").

Shoulder cap protectors must follow the contour of the shoulder cap without becoming a projection/extension beyond or above the shoulder or shoulder cap. This contoured padding must not be more than one inch (1") in thickness beyond the top ridge of the shoulder and shoulder cap.

On each side the shoulder clavicle protectors are not to exceed seven inches (7") in width. Their maximum thickness is to be one inch (1"). This protection is not to extend or project above or beyond the shoulder or shoulder cap nor extend beyond the armpit. No insert is allowed between the shoulder clavicle protector and the chest pad that would elevate the shoulder clavicle protector.

If, when the goalkeeper assumes his normal crouch position, the shoulder and/or shoulder cap protection is pushed above the contour of the shoulder, the chest pad will be considered illegal.

The chest and arm protector worn by each goalkeeper must be anatomically proportional and size specific based on the individual physical characteristics of that goalkeeper. The League's Hockey Operations Department will have the complete discretion to determine the maximum size for each goalkeeper's chest and arm protector based on measurements obtained by the League's Hockey Operations Department, which will include but not be limited to, measurements for torso and arm length. Any chest and arm protector deemed too large for a goalkeeper will be considered illegal equipment for that goalkeeper, regardless of whether or not it would have fallen within previous equipment maximums.

11.4 **Pants** – No internal or external or cheater padding is permitted on the pant leg or waist beyond that which is required to provide protection (no outside or inside ridges).

The maximum width (straight line) of the thigh pad across the front of the leg is ten inches (10"). If the groin and/or hip pads extend beyond the edge of the front thigh pad they are to be included in this ten-inch (10") measurement. This measurement is to be taken while the goalkeeper is in an upright standing position. This measurement is to be made five inches (5") up from the bottom of the pant.

All thigh pads must follow the contour of the leg. Square thigh pads are considered illegal.

Each goalkeeper must wear pants that are anatomically proportional and size specific based on the individual physical characteristics of that goalkeeper. The League's Hockey Operations

Department will have the complete discretion to determine the maximum size of each goalkeeper's pants based on measurements obtained by the League's Hockey Operations Department, which will include but not be limited to, measurements for waist circumference and length of pant above and below waist line. In determining pants sizes, whether or not a goalkeeper wears his chest and arm pads inside or outside of his pants will also be a consideration. Any pants deemed too large for a goalkeeper will be considered illegal equipment for that goalkeeper, regardless of whether or not they would have fallen within previous equipment maximums.

11.5 **Knee Pads** – All knee protection must be strapped and fit under the thigh pad of the pant leg and not exceed a contoured nine inches (9"), with no flat surfaces and must not be permanently attached or fixed to the pants.

Layering at the knee is permitted to add protection but not to add stopping area. Any layering to protect the knee, whether across the front or along the sides, shall not exceed nine inches (9").

This measurement is to be taken while the goalkeeper is in an upright standing position. In the event a goalkeeper is required to wear a medical appliance to support the knee, the measurement will be taken without the goalkeeper wearing the medical appliance.

11.6 **Catching Glove** – A maximum perimeter of forty-five inches (45") is permitted. The perimeter of the glove is the distance around the glove (see measurement procedures below).

The wrist cuff must be four inches (4") in width. The cuff of the glove is considered to be the portion of the glove protecting the wrist from the point where the thumb joint meets the wrist. Any protection joining/enhancing the cuff to the glove will be considered part of the glove rather than the cuff.

The wrist cuff is to be a maximum of eight inches (8") in length (this includes the bindings). All measurements follow the contour of the cuff.

The distance from the heel of the glove along the pocket and following the contour of the inside of the trap of the glove to the top of the "T" trap must not exceed eighteen inches (18"). The heel is considered to be the point at which the straight vertical line from the cuff meets the glove (see diagram at right).

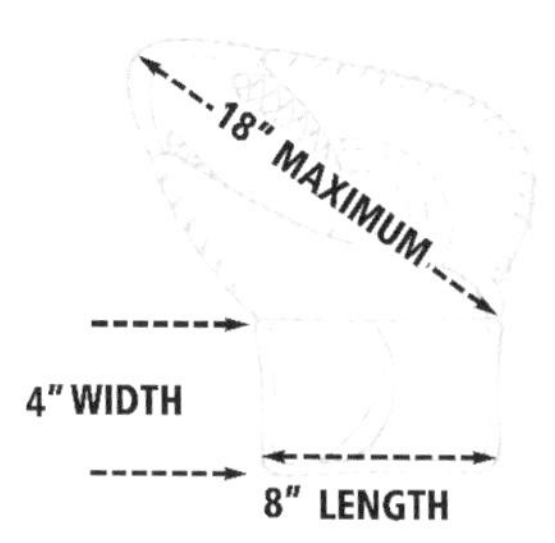


## Measuring Procedures for Goalkeepers' Catching Glove

Suggested Equipment - binder clip, pins and a 5/8" fiberglass cloth measuring tape that measures eighth of an inch.

Procedure:

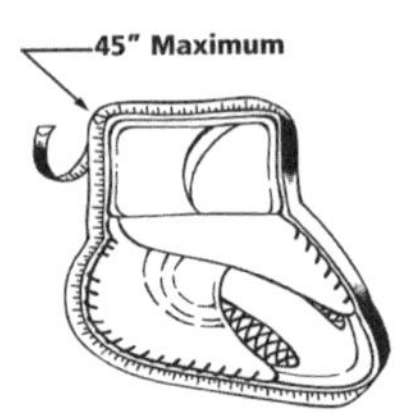


1) At the “starting point” of the measurement, anchor the tape with a pin or binder clip.

2) Ensure that the midpoint line of the measuring tape follows the outside top ridge of the edge/binding.

3) If at the junction of the cuff and catch portions of the glove there is a “jagged point,” the measurement tape will follow the imaginary perpendicular line to the glove ridge above. (A “jagged joint” anywhere else on the glove will not be allowed this “straight line” privilege, i.e. where the trap joins the main glove).

11.7 **Blocking Glove** – Protective padding attached to the back or forming part of the goalkeeper's blocking glove shall not exceed eight inches (8") in width nor more than fifteen inches (15") in length at any point (this includes the bindings). All measurements follow the contour of the back of the glove.

The blocking glove must be rectangular in shape.

The flap protecting the thumb and wrist must be fastened to the blocker and must follow the contour of the thumb and wrist. This thumb protection must not exceed seven inches (7") in extreme length when measured from the top of the blocking surface.

Raised ridges are not to be added to any portion of the blocking glove.

All goalkeepers must use one of each a blocking glove and catching glove, meeting League-approved sizing specifications.

11.8 **Masks** – Protective masks of a design approved by the League must be worn by goalkeepers. Protective masks deemed to be worn only to increase stopping area will be considered illegal.

11.9 **League Inspections** - These inspections can take place at any time, before, during, or after any game. A member of the League’s Hockey Operations, Officiating and/or Security departments may obtain equipment from any or all of the four participating goalkeepers. This equipment may be removed to a secure location for measuring.

Any violation of this rule will result in an automatic two (2) game suspension to the offending goalkeeper. Should both goalkeepers on a Club have illegal equipment, both will be suspended in sequence. The goalkeeper who played the day/night of the measurement will be suspended for the next two (2) games played by his team, and the back-up goalkeeper will be suspended for the subsequent two (2) games.

A goalkeeper who plays with equipment that has not been inspected and approved by the League's Hockey Operations Department, or who tampers with equipment after it has been inspected and approved by the League's Hockey Operations, Officiating and or Security departments will be suspended for the next two (2) League games, his Club will be fined $25,000.00 and his Equipment Manager will be fined $1000.00 (to be deducted from his pay), regardless of whether or not such equipment previously complied with League standards. Each additional violation will result in all game suspensions and fines being doubled.

Refusal to submit the equipment for League measurement will result in the same sanctions as those imposed on a goalkeeper with illegal equipment.

Any violation of this rule shall be reported to the Club involved and to the Commissioner of the League.

## Rule 12 – Illegal Equipment

12.1 **Illegal Equipment** - All protective equipment, except gloves, headgear and goalkeepers' leg guards must be worn under the uniform. For violation of this rule, after warning by the Referee, a minor penalty shall be imposed.

Players violating this rule shall not be permitted to participate in the game until such equipment has been corrected or removed.

12.2 **Gloves** - A glove from which all or part of the palm has been removed or cut to permit the use of the bare hand shall be considered illegal equipment and if any player wears such a glove in play, a minor penalty shall be imposed on him.

When a complaint is made under this rule, and such complaint is not sustained, a bench minor penalty shall be imposed against the complaining Club for delaying the game.

12.3 **Elbow Pads** - All elbow pads which do not have a soft protective outer covering of sponge rubber or similar material at least one-half inch ($^{1}/_{2}$") thick shall be considered dangerous equipment.

12.4 **Fair Play** - These equipment regulations (Section 3) are written in the spirit of "fair play." If at any time the League feels that this spirit is being abused, the offending equipment will be deemed ineligible for play until a hearing has ruled on its eligibility.

12.5 **League Inspections** - The League's Hockey Operations, Officiating and/or Security departments are specifically authorized to make a check of each team's equipment to ensure the compliance with this rule. They shall report their findings to the Commissioner for his disciplinary action.

## Rule 13 - Puck

13.1 **Dimensions** - The puck shall be made of vulcanized rubber, or other approved material, one inch (1") thick and three inches (3") in diameter and shall weigh between five and one-half ounces (5½" oz.) and six ounces (6 oz.). All pucks used in competition must be approved by the League.

13.2 **Supply** - The home team shall be responsible for providing an adequate supply of official pucks which shall be kept in a frozen condition. This supply of pucks shall be kept at the penalty bench under the control of one of the regular off-ice Officials or a special attendant.

13.3 **Illegal Puck** - If at any time while play is in progress, a puck other than the one legally in play shall appear on the playing surface, the play shall not be stopped but shall continue with the legal puck until the play then in progress is completed by change of possession.

## Rule 14 – Adjustment to Clothing or Equipment

14.1 **Adjustment to Clothing or Equipment** - Play shall not be stopped nor the game delayed by reasons of adjustments to clothing, equipment, skates or sticks.

The onus of maintaining clothing and equipment in proper condition shall be upon the player. If adjustments are required, the player shall leave the ice and play shall continue with a substitute.

No delay shall be permitted for the repair or adjustment of goalkeeper's equipment. If adjustments are required, the goalkeeper shall leave the ice and his place shall be taken by the substitute goalkeeper immediately.

# SECTION 4 – TYPES OF PENALTIES

## Rule 15 – Calling of Penalties

15.1 **Calling a Penalty** - Should an infraction of the rules which would call for a minor, major, misconduct, game misconduct or match penalty be committed by a player of the side in control of the puck, the Referee shall immediately blow his whistle and penalize the offending player.

Should an infraction of the rules which would call for a minor, major, misconduct, game misconduct or match penalty be committed by a player of the team not in control of the puck, the Referee shall raise his arm to signal the delayed calling of a penalty. When the team to be penalized gains control of the puck, the Referee will blow his whistle to stop play and impose the penalty on the offending player.

When a player, Trainer, Manager, coach or non-playing Club personnel is ejected from the game for a violation of the playing rules, that individual must vacate the players' bench area and may not, in any manner, further participate in the game. This includes directing the team from the spectator area or by radio communications. Any violations shall be reported to the Commissioner.

Refer to Reference Tables – Table 1 – Summary of Penalties to Coaches and Non-playing Club Personnel (page 134) for a list of infractions specific to those individuals.

15.2 **Calling a Minor Penalty – Goal Scored** - If the penalty to be imposed is a minor penalty and a goal is scored on the play by the non-offending side, the minor penalty shall not be imposed but major and match penalties shall be imposed in the normal manner regardless of whether or not a goal is scored.

If two or more minor penalties were to be imposed and a goal is scored on the play by the non-offending side, the Captain of the offending team shall designate to the Referee which minor penalty(ies) will be assessed and which minor penalty will be washed out as a result of the scoring of the goal.

15.3 **Calling a Double-minor Penalty – Goal Scored** - When the penalty to be imposed is applicable under Rule **47** for Head-butting or Rule **58** Butt-ending, Rule **60** High-sticking or Rule **62** Spearing, and a goal is scored, two minutes of the appropriate penalty will be assessed to the offending player. (This will be announced as a double-minor for the appropriate foul and the player will serve two (2) minutes only.)

15.4 **Calling a Penalty – Short-handed Team – Goal Scored** - If when a team is "short-handed" by reason of one or more minor or bench minor penalties, the Referee signals a further minor penalty or penalties against the "short-handed" team and a goal is scored by the non-offending side before the whistle is blown, then the goal shall be allowed. The penalty or penalties signaled shall be assessed and the first of the minor penalties already being served shall automatically terminate under Rule **16** – Minor Penalties. Major and match penalties shall be imposed in the normal manner regardless of whether or not a goal is scored.

Should a minor or bench minor penalty be signaled against a team already short-handed by reason of a major (or match) penalty, but before the play can be stopped to assess the minor or bench minor penalty, a goal is scored by the non-offending side, the signaled minor or bench minor penalty shall not be imposed due to the scoring of the goal.

Should a penalty be signaled against a team already short-handed by reason of one or more minor or bench minor penalties, and the signaled penalty would result in the awarding of a penalty shot, but before the Referee can stop play to award the penalty shot, the non-offending team scores a goal, then the signaled penalty (that would have resulted in a penalty shot) shall be assessed as a minor (double-minor, major or match) penalty and the first of the minor penalties already being served shall automatically terminate under Rule **16** – Minor Penalties.

15.5 **Face-off Locations** – When players are penalized at a stoppage of play so as to result in one or more penalties being placed on the penalty time clock to one team, the ensuing face-off shall be conducted at one of the two face-off spots in the offending team's end zone. There are only four (4) exceptions to this application:

*(i) when a penalty is assessed after the scoring of a goal – face-off at center ice;.*

*(ii) when a penalty is assessed at the end (or start) of a period – face-off at center ice;*

*(iii) when the defending team is penalized and the attacking players enter the attacking zone beyond the outer edge of the end zone face-off circle – face-off in the neutral zone (see Rule **76.2**, paragraph 10);*

*(iv) when the team not being penalized ices the puck – face-off in the neutral zone outside the blue line of the team icing the puck..*

## Rule 16 – Minor Penalties

16.1 **Minor Penalty** - For a minor penalty, any player, other than a goalkeeper, shall be ruled off the ice for two (2) minutes during which time no substitute shall be permitted.

16.2 **Short-handed** - "Short-handed" means that the team must be below the numerical strength of its opponent on the ice at the time the goal is scored. The minor or bench minor penalty which terminates automatically is the one with the least amount of time on the clock. Thus coincident minor penalties to both Teams do not cause either side to be "short-handed" (see Rule **19**).

If while a team is "short-handed" by one or more minor or bench minor penalties, the opposing team scores a goal, the first of such penalties shall automatically terminate.

This rule shall also apply when a goal is awarded.

This rule does not apply when a goal is scored on a penalty shot (i.e. offending team's penalized player(s) do not get released on the scoring of a goal on a penalty shot).

**Minor penalty expiration criteria:**

*(i) Is the team scored against short-handed?*

*(ii) Is the team scored against serving a minor penalty on the clock?*

If both criteria are satisfied, the minor penalty with the least amount of time on the clock shall terminate except when coincidental penalties are being served. Refer to Reference Tables – Table 14 – Goals Scored Against a Short-handed Team (page 141).

No penalty shall expire when a goal is scored against a team on a penalty shot.

When the minor penalties of two players of the same team terminate at the same time, the Captain of that team shall designate to the Referee which of such players will return to the ice first and the Referee will instruct the Penalty Timekeeper accordingly.

16.3 **Infractions** – Refer to Reference Tables – Table 2 – Summary of Minor Penalties (page 134), for a list of infractions that can result in a minor penalty being assessed (see specific rule numbers for complete descriptions).

## Rule 17 – Bench Minor Penalties

17.1 **Bench Minor Penalty** - A bench minor penalty involves the removal from the ice of one player of the team against which the penalty is assessed for a period of two (2) minutes. Any player except a goalkeeper of the team may be designated to serve the penalty by the Manager or Coach through the playing Captain and such player shall take his place on the penalty bench promptly and serve the penalty as if it was a minor penalty imposed upon him.

17.2 **Short-handed** – see **16.2**.

17.3 **Infractions** – Refer to Reference Tables – Table 3 – Summary of Bench Minor Penalties (page 135) for a list of infractions that can result in a bench minor penalty being assessed (see specific rule numbers for complete descriptions).

## Rule 18 – Double-minor Penalties

18.1 **Double-minor Penalty** - For a double-minor penalty, any player, other than a goalkeeper, shall be ruled off the ice for four (4) minutes during which time no substitute shall be permitted.

18.2 **Short-handed** – see **16.2**.

When a double-minor penalty has been signaled by the Referee and the non-offending team scores during the delay, one of the minor penalties shall be washed out and the penalized player will serve the remaining two minutes of the double-minor penalty. The penalty will be announced as a double-minor penalty but only two minutes would be shown on the penalty time clock.

18.3 **Infractions** – Refer to Reference Tables – Table 4 – Summary of Double-minor Penalties (page 136) for a list of infractions that can result in a double-minor penalty being assessed (see specific rule numbers for complete descriptions).

## Rule 19 – Coincidental Penalties

19.1 **Coincidental Minor Penalties** - When coincident minor penalties or coincident minor penalties of equal duration are imposed against players of both teams, the penalized players shall all take their places on the penalty benches and such penalized players shall not leave the penalty bench until the first stoppage of play following the expiry of their respective penalties. Where goalkeepers are involved, refer to **27.1**. Immediate substitution shall be made for an equal number of minor penalties or coincident minor penalties of equal duration to each team so penalized and the penalties of the players for which substitutions have been made shall not be taken into account for the purpose of the delayed penalty rule (Rule **26**). This rule only applies when at least one team is already serving a time penalty in the penalty box that causes them to be short-handed.

When one minor penalty is assessed to one player of each team at the same stoppage in play, these penalties will be served without substitution provided there are no other penalties in effect and visible on the penalty clocks. Both teams will therefore play four skaters against four skaters for the duration of the minor penalties.

Should one or both of these players (or any other players) also incur a misconduct penalty in addition to their one minor penalty, this rule shall apply and the teams would still play four skaters against four skaters (the player incurring the misconduct penalty would have to serve the entire 12 minutes – minor plus misconduct – and his team would have to place an additional player on the penalty bench to serve the minor penalty and be able to return to the ice when the minor penalty expires).

When multiple penalties are assessed to both teams, equal numbers of minor and major penalties shall be eliminated using the coincident penalty rule and any differential in time penalties shall be served in the normal manner and displayed on the penalty time clock accordingly (see **19.5**). If there is no differential in time penalties, all players will serve their allotted penalty time, but will not be released until the first stoppage of play following the expiration of their respective penalties.

For coincidental penalties that carry over into, or are assessed during regular-season overtime, refer to **84.3**, to Reference Tables – Table 17 – Penalties In Effect Prior to the Start of Overtime – Regular Season on page 157, and to Reference Tables – Table 18 – Penalties Assessed in Overtime – Regular Season on page 158.

19.2 **Coincidental Major Penalties** - When coincident major penalties or coincident penalties of equal duration, including a major and/or a match penalty, are imposed against players of both teams, the penalized players shall all take their places on the penalty benches and such penalized players shall not leave the penalty benches until the first stoppage of play following the expiry of their respective penalties. Immediate substitutions shall be made for an equal number of major penalties, or coincident penalties of equal duration including a major penalty to each team so penalized, and the penalties of the players for which substitutions have been made shall not be taken into account for the purpose of the delayed penalty rule, (Rule **26**). In such situations, if one or both players have received a game misconduct in addition to their major penalties, no substitutes are required to take their places on the penalty benches.

19.3 **Coincidental Match Penalties** - When coincident match penalties or coincident penalties of equal duration, including a major and/or a match penalty, are imposed against players of both teams, the players with the match penalties shall be immediately removed from the game. The remaining penalized players shall not leave the penalty benches until the first stoppage of play following the expiry of their respective penalties. Immediate substitutions shall be made for an equal number of major and/or match penalties, or coincident penalties of equal duration including a major or match penalty to each team so penalized, and the penalties of the players for which substitutions have been made shall not be taken into account for the purpose of the delayed penalty rule, (Rule **26**).

19.4 **Last Five Minutes and Overtime** - During the last five (5) minutes of regulation time, or at any time in overtime, when a minor penalty (or double-minor penalty) is assessed to one player of Team A, and a major (or match) penalty is assessed to one player of Team B at the same stoppage of play, the three-minute (or one-minute) differential shall be served immediately as a major penalty. This is also applicable when coincidental penalties are negated, leaving the aforementioned examples. In such instances, the team of the player receiving the major penalty must place the replacement player in the penalty bench prior to expiration of the penalty. In the case of a match penalty, the team must place the replacement player in the penalty bench immediately. The differential will be recorded on the penalty clock as a three (3) minute or a one (1) minute penalty (as applicable), and served in the same manner as a major penalty. This rule shall be applied regardless as to the on-ice strength of the two teams at the time the above outlined penalties are assessed.

19.5 **Applying the Coincidental Penalty Rule –** When multiple penalties are assessed to both teams at the same stoppage of play, the following rules are to be utilized by the Referees to determine the on-ice strength for both teams:

*(i) Cancel as many major and/or match penalties as possible*

*(ii) Cancel as many minor, bench minor and or double-minor penalties as possible*

Refer to Reference Tables - Table 15 – Coincidental Penalties on page 148.

## Rule 20 – Major Penalties

20.1 **Major Penalty** - For the first major penalty in any one game, the offender, except the goalkeeper, shall be ruled off the ice for five (5) minutes during which time no substitute shall be permitted.

When one player receives a major penalty and a minor penalty at the same time, the major penalty shall be served first by the penalized player (or substitute for the goalkeeper), except under Rule **19.2** where coincidental major penalties are in effect, in which case the minor penalty will be recorded and served first.

20.2 **Short-handed** – Although a major penalty does cause a team to be short-handed, the penalized player serving the major penalty does not leave the penalty bench when the opposing team scores. The player must wait for the entire major penalty to expire before he is permitted to exit the penalty bench.

20.3 **Substitution** – When a player has been assessed a major penalty and has been removed from the game or is injured, the offending team does not have to place a substitute player on the penalty bench immediately, but must do so at a stoppage of play prior to the expiration of the major penalty. He may then legally exit the penalty bench when the major penalty has expired. If the player has been assessed minor penalties in addition to the major penalty that must also be served on the penalty time clock, the offending team must place a substitute on the penalty bench immediately.

Failure to place a player on the penalty bench prior to the expiration of the major penalty will result in that team having to continue playing one player short (but not officially considered short-handed) until the next stoppage of play. Any replacement player who enters the game other than from the penalty bench shall constitute an illegal substitution under Rule **68** – Illegal Substitution calling for a bench minor penalty.

Furthermore, if the team fails to place a player on the penalty bench to return to the ice at the end of the major penalty, they continued to play short-handed but are not permitted to ice the puck as they are no longer short-handed by reason of a penalty.

20.4 **Automatic Game Misconduct** – An automatic game misconduct shall be applied to any player who has been assessed a third major penalty in the same game.

An automatic game misconduct shall also be applicable whenever a player is assessed a major penalty for any of the infractions listed in the Reference Tables – Table 6 – Summary of Major Penalties that Result in an Automatic Game Misconduct (page 136). See specific rule numbers for complete descriptions.

When a player has been assessed a major penalty for any of the infractions listed in the Reference Tables – Table 7 – Summary of Major Penalties that Result in an Automatic Game Misconduct When There is an Injury to the Face or Head (page 137) and his opponent has suffered an injury to the face or head, a game misconduct must also be assessed. See specific rule numbers for complete descriptions.

When a major and automatic game misconduct are assessed, the player shall be ruled off the ice for the balance of the game, but a substitute shall be permitted to replace the player so suspended after five (5) minutes have elapsed.

20.5 **Fines** - An automatic fine of one hundred dollars ($100) shall also be added when a major penalty is imposed for any foul causing injury to the face or head of an opponent by means of a stick.

When a player is assessed a major penalty plus a game misconduct as outlined in **20.4** above, he also receives an automatic fine of two hundred dollars ($200).

20.6 **Infractions** – Refer to the Reference Tables – Table 5 – Summary of Major Penalties (page 136) for a list of the infractions that can result in a major penalty being assessed (see specific rule numbers for complete descriptions).

## Rule 21 – Match Penalties

21.1 **Match Penalty** - A match penalty involves the suspension of a player for the balance of the game and the offender shall be ordered to the dressing room immediately.

A match penalty shall be imposed on any player who deliberately attempts to injure or who deliberately injures an opponent in any manner.

21.2 **Short-handed** - A substitute player is permitted to replace the penalized player after five (5) minutes playing time has elapsed.

The match penalty, plus any additional penalties, shall be served by a player (excluding a goalkeeper) to be designated by the Manager or Coach of the offending team through the playing Captain, such player to take his place in the penalty box immediately.

For all match penalties, regardless of when imposed, or prescribed additional penalties, a total of ten minutes shall be charged in the records against the offending player.

In addition to the match penalty, the player shall be automatically suspended from further competition until the Commissioner has ruled on the issue. See also Rule **28** – Supplementary Discipline.

21.3 **Reports** - The Referee is required to report all match penalties and the surrounding circumstances to the Commissioner of the League immediately following the game in which they occur.

21.4 **Infractions** – Refer to the Reference Tables – Table 8 – Summary of Match Penalties (page 137) for a list of the infractions that can result in a match penalty being assessed (see specific rule numbers for complete descriptions).

## Rule 22 – Misconduct Penalties

22.1 **Misconduct Penalty** - In the event of misconduct penalties to any players except the goalkeeper, the players shall be ruled off the ice for a period of ten (10) minutes each. A substitute player is permitted to immediately replace a player serving a misconduct penalty. A player whose misconduct penalty has expired shall remain in the penalty box until the next stoppage of play.

22.2 **Misconduct Penalty – Goalkeeper** - Should a goalkeeper on the ice incur a misconduct penalty, this penalty shall be served by another member of his team who was on the ice when the offense was committed. This player is to be designated by the Manager or Coach of the offending team through the Captain.

22.3 **Short-handed** – A player receiving a misconduct penalty does not cause his team to play short-handed unless he also receives a minor, major or match penalty in addition to the misconduct penalty.

When a player receives a minor penalty and a misconduct penalty at the same time, the penalized team shall immediately put a substitute player on the penalty bench and he shall serve the minor penalty without change. Should the opposing team score during the time the minor penalty is being served, the minor penalty shall terminate (unless **15.4** is applicable) and the misconduct to the originally penalized player shall commence immediately.

When a player receives a major penalty and a misconduct penalty at the same time, the penalized team shall place a substitute player on the penalty bench before the major penalty expires and no replacement for the penalized player shall be permitted to enter the game except from the penalty bench.

22.4 **Reporting** – All misconduct penalties assessed for abuse of officials must be reported in detail to the League office.

22.5 **Fines** - A misconduct penalty imposed on any player at any time shall be accompanied with an automatic fine of one hundred dollars ($100).

22.6 **Infractions** – Refer to the Reference Tables – Table 9 – Summary of Misconduct Penalties (page 138) for a list of the infractions that can result in a misconduct penalty being assessed (see specific rule numbers for complete descriptions).

## Rule 23 – Game Misconduct Penalties

23.1 **Game Misconduct Penalty** - A game misconduct penalty involves the suspension of a player for the balance of the game but a substitute is permitted to replace immediately the player so removed. Ten minutes are applied in the league records to the player incurring a game misconduct penalty.

23.2 **Fines and Suspensions** - A player incurring a game misconduct penalty shall incur an automatic fine of two hundred dollars ($200) and the case shall be reported to the Commissioner who shall have full power to impose such further penalties by way of suspension or fine on the penalized player or any other player involved in the altercation.

Any game misconduct penalty for which a player has been assessed an automatic suspension or supplementary discipline in the form of game suspension(s) by the Commissioner shall not be taken into account when calculating the total number of offenses under this subsection.

The automatic suspensions incurred under this subsection in respect to League games shall have no effect with respect to violations during Playoff games.

Any request by a Club to have a game misconduct reviewed and rescinded by the League must submit their request in writing to the League's Hockey Operations Department within 48 hours of the conclusion of the game in which the game misconduct was assessed. Failure to submit the written request within this time frame will automatically result in the game misconduct being upheld and no further review of the incident will be considered or entertained. This does not apply to infractions addressed under Rule **28** – Supplementary Discipline.

23.3 **Fines and Suspensions – General Category** - In regular League games, any player who incurs a total of three (3) game misconduct penalties in the "General Category" and exclusive of other designated categories, shall be suspended for the next League game of his team. For each subsequent game misconduct penalty, the automatic suspension shall be increased by one game. For each suspension of a player or goalkeeper, his Club shall be fined one thousand dollars ($1,000).

In Playoff games, any player who incurs a total of two game misconduct penalties in the "General Category" shall be suspended automatically for the next Playoff game of his team. For each subsequent game misconduct penalty during the Playoffs, the automatic suspension shall be increased by one game. For each suspension of a player during Playoffs, his club shall be fined one thousand dollars ($1,000).

*General Category*

| | | |
|---|---|---|
| *(i)* | *Fighting off the playing surface* | *Rule 46* |
| *(ii)* | *Inciting an opponent into incurring a penalty* | *Rule 75* |
| *(iii)* | *Intervening in an altercation* | *Rule 46* |
| *(iv)* | *Not properly tied down during an altercation* | *Rule 46* |
| *(v)* | *Obscene language or gestures* | *Rule 75* |
| *(vi)* | *Persists in continuing an altercation* | *Rule 46* |
| *(vii)* | *Removing jersey prior to an altercation* | *Rule 46* |
| *(viii)* | *Secondary altercation* | *Rule 46* |
| *(ix)* | *Third major penalty in a game* | *Rule 20* |
| *(x)* | *Throwing stick outside playing area* | *Rule 53* |

23.4 **Fines and Suspensions – Abuse of Officials Category** - In regular season League or Playoff games, any player who incurs a total of two (2) game misconduct penalties for abuse of officials related infractions penalized under Rule **39** - Abuse of Officials, shall be suspended automatically for the next League or Playoff game of his team. For each subsequent game misconduct penalty, the automatic suspension shall be increased by one game.

23.5 **Fines and Suspensions – Stick Infractions Category** - In regular season League games, any player who incurs a total of two (2) game misconduct penalties for stick-related infractions in the "Stick Infractions Category", before playing in 41 consecutive regular season

League games without such penalty, shall be suspended automatically for the next regular season League game of his team. For each subsequent game misconduct penalty, the automatic suspension shall be increased by one game.

In Playoff games any player who incurs a total of two (2) game misconduct penalties in the "Stick Infractions Category", shall be suspended automatically for the next Playoff game of his team. For each subsequent game misconduct penalty in this category during the Playoffs the automatic suspension shall be increased by one game.

Prior to the commencement of each Stanley Cup Finals, a player will have his current "Stick Infractions Category" game misconducts removed from his current playoff record. They will remain part of his historical record.

*Stick Infractions Category*

| | | |
|---|---|---|
| *(i)* | *Butt-ending* | *Rule 58* |
| *(ii)* | *Cross-checking* | *Rule 59* |
| *(iii)* | *Hooking* | *Rule 55* |
| *(iv)* | *Slashing* | *Rule 61* |
| *(v)* | *Spearing* | *Rule 62* |

When a player has played in 41 consecutive regular season League games without being assessed a stick-related major and a game misconduct penalty in the "Stick Infractions Category", he will have the previous game misconduct penalties removed from his current record. They will remain part of his historical record.

A player's total games played will cover a two-year time period from the date of the first game misconduct penalty for each category of foul.

23.6 **Fines and Suspensions – Physical Fouls Category** – In regular season League games, any player who incurs a total of two (2) game misconduct penalties in the "Physical Fouls Category", before playing in 41 consecutive regular season League games without such penalty, shall be suspended automatically for the next League game of his team. For each subsequent game misconduct penalty, the automatic suspension shall be increased by one game.

In Playoff games, any player who incurs a total of two (2) game misconduct penalties in the "Physical Fouls Category" shall be suspended automatically for the next Playoff game of his team. For each subsequent game misconduct penalty in this category during the Playoffs the automatic suspension shall be increased by one game.

Prior to the commencement of each Stanley Cup Finals, a player will have his current "Physical Fouls Category" game misconducts removed from his current playoff record. They will remain part of his historical record.

*Physical Fouls Category*

| | | |
|---|---|---|
| *(i)* | *Boarding* | *Rule 41* |
| *(ii)* | *Charging* | *Rule 42* |
| *(iii)* | *Checking from Behind* | *Rule 43* |
| *(iv)* | *Clipping* | *Rule 44* |
| *(v)* | *Elbowing* | *Rule 45* |
| *(vi)* | *Head-butting* | *Rule 47* |
| *(vii)* | *Interference* | *Rule 56* |
| *(viii)* | *Kneeing* | *Rule 50* |

When a player has played in 41 consecutive regular League games without being assessed a major and a game misconduct in the "Physical Fouls Category", he will have the previous game misconduct penalties removed from his current record. They will remain part of his historical record.

A player's total games played will cover a two-year time period from the date of the first game misconduct penalty for each category of foul.

23.7 **Automatic Game Misconduct** – See **20.4**.

23.8 **Other Infractions That Could Result in a Game Misconduct** – Refer to the Reference Tables – Table 10 – Summary of Game Misconduct Penalties (page 139) for a list of the infractions that can result in a game misconduct penalty being assessed (see specific rule numbers for complete descriptions).

In addition, the following list of infractions can also result in a game misconduct penalty being assessed:

*(i) interfering with or striking a spectator.*

*(ii) racial taunts or slurs*

*(iii) spitting on or at an opponent or spectator*

Any player or non-playing Club personnel who physically interferes with the spectators, becomes involved in an altercation with a spectator, or throws any object at a spectator, shall automatically incur a game misconduct penalty and the Referee shall report all such infractions to the Commissioner who shall have full power to impose such further penalty as he shall deem appropriate.

## Rule 24 – Penalty Shot

24.1 **Penalty Shot** – A penalty shot is designed to restore a scoring opportunity which was lost as a result of a foul being committed by the offending team, based on the parameters set out in these rules.

24.2 **Procedure** - The Referee shall ask to have announced over the public address system the name of the player designated by him or selected by the team entitled to take the shot (as appropriate). He shall then place the puck on the center face-off spot and the player taking the shot will, on the instruction of the Referee (by blowing his whistle), play the puck from there and shall attempt to score on the goalkeeper. The puck must be kept in motion towards the opponent's goal line and once it is shot, the play shall be considered complete. No goal can be scored on a rebound of any kind (an exception being the puck off the goal post or crossbar, then the goalkeeper and then directly into the goal), and any time the puck crosses the goal line or comes to a complete stop, the shot shall be considered complete.

The lacrosse-like move whereby the puck is picked up on the blade of the stick and "whipped" into the net shall be permitted provided the puck is not raised above the height of the shoulders at any time and when released, is not carried higher than the crossbar. See also **80.1**.

The spin-o-rama type move where the player completes a 360° turn as he approaches the goal, shall not be permitted. Should a player perform such a move during the penalty shot, the shot shall be stopped by the Referee and no goal will be the result.

Only a player designated as a goalkeeper or alternate goalkeeper may defend against the penalty shot.

The goalkeeper must remain in his crease until the player taking the penalty shot has touched the puck.

If at the time a penalty shot is awarded, the goalkeeper of the penalized team has been removed from the ice to substitute another player, the goalkeeper shall be permitted to return to the ice before the penalty shot is taken.

The team against whom the penalty shot has been assessed may replace their goalkeeper to defend against the penalty shot, however, the substitute goalkeeper is required to remain in the game until the next stoppage of play.

While the penalty shot is being taken, players of both sides shall withdraw to the sides of the rink and in front of their own player's bench.

24.3 **Designated Player** – In cases where a penalty shot has been awarded to a player specifically fouled, that player shall be designated by the Referee to take the penalty shot.

In all other cases where a penalty shot has been awarded, the penalty shot shall be taken by a player selected by the Captain of the non-offending team from the players on the ice at the time when the foul was committed. Such selection shall be reported to the Referee and cannot be changed.

If by reason of injury, the player designated by the Referee to take the penalty shot is unable to do so within a reasonable time, the shot may be taken by a player selected by the Captain of the non-offending team from the players on the ice when the foul was committed. Such selection shall be reported to the Referee and cannot be changed.

Should the player in respect to whom a penalty shot has been awarded himself commit a foul in connection with the same play or circumstances, either before or after the penalty shot has been awarded, be designated to take the shot, he shall first be permitted to do so before being sent to the penalty bench to serve the penalty except when such penalty is for a game misconduct or match penalty in which case the penalty shot shall be taken by a player selected by the Captain of the non-offending team from the players on the ice at the time when the foul was committed.

24.4 **Violations During the Shot** – Should the goalkeeper leave his crease prior to the player taking the penalty shot has touched the puck, and in the event of violation of this rule or any foul committed by a goalkeeper, the Referee shall allow the shot to be taken and if the shot fails, he shall permit the penalty shot to be taken over again. When an infraction worthy of a minor penalty is committed by the goalkeeper during the penalty shot that causes the shot to fail, no penalty is to be assessed but the Referee shall permit the shot to be taken over again. Should a goalkeeper commit a second violation during the penalty shot and the shot fails, he shall be assessed a misconduct penalty and the Referee shall permit the penalty shot to be taken over again. A third such violation shall result in the goalkeeper being assessed a game misconduct penalty.

When a major or match penalty is committed by the goalkeeper that causes the shot to fail, the Referee shall permit the shot to be taken over again and the appropriate penalties shall be assessed to the goalkeeper.

The goalkeeper may attempt to stop the shot in any manner except by throwing his stick or any object, or by deliberately dislodging the goal, in which case a goal shall be awarded.

During the shot, should the goalkeeper, in an attempt at making a save, dislodge the goal accidentally, the Referee shall make one of the following determinations:

*(i) Award a goal if he deems the player would have scored into the area normally occupied by the net had it not been dislodged.*

*(ii) Allow the shot to be re-taken if he does not score or it could not be determined if the puck would have entered the area normally occupied by the net.*

*(iii) If the goal becomes dislodged after the puck has crossed the goal line thus ending the shot, the above determinations do not apply, the shot is complete.*

If, while the penalty shot is being taken, any player, Coach or non-playing Club personnel of the opposing team shall have by some action interfered with or distracted the player taking the shot and, because of such action, the shot should have failed, a second attempt shall be permitted and the Referee shall impose a bench minor penalty to the offending team, and if a player on the bench is responsible, a misconduct penalty on the player so interfering or distracting shall be assessed. When a Coach or non-playing Club personnel is guilty of such an act, he shall be automatically suspended from the game, ordered to the dressing room and the matter will be reported to the Commissioner for possible further disciplinary action.

If, while the penalty shot is being taken, any player, goalkeeper, Coach or non-playing Club personnel of the team taking the shot shall have by some action interfered with or distracted the goalkeeper defending the shot and, because of such action, the shot was successful, the Referee shall rule no goal and shall impose a bench minor penalty to the offending team, and if a player or goalkeeper on the bench is responsible, a misconduct penalty on the player or goalkeeper so interfering or distracting shall be assessed. When a Coach or non-playing Club personnel is guilty of such an act, he shall be automatically suspended from the game, ordered to the dressing room and the matter will be reported to the Commissioner for possible further disciplinary action.

If, while the penalty shot is being taken, a spectator throws any object onto the ice or, in the judgment of the Referee, interferes with the player taking the shot or the goalkeeper defending the shot, he shall permit the shot be taken again.

If, after a player's stick has been ruled illegal, he attempts to take a penalty shot with a second stick that is also ruled illegal prior to taking the penalty shot, the opportunity to take the penalty shot shall be disallowed. The player shall be assessed one minor penalty for the first illegal stick.

24.5 **Face-Off Location** - If a goal is scored from a penalty shot, the puck shall be faced-off at center ice. If a goal is not scored, the puck shall be faced-off at either of the end face-off spots in the zone in which the penalty shot was tried, except when another rule dictates the face-off location should be in an alternate location, such as when the point men enter the zone beyond the outer edge of the end zone face-off circle or when the attacking team has been penalized on the same play (see Rule **76.2**).

24.6 **Results** - Should a goal be scored from a penalty shot, a further penalty to the offending player or goalkeeper shall not be applied unless the offense for which the penalty shot was awarded was such as to incur a major, match or misconduct penalty, in which case the penalty prescribed for the particular offense shall be imposed.

If the offense for which the penalty shot was awarded was such as to normally incur a minor penalty, then regardless of whether the penalty shot results in a goal or not, no further minor penalty shall be served.

If the offense for which the penalty shot was awarded was such as to incur a double-minor penalty, or where the offending team is assessed an additional minor penalty on the same play in which a penalty shot was awarded, the first minor penalty is not assessed since the penalty shot was awarded to restore the lost scoring opportunity. The second minor penalty would be assessed and served regardless of whether the penalty shot results in a goal. This will be announced as a double-minor penalty for the appropriate foul and the player will serve two (2) minutes only.

No penalty shall expire when a goal is scored against a team on a penalty shot.

Should two penalty shots be awarded to the same team at the same stoppage of play (two separate fouls), only one goal can be scored or awarded at a single stoppage of play. Should the first penalty shot result in a goal, the second shot would not be taken but the appropriate penalty would be assessed and served for the infraction committed.

24.7 **Timing** - If the foul upon which the penalty shot is based occurs during actual playing time, the penalty shot shall be awarded and taken immediately in the usual manner notwithstanding any delay occasioned by a slow whistle by the Referee to allow play to continue until the attacking side has lost possession of the puck to the defending side, which delay results in the expiry of the regular playing time in any period.

The time required for the taking of a penalty shot shall not be included in the regular playing time or overtime.

24.8 **Infractions** – Refer to the Reference Tables – Table 11 – Summary of Penalty Shots (page 140) for a list of the infractions that shall result in a penalty shot being awarded (see specific rule numbers for complete descriptions).

There are four (4) specific conditions that must be met in order for the Referee to award a penalty shot for a player being fouled from behind. They are:

*(i) The infraction must have taken place in the neutral zone or attacking zone, (i.e. over the puck carrier's own blue line);*

*(ii) The infraction must have been committed from behind;*

*(iii) The player in possession and control (or, in the judgment of the Referee, clearly would have obtained possession and control of the puck) must have been denied a reasonable chance to score (the fact that he got a shot off does not automatically eliminate this play from the penalty shot consideration criteria. If the foul was from behind and he was denied a "more" reasonable scoring opportunity due to the foul, then the penalty shot should be awarded);*

*(iv) The player in possession and control (or, in the judgment of the Referee, clearly would have obtained possession and control of the puck) must have had no opposing player between himself and the goalkeeper.*

## Rule 25 – Awarded Goals

25.1 **Awarded Goal –** A goal will be awarded to the attacking team when the opposing team has taken their goalkeeper off the ice and an attacking player has possession and control of the puck in the neutral or attacking zone, without a defending player between himself and the opposing goal, and he is prevented from scoring as a result of an infraction committed by the defending team (see **25.3** Infractions – When Goalkeeper is Off the Ice, below).

25.2 **Infractions – When Goalkeeper is On the Ice** – A goal will be awarded when an attacking player, in the act of shooting the puck into the goal (between the normal position of the posts and completely across the goal line), is prevented from scoring as a result of a defending player or goalkeeper displacing the goal post, either deliberately or accidentally.

25.3 **Infractions – When Goalkeeper is Off the Ice** – Refer to the Reference Tables – Table 12 – Summary of Awarded Goals (When Goalkeeper has been Removed for an Extra Attacker) (page 140) for a list of the infractions that shall result in an awarded goal being awarded when the goalkeeper has been removed for an extra attacker (see specific rule numbers for complete descriptions).

25.4 **Infractions – During the Course of a Penalty Shot** - A goal will be awarded when a goalkeeper attempts to stop a penalty shot by throwing his stick or any other object at the player taking the shot or by dislodging the goal (either deliberately or accidentally) (see Rule **63.6**).

## Rule 26 – Delayed Penalties

26.1 **Delayed Penalty** - If a third player of any team shall be penalized while two players of the same team are serving penalties, the penalty time of the third player shall not commence until the penalty time of one of the two players already penalized has elapsed. Nevertheless, the third penalized player must at once proceed to the penalty bench. He may be substituted for on the ice so as to keep the on-ice strength at no less than three skaters for his team.

26.2 **Penalty Expiration** - When any team shall have three players serving penalties at the same time and because of the delayed penalty rule, a substitute for the third offender is on the ice, none of the three penalized players on the penalty bench may return to the ice until play has stopped. When play has been stopped, the player whose full penalty has expired may return to the ice.

During the play, the Penalty Timekeeper shall permit the return to the ice of the penalized players, in the order of expiry of their penalties, but only when the penalized team is entitled to have more than four players on the ice. Otherwise, these players must wait until the first stoppage of play after the expiration of their penalties in order to be released from the penalty bench.

When the penalties of two players of the same team will expire at the same time, the Captain of that team will designate to the Referee which of such players will return to the ice first and the Referee will instruct the Penalty Timekeeper accordingly (this is done to expedite the release of a player from the penalty bench when the opposing team scores on the power-play).

26.3 **Major and Minor Penalty** - When a major and a minor penalty are imposed at the same time on different players of the same team, the Penalty Timekeeper shall record the minor as being the first of such penalties.

## Rule 27 – Goalkeeper's Penalties

27.1 **Minor Penalty to Goalkeeper** – A goalkeeper shall not be sent to the penalty bench for an offense which incurs a minor penalty, but instead, the minor penalty shall be served by another member of his team who was on the ice when the offense was committed. This player is to be designated by the Manager or Coach of the offending team through the playing Captain and such substitute shall not be changed.

A penalized player may not serve a goalkeeper's penalty.

If the goalkeeper is involved in coincidental penalties being assessed and as a result, his team is required to play shorthanded due to additional penalties assessed to the goalkeeper, the player designated to serve the additional time penalties assessed to the goalkeeper may be any player as designated by the Manager or Coach of the offending team through the playing Captain.

27.2 **Major Penalty to Goalkeeper** – A goalkeeper shall not be sent to the penalty bench for an offense which incurs a major penalty, but instead, the major penalty shall be served immediately by another member of his team who was on the ice when the offense was committed. This player is to be designated by the Manager or Coach of the offending team through the playing Captain and such substitute shall not be changed.

When a goalkeeper is assessed a major penalty plus a game misconduct, which is coincidental with a major or match penalty to the opposing team, no player is required to serve the goalkeeper's penalties in the penalty box, since he has been ejected from the game.

Should a goalkeeper incur three major penalties in one game, he shall be ruled off the ice for the balance of the playing time and his place shall be taken by a member of his own Club, or by a regular substitute goalkeeper who is available. Such player will be allowed the goalkeeper's equipment. (Major penalty plus game misconduct penalty and automatic fine of two hundred dollars ($200).)

27.3 **Misconduct Penalty to Goalkeeper** – Should a goalkeeper on the ice incur a misconduct penalty, this penalty shall be served by another member of his team who was on the ice when the offense was committed. This player is to be designated by the Manager or Coach of the offending team through the Captain and, in addition, the goalkeeper shall be fined one hundred dollars ($100).

27.4 **Game Misconduct Penalty to Goalkeeper** – Should a goalkeeper incur a game misconduct penalty, his place will then be taken by a member of his own Club, or by a regular substitute goalkeeper who is available, and such player will be allowed the goalkeeper's full equipment. In addition, the goalkeeper shall be fined two hundred dollars ($200).

27.5 **Match Penalty to Goalkeeper** – Should a goalkeeper incur a match penalty, his place will then be taken by a member of his own Club, or by a substitute goalkeeper who is available, and such player will be allowed the goalkeeper's full equipment.

The match penalty, and any additional penalties assessed to the goalkeeper, shall be served immediately by a member of the team on the ice when the offenses were committed. This player shall be designated by the Manager or Coach of the offending team through the Captain. However, when the match penalty is coincidental with a match or major penalty to the opposing team, no player is required to proceed to the penalty bench to serve the goalkeeper's match penalty.

27.6 **Leaving Goal Crease** – A minor penalty shall be imposed on a goalkeeper who leaves the immediate vicinity of his crease during an altercation. In addition, he shall be subject to a fine of two hundred dollars ($200) and this incident shall be reported to the Commissioner for such further disciplinary action as may be required. However, should the altercation occur in or near the goalkeeper's crease, the Referee should direct the goalkeeper to a neutral location and not assess a penalty for leaving the immediate vicinity of the goal crease. Equally, if the goalkeeper is legitimately outside the immediate vicinity of the goal crease for the purpose of proceeding to the players' bench to be substituted for an extra attacker, and he subsequently becomes involved in an altercation, the minor penalty for leaving the crease would not be assessed.

In addition, during stoppages of play in the game, he must not proceed to his players' bench for the purpose of receiving a replacement stick or equipment or repairs thereto, or due to an injury, or to receive instructions, without first obtaining permission to do so from the Referee. Otherwise, he must be replaced by the substitute goalkeeper immediately (without any delay) or be assessed a bench minor penalty for delay of game.

27.7 **Participating in the Play Over the Center Red Line** - If a goalkeeper participates in the play in any manner (intentionally plays the puck or checks an opponent) when he is beyond the center red line, a minor penalty shall be imposed upon him. The position of the puck is the determining factor for the application of this rule.

27.8 **Restricted Area** – A goalkeeper shall not play the puck outside of the designated area behind the net. This area shall be defined by lines that begin six feet (6') from either goal post and extend diagonally to points twenty-eight feet (28') apart at the end boards. Should the goalkeeper play the puck outside of the designated area behind the goal line, a minor penalty for delay of game shall be imposed. The determining factor shall be the position of the puck. The minor penalty will not be assessed when a goalkeeper plays the puck while maintaining skate contact with his goal crease.

27.9 **Infractions – Unique to Goalkeepers** – Refer to the Reference Tables – Table 13 – Summary of Goalkeeper Penalties (page 141) for a list of the infractions that shall result in a penalty to the goalkeeper (see specific rule numbers for complete descriptions).

## Rule 28 – Supplementary Discipline

28.1 **Supplementary Discipline** - In addition to the automatic fines and suspensions imposed under these rules, the Commissioner may, at his discretion, investigate any incident that occurs in connection with any Pre-season, Exhibition, League or Playoff game and may assess additional fines and/or suspensions for any offense committed during the course of a game or any aftermath thereof by a player, goalkeeper, Trainer, Manager, Coach or non-playing Club personnel or Club executive, whether or not such offense has been penalized by the Referee.

If an investigation is requested by a Club or by the League on its own initiative, it must be initiated within twenty-four (24) hours following the completion of the game in which the incident occurred.

28.2 **Pre-Season and Exhibition Games** - Whenever suspensions are imposed as a result of infractions occurring during pre-season and exhibition games, the Commissioner shall exercise his discretion in scheduling the suspensions to ensure that no team shall be short more players in any regular League game than it would have been had the infractions occurred in regular League games.

## Rule 29 – Signals

| | | | |
|---|---|---|---|
| 29.1 | Boarding | Striking the clenched fist of one hand into the open palm of the opposite hand in front of the chest. |  |
| 29.2 | Butt-ending | Moving the forearm, fist closed, under the forearm of the other hand held palm down. | |
| 29.3 | Charging | Rotating clenched fists around one another in front of the chest. |  |
| 29.4 | Checking from behind | A forward motion of both arms, with the palms of the hands open and facing away from the body, fully extended from the chest at shoulder level. |  |

| | | | |
|---|---|---|---|
| 29.5 | Clipping | Striking leg with either hand behind the knee, keeping both skates on the ice. |  |
| 29.6 | Cross-checking | A forward and backward motion of the arms with both fists clenched, extending from the chest for a distance of about one foot. |  |
| 29.7 | Delayed off-side | Non-whistle arm fully extended above the head. To nullify a delayed off-side, the Linesman shall drop the arm to the side. |  |
| 29.8 | Delayed penalty | Extending the non-whistle arm fully above the head. |  |
| 29.9 | Delaying the game | The non-whistle hand, palm open, is placed across the chest and then fully extended directly in front of the body. |  |
| 29.10 | Elbowing | Tapping either elbow with the opposite hand. |  |
| 29.11 | Goal scored | A single point directed at the goal in which the puck legally entered. |  |

| | | | |
|---|---|---|---|
| 29.12 | Hand pass | With the palm open and facing forward, a pushing motion towards the front of the body once or twice to indicate the puck was moved ahead with the hand. |  |
| 29.13 | Head-butting | No signal in the National Hockey League. | NO SIGNAL |
| 29.14 | High-sticking | Holding both fists clenched, one slightly above the other (as if holding a stick) at the height of the forehead. |  |
| 29.15 | Holding | Clasping either wrist with the other hand in front of the chest. |  |
| 29.16 | Holding the stick | Two stage signal involving the holding signal (29.15) followed by a signal indicating you are holding onto a stick with two hands in a normal manner. |  |
| 29.17 | Hooking | A tugging motion with both arms as if pulling something from in front toward the stomach. |  |
| 29.18 | Icing (a) | The back Linesman signals a possible icing by fully extending either arm over his head. The arm should remain raised until the front Linesman either blows the whistle to indicate an icing or until the icing is washed out |  |

| | | | |
|---|---|---|---|
| | Icing (b) | Once the icing has been completed, the back Linesman will then point to the appropriate face-off spot and skate to it, turning backwards somewhere near the blue line and crossing his arms across his chest to indicate icing. |  |
| 29.19 | Illegal check to the head | Patting flat (open palm) of the non-whistle hand on this side of the head. |  |
| 29.20 | Interference | Crossing arms stationary in front of the chest in an "X" formation. |  |
| 29.21 | Kicking | No signal in the National Hockey League. | NO SIGNAL |
| 29.22 | Kneeing | Slapping either knee with the palm of the hand, while keeping both skates on the ice. |  |
| 29.23 | Match penalty | No signal in the National Hockey League. | NO SIGNAL |
| 29.24 | Misconduct | Both hands on hips. |  |

| | | | |
|---|---|---|---|
| 29.25 | Penalty shot | Non-whistle arm fully extended pointing to the center ice face-off spot. | |
| 29.26 | Roughing | Fist clenched and arm extended out to the side of the body. | |
| 29.27 | Slashing | A chopping motion with the edge of one hand across the opposite forearm. | |
| 29.28 | Spearing | Jabbing motion with both hands thrust out immediately in front of the body and then hands dropped to the side of the body (essentially the opposite to the hooking signal – away from the body rather than towards the body). |  |
| 29.29 | Throwing equipment | No signal in the National Hockey League. | NO SIGNAL |
| 29.30 | Time-out | Using both hands to form a "T" in front of the chest. |  |
| 29.31 | Too many men on the ice | No signal in the National Hockey League. | NO SIGNAL |

| | | | |
|---|---|---|---|
| 29.32 | Tripping | Striking leg with either hand below the knee, keeping both skates on the ice. |  |
| 29.33 | Unsports-manlike conduct | Using both hands to form a "T" in front of the chest (same as time-out). |  |
| 29.34 | Wash out | A sweeping sideways motion of both arms across the front of the body at shoulder level with palms down. This signal is used by Referees to signal no goal; by the Linesmen to signal no icing and no off-side; and by all Officials to wash out a hand pass or a high-sticking the puck violation. |  |

# SECTION 5 - OFFICIALS

## Rule 30 – Appointment of Officials

30.1 **Appointment of Officials by Commissioner** - The Commissioner shall appoint the Referees, the Linesmen, Video Goal Judge and all Off-ice Officials for each game.

The Commissioner shall forward to all Clubs a list of Referees, Linesmen, and Off-ice Officials, all of whom must be treated with proper respect at all times during the season by all players and officials of Clubs.

## Rule 31 – Referees

31.1 **Attire and Equipment** - All Referees shall be dressed in black trousers, official sweaters and a League-approved black helmet.

They shall be equipped with approved whistles, tape measure and an official stick-measuring gauge.

31.2 **Disputes** - The Referees shall have general supervision of the game and shall have full control of all game officials and players during the game, including stoppages; and in case of any dispute, their decision shall be final.

As there is a human factor involved in blowing the whistle to stop play, the Referee may deem the play to be stopped slightly prior to the whistle actually being blown. The fact that the puck may come loose or cross the goal line prior to the sound of the whistle has no bearing if the Referee has ruled that the play had been stopped prior to this happening.

In the event of any dispute regarding time or the expiration of penalties, the matter shall be referred to the Referee for adjustment and his decision shall be final. He may use the Video Goal Judge to assist in rendering the final decision. See Rule **38** – Video Goal Judge.

31.3 **Face-offs** – One of the Referees shall face-off the puck to start each period and following the scoring of a goal. Linesmen are responsible for all other face-offs.

31.4 **General Duties** - It shall be the duty of the Referees to impose such penalties as are prescribed by the rules for infractions thereof and they shall give the final decision in matters of disputed goals. The Referees may consult with the Linesmen, Goal Judge or Video Goal Judge before making their decision.

The Referees shall not halt the game for any infractions of the rules concerning Rule **83** - Off-side, or any violation of Rule **81** - Icing. Determining infractions of these rules is the duty of the Linesmen unless, by virtue of some accident, the Linesman is prevented from doing so in which case the duties of the Linesman shall be assumed by a Referee until play is stopped.

31.5 **Goals** - The Referees shall have announced over the public address system information regarding the legality of an apparent goal. The

Official Scorer, with the assistance of the Video Goal Judge, will confirm the goal scorer and any players deserving of an assist. See also Rule **78** – Goals.

The Referees shall have announced over the public address system the reason for not allowing a goal every time the goal signal light is turned on in the course of play. This shall be done at the first stoppage of play regardless of any standard signal given by the Referees when the goal signal light was put on in error.

The Referees shall report to the Official Scorer the name or number of the goal scorer but he shall not give any information or advice with respect to the awarding of assists.

The name of the scorer and any player entitled to an assist will be announced over the public address system. In the event that the Referee disallows a goal for any violation of the rules, he shall report the reason for the disallowance to the Official Scorer who shall have announced the Referee's decision correctly over the public address system.

31.6 **Off-ice Officials** - The Referees shall, before starting the game, see that the appointed off-ice officials, including the Game Timekeeper and the Goal Judges are in their respective places and ensure that the timing and signaling equipment are in order.

31.7 **Penalties** - The infraction of the rules for which each penalty has been imposed will be announced correctly, as reported by the Referee, over the public address system. Where players of both teams are penalized on the same play, the penalty to the visiting player will be announced first.

When a penalty is imposed by the Referee which calls for a mandatory or automatic fine, only the time portion of the penalty will be reported by the Referee to the Official Scorer and announced over the public address system, and the fine will be collected through the League office.

31.8 **Players' Uniforms** - It shall be the duty of the Referees to see to it that all players are properly dressed, and that the approved regulation equipment (including the approved on-ice branded exposure program) is in use at all times during the game.

31.9 **Reports** - The Referee shall report to the Commissioner promptly and in detail the circumstances surrounding the following:

*(i) The assessment of misconduct penalties for abuse of officials;*
*(ii) The assessment of game misconduct penalties;*
*(iii) The assessment of match penalties;*
*(iv) The assessment of an instigator penalty;*
*(v) Any time a goalkeeper leaves his crease during an altercation;*
*(vi) Any time a stick or other object is thrown outside the playing area;*
*(vii) Any time a player, goalkeeper or non-playing Club personnel are involved in an altercation with a spectator;*
*(viii) Any unusual occurrence that takes place on or off the ice, before, during or after the game.*

31.10 **Start and End of Game and Periods** - The Referees shall order the teams on the ice at the appointed time for the beginning of a game and at the commencement of each period. If for any reason, there is more than a fifteen (15) minute delay in the commencement of the game or any undue delay in resuming play after the League approved intermission length between periods, the Referees shall state in their report to the Commissioner the cause of the delay and the Club or Clubs which were at fault.

The Referees shall remain on the ice at the conclusion of each period until all players have proceeded to their dressing rooms.

The Referees shall check club rosters and all players in uniform before signing the Official Report of Match form.

31.11 **Unable to Continue** - Should a Referee accidentally leave the ice or receive an injury which incapacitates him from discharging his duties while play is in progress, the game shall be automatically stopped. If the Referee is unable to continue, the game shall continue using the one Referee, two Linesmen system.

If, owing to illness or accident, one of the Referees is unable to continue to officiate, the remaining Referee shall perform the duties of the ill or injured Referee during the balance of the game. In the event that a member of the League's Hockey Operations or Officiating departments is in attendance at a game where a spare official is present, he shall have the authority to substitute the injured Referee with the spare official.

If, through misadventure or sickness, the Referees and Linesmen appointed are prevented from appearing, the League will make every attempt to find suitable replacement officials, otherwise, the Managers or Coaches of the two Clubs shall agree on Referee(s) and Linesman(men). If they are unable to agree, they shall appoint a player from each side who shall act as Referee and Linesman; the player of the home Club acting as Referee and the player of the visiting Club as Linesman.

If the regularly appointed officials appear during the progress of the game, they shall at once replace the temporary officials.

## Rule 32 – Linesmen

32.1 **Attire and Equipment** – All Linesmen shall be dressed in black trousers, official sweaters and a League-approved black helmet.

They shall be equipped with approved whistles, tape measure and an official stick-measuring gauge.

32.2 **Face-offs** - The Linesman shall face-off the puck at all times except at the start of each period and following the scoring of a goal.

32.3 **General Duties –** The Linesmen are generally responsible for calling violations of off-side (Rule **83**) and icing (Rule **81**). They may stop play for a variety of other situations as noted in sections **32.4** and **33.5** below.

32.4 **Reporting to Referee** - The Linesman shall give to the Referees his interpretation of any incident that may have taken place during the game.

The Linesman may stop play and report what he witnessed to the Referees when:

| | | |
|---|---|---|
| *(i)* | *There are too many men on the ice* | *Rule 74* |
| *(ii)* | *Articles are thrown on the ice from the players' bench or penalty bench* | *Rule 75* |
| *(iii)* | *When team personnel interfere with a game official* | *Rule 39* |
| *(iv)* | *When a player who has lost or broken his stick receives one illegally* | *Rule 10* |

The Linesman must report upon completion of play, any circumstances pertaining to:

| | | |
|---|---|---|
| *(v)* | *Major penalties* | *Rule 20* |
| *(vi)* | *Match penalties* | *Rule 21* |
| *(vii)* | *Misconduct penalties* | *Rule 22* |
| *(viii)* | *Game Misconduct penalties* | *Rule 23* |
| *(ix)* | *Abuse of Officials* | *Rule 39* |
| *(x)* | *Physical Abuse of Officials* | *Rule 40* |
| *(xi)* | *Unsportsmanlike Conduct* | *Rule 75* |

Should a Linesman witness a foul (above) committed by an attacking player (undetected by the Referees) prior to the attacking team scoring a goal, the Linesman shall report what he witnessed to the Referees, the goal shall be disallowed and the appropriate penalty assessed.

The Linesman must stop play immediately and report to the Referees when:

| | | |
|---|---|---|
| *(xii)* | *When it is apparent that an injury has resulted from a high-stick that has gone undetected by the Referees and requires the assessment of a double-minor penalty.* | *Rule 60* |

32.5 **Stopping Play** - The Linesman shall stop play:

| | | |
|---|---|---|
| *(i)* | *When premature substitution of the goalkeeper has occurred* | *Rule 71* |
| *(ii)* | *When he deems that a player has sustained a serious injury and this has gone undetected by either of the Referees* | *Rule 8* |
| *(iii)* | *For encroachment into the face-off area* | *Rule 76* |
| *(iv)* | *When the puck has been directed with a hand to a teammate in any zone other than the defending zone and this has gone undetected by either of the Referees* | *Rule 79* |

| | | | |
|---|---|---|---|
| *(v)* | *When the puck has been batted with the hand by either center in an attempt to win the face-off in any zone* | *Rule 76* | |
| *(vi)* | *When the puck is struck by a stick above the normal height of the shoulders and this has gone undetected by either of the Referees* | *Rule 80* | |
| *(vii)* | *When either team ices the puck* | *Rule 81* | |
| *(viii)* | *When there has been interference by/with spectators* | *Rule 24* | |
| *(ix)* | *For any infraction of the rules concerning off-side play at the blue line* | *Rule 83* | |
| *(x)* | *When the puck is out of bounds or unplayable* | *Rule 85* | |
| *(xi)* | *When a goal has been scored that has not been observed by the Referees* | *Rule 78* | |
| *(xii)* | *When the puck is interfered with by an ineligible player/person* | *Rule 5*<br>*Rule 74* | *Rule 78*<br>*Rule 84* |
| *(xiii)* | *The calling of a penalty shot under* | *Rule 53* | |

32.6 **Unable to Continue** - Should a Linesman appointed be unable to act at the last minute or through sickness or accident be unable to finish the game, the Referees shall have the power to appoint another in his stead, if they deem it necessary, or if required to do so by the Manager or Coach of either of the competing teams. If no replacement Linesman is available, the two Referees will assist the remaining Linesman with his duties while still retaining their ability to assess penalties when deemed appropriate.

## Rule 33 – Official Scorer

33.1 **General Duties** - Before the start of the game, the Official Scorer shall obtain from the Manager or Coach of both teams a list of all eligible players and the starting line-up of each team, which information shall be made known to the opposing Manager or Coach before the start of play.

The Official Scorer shall secure the names of the Captain and Alternate Captains from the Manager or Coach at the time the line-ups are collected and will indicate those nominated by placing the letter "C" or "A" opposite their names on the Official Report of Match form.

The Official Scorer shall keep a record of the goals scored, the scorers, and players to whom assists have been credited and shall indicate those players on the lists who have actually taken part in the game.

At the conclusion of the game, the Official Scorer shall complete and sign the Score Sheet form and forward same to the League office.

The Official Scorer shall prepare the Official Report of Match form for signature by the Referees and forward it to the League office together with the Score Sheet and the Penalty Record forms.

Under the Report of Match section, the Official Scorer must

explain if the start of the game is delayed for any reason, any goalkeeper substitutions, time-outs, empty net goals, any delays in the playing of the game due to injury or television, etc.

33.2 **Goals and Assists** - The Official Scorer shall award the points for goals and assists and his decision shall be final. The Official Scorer shall use the Video Goal Judge system to verify the proper awarding of goals and assists. The awards of points for goals and assists shall be announced twice over the public address system and all changes in such awards shall also be announced in the same manner.

No requests for changes in any award of points shall be considered unless they are made at or before the conclusion of actual play in the game by the Team Captain, or immediately following the game by a Team representative.

In the event that the Video Goal Judge reviews a play and a goal is awarded even though play went for any period of time, the Official Scorer awards the goal and any assists at the time the goal was scored. If he is unsure, he must check with the Video Goal Judge. The Game Timekeeper and the Penalty Timekeeper must also be informed in order to adjust the clock and the penalty clocks accordingly.

A goal is awarded to the last player on the scoring team to touch the puck prior to the puck entering the net. (A puck entering the net is considered to be between the posts, from in front of, and below the crossbar, and entirely across the goal line.)

An assist is awarded to the player or players (maximum two) who touches the puck prior to the goal scorer, provided no defender plays or possesses the puck in between.

Assists can be given to deserving players on a goal that has been awarded by the Referee, if the Official Scorer deems that assists would have been given on the eventual goal anyway.

When goals are scored in the final minute of a period where tenths of seconds are shown on the clock, the time of the goal shall be rounded up to the nearest second for the official records.

33.3 **Line-ups** - It is the policy of the National Hockey League that the Coach of the visiting club provide to the Official Scorer, a list of eligible players, his starting line-up and designated Captain and Alternates, within five (5) minutes of the completion of the warm-up (twenty (20) minutes prior to face-off).

This twenty (20) minutes gives the Official Scorer time to obtain the completed home team line-up, return it to the visiting Coach and provide a copy of both line-ups to the Referees.

The Official Scorer should have an off-ice crew member assist him in order to save time and complete these duties.

The Official Scorer must file a report to the Commissioner or his designate if either Coach fails to cooperate within these recommended guidelines. This report should be forwarded to the National Hockey League Toronto office.

33.4 **Location** - The Official Scorer should view the game from an elevated position, well away from the players' benches, with house telephone communication to the public address announcer. He should also have access to a television monitor along with a recording device with simultaneous play and record capabilities to aid in the awarding of points. He must have access to the Video Goal Judge.

33.5 **Penalties** - The Official Scorer must help the Penalty Timekeeper with the numbers of the players on the ice, in the event a goalkeeper is assessed a penalty or a player is ejected from a game. He must also keep an eye on the players' benches during an altercation and record the numbers of any players who leave their respective players' or penalty benches and in the order that they so leave.

## Rule 34 – Game Timekeeper

34.1 **General Duties** – The Game Timekeeper shall record the time of starting and finishing of each period in the game. During the game the Game Timekeeper will start the clock with the drop of the puck and stop the clock upon hearing the officials' whistle or the scoring of a goal.

The Game Timekeeper shall cause to be announced over the public address system at the nineteenth minute in each period that there is one minute remaining to be played in the period.

34.2 **Intermissions** - For the purpose of keeping the spectators informed as to the time remaining during intermissions, the Game Timekeeper will use the electronic clock to record the length of intermissions. The clock will start for the intermission immediately at the conclusion of the period.

Intermissions are eightteen minutes (18:00) in length, unless otherwise notified. If there are unusual delays for any reason, (e.g. altercation, building, ice, or ice resurfacing problems) it is important to use discretion in starting the clock.

34.3 **Overtime** - In the event of overtime in the regular season, the Game Timekeeper shall reset the clock to five (5) minutes in preparation for the overtime period. The overtime period will commence promptly following the shoveling of the entire ice surface.

During overtime in the play-offs, each intermission will be completed in a normal manner.

34.4 **Signal Devices** - If the arena is not equipped with an automatic signaling device or, if such device fails to function, the Game Timekeeper shall signal the end of each period by blowing a whistle.

34.5 **Start of Periods** - The Game Timekeeper shall signal the Referees and the competing teams for the start of the game and each succeeding period and the Referees shall start the play promptly in accordance with Rule **77** – Game and Intermission Timing.

34.6 **Television** - The Game Timekeeper is required to synchronize his timing device with the television producer of the originating broadcast.

34.7 **Verification of Time** - Any loss of time on the game or penalty clocks due to a false face-off must be replaced as appropriate. The Video Goal Judge may be consulted to ensure the time is accurately replaced.

In the event of any dispute regarding time, the matter shall be referred to the Referees for adjudication and their decision shall be final. They may use the Video Goal Judge to assist in rendering their final decision. (See Rule **38** – Video Goal Judge.) The Game Timekeeper shall assist to verify game time using an additional timing device (League-approved stopwatch).

In the event that clock fails to operate when play resumes, the on-ice officials may elect to stop play provided there is no imminent scoring opportunity or wait until the next legitimate stoppage of play. In cooperation with the Game Timekeeper and the Video Goal Judge, the clock is to be re-set to the appropriate time.

In the event that a video replay shows a goal was scored prior to the play being stopped, the Video Goal Judge will inform the Game Timekeeper and Official Scorer of the time of goal and the amount of playing time left to be reset on the game clock.

## Rule 35 – Penalty Timekeeper

35.1 **General Duties** – The Penalty Timekeeper shall keep, on the Penalty Record form, a correct record of all penalties imposed by the Referees including the names of the players penalized, the penalties assessed, the duration of each penalty and the time at which each penalty was imposed.

The Penalty Timekeeper shall inform penalized players and the Penalty Box Attendants as to the correct expiration time of all penalties. In the event of a dispute regarding the time a player is permitted to return to the ice, the game clock is the determining time clock. For example, a player is assessed a minor penalty at the 12:00 mark. A stoppage of play occurs at the 10:00 mark, however, the penalty time clock shows one second remaining in the penalty. Since the game clock is the determining time clock, the penalized player shall be permitted to return to the ice.

The infraction of the rules for which each penalty has been imposed will be announced twice over the public address system as reported by the Referee. Where players of both teams are penalized at the same time, the penalty to the visiting player will be announced first. In situations where multiple game misconducts have been assessed to any one player at the same stoppage of play, only one game misconduct should be announced.

Misconduct penalties and coincident major penalties should not be recorded on the timing device (penalty time clock) but such penalized players should be alerted and released at the first stoppage of play following the expiration of their penalties.

When a player is assessed a misconduct in addition to other penalties, the misconduct shall only commence after all other penalties have been served (or washed out by the scoring of a goal).

If a player leaves the penalty bench before the time has expired, the Penalty Timekeeper must note the time and notify the Referees at his first opportunity.

It is the responsibility of the Penalty Timekeeper to ensure that penalized players return to the penalty box before the puck is dropped for the start of a new period. In the event that a penalized player is not in the penalty box, the Penalty Timekeeper should notify the Referees and prevent the game from resuming until the player is there.

35.2 **Equipment** - The Penalty Timekeeper shall have an official stick-measuring gauge and tape measure available for the Referees use during the game.

35.3 **Goalkeeper's Penalties** - In the event that a goalkeeper is penalized, the penalty shall be served by another member of his team who was on the ice when the offense was committed. Communication with the Official Scorer and/or Real Time Scorers is important at this time as they can inform the Penalty Timekeeper who was actually on the ice to ensure only the proper players can serve the time.

35.4 **Penalty Shot** - He shall report on the Penalty Record form each penalty shot awarded, the name of the player taking the shot and the result of the shot.

35.5 **Penalty Time Clock** - He shall be responsible for the correct posting of penalties on the scoreboard at all times and shall promptly call to the attention of the Referees any discrepancy between the time recorded on the clock and the official correct time and he shall be responsible for making any adjustments ordered by the Referees.

In the event that two players from one team and one player from the opposing team are penalized at the same time, the Penalty Timekeeper shall request through the Referee or the offending team's Captain, which penalty they prefer to have on the timing device.

35.6 **Reports** – Prior to each game, the Penalty Timekeeper shall obtain copies of the Instigator, Aggressor & Game Misconduct List provided by the League, retain one copy and provide one to the Referees. Should a player be assessed a penalty that would result in an automatic suspension, this must be conveyed to the Referee at the time the penalty is assessed to ensure a Game Misconduct penalty is applied.

Upon the completion of each game, the Penalty Timekeeper shall complete and sign the Penalty Record form and forward same to the League office.

When penalties are assessed in the final minute of a period where tenths of seconds are shown on the clock, the time of the penalty shall be rounded up to the nearest second for the official records.

The Officiating Department shall be entitled to inspect, collect and forward to the League office the actual worksheets used by the Penalty Timekeeper in any game.

When a player is ejected from a game, the Penalty Timekeeper must complete a report of the incident (Off-Ice Officials Report of Game Misconduct/Match Penalties). When there are more than one of these incidents, it is imperative to provide the Referee with accurate information for each incident so that his report(s) to the League office is correct.

35.7 **Stick Measurements** - He shall also record on the Penalty Record form the details and the result of any stick measurement performed by the Referees during the game.

35.8 **Verification of Time** - In the event that a goal is awarded by video review even though play continued, the Penalty Timekeeper must adjust any existing penalties, according to the situation. The clock must revert back to the original time the goal was scored. If a penalty was in the process of being called, it will revert back to that time also.

## Rule 36 – Goal Judge

36.1 **General Duties** - He shall signal, normally by means of red light, his decision as to whether the puck passed between the goal posts and entirely over the goal line. His only decision is whether the puck actually entered the net, not how or when it went in. The light must be illuminated for a period of five (5) seconds each time the puck enters the net regardless of circumstances. It is up to the Referees and/or Video Goal Judge to decide if it is a goal.

36.2 **Location** - There shall be one Goal Judge situated behind each goal (or in an area designated and approved by NHL Hockey Operations), in properly protected areas, if possible, so that there can be no interference with their activities. They shall not change goals during the game.

## Rule 37 – Real Time Scorers

37.1 **General Duties** – The duty of the Real Time Scorers is to electronically record all official statistics for the game played.

This data shall be compiled and recorded in strict conformity with the instructions provided by the League.

37.2 **Real Time Scorers** – There shall be appointed for duty at every game played in the League the following Real Time Scorers:

*(i) Stats Entry Scorer*
*(ii) Stats Entry Scorer*
*(iii) Time on ice Scorer – Home*
*(iv) Time on ice Scorer – Visitor*
*(v) Event Analyst*

Assigned by the League to oversee the Real Time Scorers and the data collected is a Scoring System Manager (SSM), an off-ice official who is required to work one of the five (5) positions noted above in each game played.

37.3 **Reports** – Reports shall be generated during the first and second intermissions (and subsequent intermissions during the playoffs) and post-game for each game played. Reports are distributed to the home club's Public Relations representative by the Scoring System Manager or his/her designate. The home club's Public Relations representative shall distribute reports to the media (print/radio/tv) and to each club's Coaches.

## Rule 38 – Video Goal Judge

38.1 **General Duties** – The following are the general duties of the Video Goal Judge:

*(i) He will review replays of disputed goals when requested to do so by the Referees.*

*(ii) He will review replays of disputed goals when he observes an incident that was undetected by on-ice officials.*

*(iii) After viewing the incident he will promptly convey his decision directly to the Referee at the penalty bench. When a play has been referred to the Video Goal Judge, his decision shall be final.*

*(iv) During the review he may consult with a member of the League's Hockey Operations or Officiating department staff if latter is in attendance at the game (or via telephone).*

*(v) Any potential goal requiring video review must be reviewed prior to or during the next stoppage of play. No goal may be awarded (or disallowed) as a result of video review once the puck has been dropped and play has resumed.*

38.2 **Goals** – Every goal is to be reviewed by the Video Goal Judge.

Upon making contact with the off-ice official at ice level, the Video Goal Judge should say initially that he is "looking at the play". If there is a need to delay the resumption of the play, the off-ice official at ice level should signal one of the Referees to delay the center ice face-off for a moment. Once the Video Goal Judge has reviewed the video and confirmed that the goal is valid, he should say that "it is a good goal". The off-ice official will then signal to the Referee to resume play.

If there is a need to expand the review, the Video Goal Judge will advise the off-ice official at ice level and the Public Address Announcer that the "play is under review". Once the play has been reviewed and deemed a goal, the goal will be announced in the normal manner. If the review reveals that the goal must be disallowed, the Public Address Announcer shall announce the reason for the disallowed goal as reported by the Referee.

When the Video Goal Judge observes an incident involving a potential goal that was undetected by the on-ice officials he will contact the Referee at the first stoppage of play and inform him that a review of the play is in progress.

When a review is requested by either the Referee or Video Goal Judge, the Public Address Announcer shall make the following announcement: "The play is under review".

The Video Goal Judge will use all the facilities at his disposal to review the incident and reach a conclusion as to the accurate time of the goal. It is the responsibility of the Video Goal Judge to record the time of the disputed goal and the clock is to be reset accordingly.

He will report his findings to the Referee as quickly as possible ensuring all available video feeds and angles have been reviewed.

When the Referee indicates there is to be a video review, all players (with the exception of the goalkeepers) will go to their respective players' bench immediately and failure to do so would result in a game misconduct penalty with a fine to the Coach.

38.3 **Reports** - Following every game, the Video Goal Judge must call the National Hockey League Toronto office and provide a verbal report of all video reviews conducted during the game.

Video Goal Judge reports are to be faxed or sent electronically to the National Hockey League Toronto office immediately following the game.

38.4 **Situations Subject to Video Review** - The following situations are subject to review by the Video Goal Judge:

*(i) Puck crossing the goal line.*

*(ii) Puck in the net prior to the goal frame being dislodged.*

*(iii) Puck in the net prior to, or after expiration of time at the end of the period.*

*(iv) Puck directed or batted into the net by a hand or foot or deliberately batted with any part of the attacking player's body. With the use of a foot/skate, was a distinct kicking motion evident? If so, the apparent goal must be disallowed. A DISTINCT KICKING MOTION is one which the player propels the puck with his skate into the net. If the Video Goal Judge / League Office Video Room determines that it was put into the net by an attacking player using a distinct kicking motion, it must be ruled NO GOAL. This would also be true even if the puck, after being kicked, deflects off any other player of either team and then into the net. This is still NO GOAL. However, a puck that enters the goal after deflecting off an attacking player's skate or that deflects off his skate while he is in the process of stopping, shall be ruled a good goal.* *See also **49.2**.*

*(v) Puck deflected directly into the net off an Official.*

*(vi) Puck struck with a high-stick, above the height of the crossbar, by an attacking player prior to entering the goal. The determining factor is where the puck makes contact with the stick in relation to the crossbar. If the puck makes contact with the portion of the stick that is at or below the level of the crossbar and enters the goal, this goal shall be allowed.*

*(vii) To establish the correct time on the official game clock, provided the game time is visible on the Video Goal Judge's monitors.*

*(viii) The video review process shall be permitted to assist the Referees in determining the legitimacy of all potential goals (e.g. to ensure they are "good hockey goals"). For example (but not limited to), pucks that enter the net by going through the net meshing, pucks that enter the net from underneath the net frame, pucks that hit the spectator netting prior to being directed immediately into the goal, pucks that enter the net undetected by the Referee, etc. This would also include situations whereby the Referee stops play or is in the process of stopping the play because he has lost sight of the puck and it is subsequently determined by video review that the puck crosses (or has crossed) the goal line and enters the net as the culmination of a continuous play where the result was unaffected by the whistle (i.e., the timing of the whistle was irrelevant to the puck entering the net at*

*the end of a continuous play).*

*NOTE: For pucks that hit the spectator netting undetected by the On-Ice Officials, "immediately" shall mean the following:*

*a) When the puck strikes the spectator netting and deflects directly into the goal off of any player;*

*b) When the puck strikes the spectator netting and falls to the ice and is then directed into the goal by the player who retrieves the puck.*

*In both of the above scenarios, the Toronto Video Room must have definitive video evidence of the puck striking the netting in order to disallow the goal.*

38.5 **Coach's Challenge** – Refer also to Rule 78.7.

The League will make available in all arenas, technology (either a handheld tablet or a television or computer monitor) that will allow On-Ice Officials, in conjunction with the Toronto Video Room, to view replays if, and only to the extent, a formal Coach's Challenge has been initiated (or, in the final minute of play or in Overtime, a review by Hockey Operations is initiated). To the extent practical, the replays made available to the Officials on the ice will be the same replays that are being utilized by the Toronto Video Room.

Once a Challenge has been initiated (or, in the final minute of play or in Overtime, a review is initiated by Hockey Operations), the Toronto Video Room will immediately establish contact with the Referee (or Linesman) responsible for the call on the ice via the headset and will inquire and discuss with the Referee (or Linesman), prior to the Referee (or Linesman) examining any video, the following: (a) the Referee's (or Linesman's) "final" call on the ice; and (b) what the Referee (or Linesman) observed on the play.

The on-ice call will then be reviewed simultaneously by the appropriate On-Ice Officials at ice level and by Hockey Operations in the Toronto Video Room using any and all replays at their disposal. After reviewing the play and consulting with the Toronto Video Room, the appropriate On-Ice Officials will then make the "final" decision on whether to uphold or overturn the original call on the ice. Once the decision is made, the Referee will inform the Penalty Timekeeper/PA Announcer and will make the announcement on the ice.

38.6 **Logistics and Equipment** - The Video Goal Judge must be located in a secluded area in the upper level of the building with an unobstructed view of both goals. The location must be large enough to seat three people (Video Goal Judge, Video Technician and Supervisor of Officials) and have space for necessary monitors, replay and recording equipment.

The Video Goal Judge shall have access to all replays that may be available by reason of any telecasts of the game and if there is no scheduled telecast the Club's internal telecast of the game will be used.

The Video Goal Judge must be supplied with a phone or communication system with direct contact to the penalty bench.

The "burn in" of the game clock is mandatory for the two overhead goal video feeds, and should be available on all feeds if such can be provided by the host broadcaster.

38.7 **Verification of Time** - Any loss of time on the game or penalty clocks due to a false face-off must be replaced. The Video Goal Judge may be consulted to ensure the time is accurately replaced.

In the event of any dispute regarding time, the matter shall be referred to the Referee for adjustment and his decision shall be final. The Game Timekeeper shall assist to verify game time via an additional timing device. (NHL approved stop watch)

In accordance with Rule **38** – Video Goal Judge, the Officials may use the Video Goal Judge system to establish the correct time on the official game clock, provided the game time is visible on the Video Goal Judge's monitors.

In the event that a video replay shows a goal was scored prior to the play being stopped, the Video Goal Judge will inform the Game Timekeeper and Official Scorer of the time of goal and the amount of playing time left to be reset on the game clock and penalty time clocks (if applicable).

Should the Toronto Video Room (in coordination with the Video Goal Judge) be able to determine that a goal was legitimately scored through the use of video replay prior to the next stoppage of play, the in arena horn shall be sounded to stop the play. The game clock (and penalty clocks, if applicable) shall be reset to the time of the goal.

Should the first stoppage of play following an apparent goal coincide with the end of a period, the on-ice officials must instruct both teams to remain at their respective players' benches until the video review has been completed.

## Rule 39 – Abuse of Officials

39.1 **General Description** – A player, goalkeeper, Coach or non-playing person shall not challenge or dispute the rulings of an official before, during or after a game. A player, goalkeeper, Coach or non-playing person shall not display unsportsmanlike conduct including, but not limited to, obscene, profane or abusive language or gestures, comments of a personal nature intended to degrade an official, or persist in disputing a ruling after being told to stop or after being penalized for such behavior.

NOTE: When such conduct is directed at anyone other than an official, Rule **75** – Unsportsmanlike Conduct shall be applied.

39.2 **Minor Penalty** – A minor penalty for unsportsmanlike conduct shall be assessed under this rule for the following infractions:

*(i)* *Any player who challenges or disputes the ruling of an official.*

*(ii)* *Any identifiable player who uses obscene, profane or abusive language or gestures directed at any on or off-ice official.*

*(iii)* *Any player or players who bang the boards with their sticks or other objects at any time, or who, in any manner show disrespect for an official's decision. If this is done in order to get the attention of the on-*

*ice officials for a legitimate reason (i.e. serious injury, illness, etc.), then discretion must be exercised by the Referees.*

(iv) *When a Captain, Alternate Captain or any other player comes off the players' bench to question or protest a ruling by an official on the ice.*

(v) *If a player bangs the glass in protest of the Goal Judge's ruling. If he persists, a misconduct penalty would then be assessed.*

(vi) *If a penalized player is assessed an additional unsportsmanlike conduct penalty either before or after he begins serving his original penalty(ies), the additional minor penalty is added to his unexpired time and served consecutively.*

39.3 **Bench Minor Penalty** - A bench minor penalty for unsportsmanlike conduct shall be assessed under this rule for the following infractions:

(i) *Any Coach or non-playing person who bangs the boards with a stick or other object at any time, showing disrespect for an official's decision. If this is done in order to get the attention of the on-ice officials for a legitimate reason (i.e. serious injury, illness, etc.), then discretion must be exercised by the Referees.*

(ii) *Any unidentifiable player or any Coach or non-playing person who uses obscene, profane or abusive language or gesture directed at an on or off-ice official or uses the name of any official coupled with any vociferous remarks. (see also* ***39.5 (ii)****)*

(iii) *Any player, Coach, or non-playing person interferes in any manner with any game official including the Referees, Linesmen, Game or Penalty Timekeepers or Goal Judges in the performance of their duties.*

39.4 **Misconduct Penalty** – Misconduct penalties shall be assessed under this rule for the following infractions:

(i) *Any player who persists in the use of obscene, profane or abusive language towards any on or off-ice official for which he has already been assessed a minor or bench minor penalty for unsportsmanlike conduct.*

(ii) *Any player who intentionally knocks or shoots the puck out of the reach of an official who is retrieving it.*

(iii) *Any player who, after being assessed an unsportsmanlike conduct minor penalty, persists in challenging or disputing the ruling of an official.*

(iv) *Any player or players who bang the boards with their sticks or other objects at any time, showing disrespect for an official's decision, for which they have already been assessed a minor or bench minor penalty for unsportsmanlike conduct.*

(v) *Any player or players who, except for the purpose of taking their positions on the penalty bench, enter or remain in the Referee's crease while he is reporting to or consulting with any game official including the other Referee, the Linesmen, Game Timekeeper, Penalty Timekeeper, Official Scorer or Public Address Announcer.*

(vi) *A misconduct penalty (or game misconduct penalty at the discretion of the Referee) shall be imposed on any player who deliberately throws any equipment out of the playing area. When this is done in protest of an official's ruling, a minor penalty plus a game misconduct shall be assessed (see* ***39.5****).*

(vii) *Any player who, after previously being assessed a minor penalty for unsportsmanlike conduct for banging the glass in protest of the Goal*

*Judge's ruling.*

(viii) *In general, participants displaying this type of behaviour are assessed a minor penalty, then a misconduct penalty and then a game misconduct penalty if they persist.*

39.5 **Game Misconduct Penalty** – Game misconduct penalties shall be assessed under this rule for the following infractions:

(i) *Any player who, after being assessed a misconduct penalty, persists in challenging or disputing the ruling of an official.*

(ii) *When a player, Coach or non-playing person uses obscene, profane or abusive language or gesture directed at any on or off-ice official or uses the name of any official coupled with any vociferous remarks, after already being assessed a bench minor penalty (**39.3 (ii)**), this Coach or non-playing person is to be assessed a game misconduct and the situation reported to the Commissioner for further action. When this type of conduct occurs after the expiration of the game, on or off the ice, the game misconduct shall be applied without the necessity of having been assessed a bench minor penalty previously.*

(iii) *Any player who deliberately applies physical force in any manner against an official, in any manner attempts to injure an official, physically demeans, or deliberately applies physical force to an official solely for the purpose of getting free of such an official during or immediately following an altercation shall receive a game misconduct penalty and the guidelines set out in Rule **40** – Physical Abuse of Officials are to be applied.*

(iv) *Any player who, having entered the penalty bench, leaves the penalty bench prior to the expiration of his penalty for the purpose of challenging an official's ruling, shall be assessed a game misconduct penalty. He shall also be automatically suspended for the next three (3) regular League and/or Play-off games of his Club. This rule does not replace any other more severe penalty that may be imposed for leaving the penalty bench for the purpose of starting or participating in an altercation. See Rule **70** – Leaving the Bench.*

(v) *A minor penalty for unsportsmanlike conduct plus a game misconduct shall be imposed on a player who throws his stick or any part thereof, or any other piece of equipment or object outside the playing area in protest of an official's decision.*

(vi) *Any player, Coach or non-playing person who throws or shoots any equipment or other object in the general direction of an official but does not come close to making any contact. This action may occur on or off the ice.*

(vii) *In general, participants displaying this type of behaviour are assessed a minor penalty, then a misconduct penalty and then a game misconduct penalty if they persist.*

Any player, Coach or non-playing Club personnel penalized under this section may be subject to supplemental discipline under Rule **28.**

39.6 **Reports** - It is the responsibility of all game officials and all club officials to send a confidential report to the Commissioner setting out the full details concerning the use of obscene gestures or language by any player, Coach or non-playing Club personnel. The Commissioner shall take such further disciplinary action as he shall deem appropriate.

## Rule 40 – Physical Abuse of Officials

40.1 **Game Misconduct** - Any player who deliberately applies physical force in any manner against an official, in any manner attempts to injure an official, physically demeans, or deliberately applies physical force to an official solely for the purpose of getting free of such an official during or immediately following an altercation shall receive a game misconduct penalty. In addition, the following (**40.2, 40.3, 40.4**) disciplinary penalties shall apply.

40.2 **Automatic Suspension – Category I** - Any player who deliberately strikes an official and causes injury or who deliberately applies physical force in any manner against an official with intent to injure, or who in any manner attempts to injure an official shall be automatically suspended for not less than twenty (20) games. (For the purpose of the rule, "intent to injure" shall mean any physical force which a player knew or should have known could reasonably be expected to cause injury.)

40.3 **Automatic Suspension – Category II** - Any player who deliberately applies physical force to an official in any manner (excluding actions as set out in Category I), which physical force is applied without intent to injure, or who spits on an official, shall be automatically suspended for not less than ten (10) games.

40.4 **Automatic Suspension – Category III** - Any player who, by his actions, physically demeans an official or physically threatens an official by (but not limited to) throwing a stick or any other piece of equipment or object at or in the general direction of an official, shooting the puck at or in the general direction of an official, spitting at or in the general direction of an official, or who deliberately applies physical force to an official solely for the purpose of getting free of such an official during or immediately following an altercation shall be suspended for not less than three (3) games.

40.5 **Automatic Suspension – Process** - Immediately after the game in which such game misconduct penalty is imposed, the Referees shall, in consultation with the Linesmen, decide the category of the offense. They shall make a verbal report to the League's Director of Hockey Operations and advise of the category and of the offense. In addition, they shall file a written report to the Director of Hockey Operations in which they may request a review as to the adequacy of the suspension. The NHLPA, the player and the Club involved shall be notified of the decision of the Referees on the morning following the game. The League will then hold a conference call with the NHLPA to review the Referees application of this rule, and will refrain from issuing public comment affirming the Referees application of Rule **40** until that call is complete.

The player or the officials may request the Commissioner to review, subject to the provisions of this rule, the penalty imposed by the Referees. Such request must be filed with the Commissioner in writing not later than seventy-two (72) hours following notification of the penalty.

If a review of the incident is requested by either the player or by the officials, a hearing will be conducted by the Commissioner on an expedited basis, and best efforts will be used to provide a hearing before the second game missed by the player due to the automatic suspension imposed under this rule. The player's suspension shall continue pending the outcome of the hearing by the Commissioner.

For Category III offenses only, the Commissioner may conduct the hearing by telephone. For Category I and II offenses, the hearing shall be conducted in person.

After any review as called for hereby, the Commissioner shall issue an order that:

*(i)* *sustaining the minimum suspension, or*

*(ii)* *increasing the number of games within the category, or*

*(iii)* *changing to a lower category, or*

*(iv)* *changing to a lower category and increasing the number of games within this category, or*

*(v)* *in the case of a Category III suspension only, reducing the number of games of the suspension.*

The penalties imposed under this rule shall not be deemed to limit the right of the Commissioner with respect to any action that he might otherwise take pursuant to Article 18 of the CBA.

40.6 **Supplementary Discipline** - In the event that the player has committed more than one offense under this rule, in addition to the penalties imposed under this offense, his case shall be referred to the Commissioner of the League for consideration of supplementary disciplinary action.

40.7 **Coach or Non-Playing Club Personnel** - Any Manager, Coach or non-playing Club personnel who holds or strikes an official shall be automatically suspended from the game, ordered to the dressing room and the matter will be reported to the Commissioner for further disciplinary action.

40.8 **Police Protection and Security** - All Clubs shall provide adequate police or other protection for all players, goalkeepers and officials at all times.

The Referee shall report to the Commissioner any failure of this protection observed by him or reported to him with particulars of such failure.

# SECTION 6 – PHYSICAL FOULS

## Rule 41 - Boarding

41.1 **Boarding** – A boarding penalty shall be imposed on any player who checks or pushes a defenseless opponent in such a manner that causes the opponent to hit or impact the boards violently or dangerously. The severity of the penalty, based upon the impact with the boards, shall be at the discretion of the Referee.

There is an enormous amount of judgment involved in the application of this rule by the Referees. The onus is on the player applying the check to ensure his opponent is not in a defenseless position and if so, he must avoid or minimize contact. However, in determining whether such contact could have been avoided, the circumstances of the check, including whether the opponent put himself in a vulnerable position immediately prior to or simultaneously with the check or whether the check was unavoidable can be considered. This balance must be considered by the Referees when applying this rule.

Any unnecessary contact with a player playing the puck on an obvious "icing" or "off-side" play which results in that player hitting or impacting the boards is "boarding" and must be penalized as such. In other instances where there is no contact with the boards, it should be treated as "charging."

41.2 **Minor Penalty** – The Referee, at his discretion, may assess a minor penalty, based on the degree of violence of the impact with the boards, to a player guilty of boarding an opponent.

41.3 **Major Penalty** – The Referee, at his discretion, may assess a major penalty, based on the degree of violence of the impact with the boards, to a player guilty of boarding an opponent (see **41.5**).

41.4 **Match Penalty** – The Referee, at his discretion, may assess a match penalty if, in his judgment, the player attempted to or deliberately injured his opponent by boarding.

41.5 **Game Misconduct Penalty** - When a major penalty is imposed under this rule for a foul resulting in an injury to the face or head of an opponent, a game misconduct shall be imposed.

41.6 **Fines and Suspensions** – Refer to Rule 23.6 – Fines and Suspensions – Physical Fouls Category.

When a major penalty is imposed under this rule, an automatic fine of one hundred dollars ($100) shall be imposed.

If deemed appropriate, supplementary discipline can be applied by the Commissioner at his discretion (refer to Rule **28**).

## Rule 42 - Charging

42.1 **Charging** - A minor or major penalty shall be imposed on a player who skates or jumps into, or charges an opponent in any manner.

Charging shall mean the actions of a player who, as a result of distance traveled, shall violently check an opponent in any manner. A "charge" may be the result of a check into the boards, into the goal frame or in open ice.

A minor, major or a major and a game misconduct shall be imposed on a player who charges a goalkeeper while the goalkeeper is within his goal crease.

A goalkeeper is not "fair game" just because he is outside the goal crease area. The appropriate penalty should be assessed in every case where an opposing player makes unnecessary contact with a goalkeeper. However, incidental contact, at the discretion of the Referee, will be permitted when the goalkeeper is in the act of playing the puck outside his goal crease provided the attacking player has made a reasonable effort to avoid such contact.

42.2 **Minor Penalty** - The Referee, at his discretion, may assess a minor penalty, based on the degree of violence of the check, to a player guilty of charging an opponent.

42.3 **Major Penalty** – The Referee, at his discretion, may assess a major penalty, based on the degree of violence of the check, to a player guilty of charging an opponent (see **42.5**).

42.4 **Match Penalty** – The Referee, at his discretion, may assess a match penalty if, in his judgment, the player attempted to or deliberately injured his opponent by charging.

42.5 **Game Misconduct Penalty** - When a major penalty is imposed under this rule for a foul resulting in an injury to the face or head of an opponent, a game misconduct shall be imposed.

42.6 **Fines and Suspensions** – Refer to Rule 23.6 – Fines and Suspensions – Physical Fouls Category.

When a major penalty and a game misconduct is assessed for a foul resulting in an injury to the face or head of an opponent, an automatic fine of one hundred dollars ($100) shall be imposed.

If deemed appropriate, supplementary discipline can be applied by the Commissioner at his discretion (refer to Rule **28**).

## Rule 43 – Checking from Behind

43.1 **Checking from Behind** – A check from behind is a check delivered on a player who is not aware of the impending hit, therefore unable to protect or defend himself, and contact is made on the back part of the body. When a player intentionally turns his body to create contact with his back, no penalty shall be assessed.

43.2 **Minor Penalty** - There is no provision for a minor penalty for checking from behind.

43.3 **Major Penalty** – Any player who cross-checks, pushes or charges from behind an opponent who is unable to protect or defend himself,

shall be assessed a major penalty. This penalty applies anywhere on the playing surface (see **43.5**).

43.4 **Match Penalty** - The Referee, at his discretion, may assess a match penalty if, in his judgment, the player attempted to or deliberately injured his opponent by checking from behind.

43.5 **Game Misconduct** – A game misconduct penalty must be assessed anytime a major penalty is applied for checking from behind.

43.6 **Fines and Suspensions** – Refer to Rule 23.6 – Fines and Suspensions – Physical Fouls Category.

If deemed appropriate, supplementary discipline can be applied by the Commissioner at his discretion (refer to Rule **28**).

## Rule 44 - Clipping

44.1 **Clipping** - Clipping is the act of throwing the body, from any direction, across or below the knees of an opponent.

A player may not deliver a check in a "clipping" manner, nor lower his own body position to deliver a check on or below an opponent's knees.

An illegal "low hit" is a check that is delivered by a player who may or may not have both skates on the ice, with his sole intent to check the opponent in the area of his knees. A player may not lower his body position to deliver a check to an opponent's knees.

44.2 **Minor Penalty** - A player who commits these fouls will be assessed a minor penalty for "clipping."

44.3 **Major Penalty** - If an injury occurs as a result of this "clipping" check, the player must be assessed a major penalty (see **44.5**).

44.4 **Match Penalty** - The Referee, at his discretion, may assess a match penalty if, in his judgment, the player attempted to or deliberately injured his opponent by clipping.

44.5 **Game Misconduct Penalty** - A game misconduct penalty must be assessed anytime a major penalty is applied for injuring an opponent by clipping.

44.6 **Fines and Suspensions** – Refer to Rule 23.6 – Fines and Suspensions – Physical Fouls Category.

There are no specified fines or suspensions for clipping, however, supplementary discipline can be applied by the Commissioner at his discretion (refer to Rule **28**).

## Rule 45 - Elbowing

45.1 **Elbowing** - Elbowing shall mean the use of an extended elbow in a manner that may or may not cause injury.

45.2 **Minor Penalty** - The Referee, at his discretion, may assess a minor penalty, based on the degree of violence, to a player guilty of elbowing an opponent.

45.3 **Major Penalty** - A major penalty, at the discretion of the Referee, shall be imposed on any player who uses his elbow to foul an opponent. A major penalty must be imposed under this rule for a foul resulting in an injury to the face or head of an opponent (see **45.5**).

45.4 **Match Penalty** - The Referee, at his discretion, may assess a match penalty if, in his judgment, the player attempted to or deliberately injured his opponent by elbowing.

45.5 **Game Misconduct Penalty** - When a major penalty is imposed under this rule for a foul resulting in an injury to the face or head of an opponent, a game misconduct penalty shall also be imposed.

45.6 **Fines and Suspensions** – Refer to Rule 23.6 – Fines and Suspensions – Physical Fouls Category.

When a major penalty and a game misconduct is assessed for a foul resulting in an injury to the face or head of an opponent, an automatic fine of one hundred dollars ($100) shall be imposed.

If deemed appropriate, supplementary discipline can be applied by the Commissioner at his discretion (refer to Rule **28**).

## Rule 46 - Fighting

46.1 **Fighting** – A fight shall be deemed to have occurred when at least one player punches or attempts to punch an opponent repeatedly or when two players wrestle in such a manner as to make it difficult for the Linesmen to intervene and separate the combatants.

The Referees are provided very wide latitude in the penalties with which they may impose under this rule. This is done intentionally to enable them to differentiate between the obvious degrees of responsibility of the participants either for starting the fighting or persisting in continuing the fighting. The discretion provided should be exercised realistically.

46.2 **Aggressor** – The aggressor in an altercation shall be the player who continues to throw punches in an attempt to inflict punishment on his opponent who is in a defenseless position or who is an unwilling combatant.

A player must be deemed the aggressor when he has clearly won the fight but he continues throwing and landing punches in a further attempt to inflict punishment and/or injury on his opponent who is no longer in a position to defend himself.

A player who is deemed to be the aggressor of an altercation shall be assessed a major penalty for fighting and a game misconduct.

A player who is deemed to be the aggressor of an altercation will have this recorded as an aggressor of an altercation for statistical and suspension purposes.

A player who is deemed to be both the instigator and aggressor of an altercation shall be assessed an instigating minor penalty, a major penalty for fighting, a ten-minute misconduct (instigator) and a game misconduct penalty (aggressor).

46.3 **Altercation** - An altercation is a situation involving two players with at least one to be penalized.

46.4 **Clearing the Area of a Fight** - When a fight occurs, all players not engaged shall go immediately to the area of their players' bench and in the event the altercation takes place at a players' bench, the players on the ice from that team shall go to their defending zone. Goalkeepers shall remain in their goal crease, except in the event the altercation takes place in the vicinity of the goal crease, and therefore shall obey the directions of the Referee. Failure to comply can result in penalties incurred for their involvement in and around the area and fines as outlined in **46.18.**

46.5 **Continuing or Attempting to Continue a Fight** - Any player who persists in continuing or attempting to continue a fight or altercation after he has been ordered by the Referee to stop, or who resists a Linesman in the discharge of his duties shall, at the discretion of the Referee, incur a misconduct or game misconduct penalty in addition to any penalties imposed.

46.6 **Helmets** - No player may remove his helmet prior to engaging in a fight. If he should do so, he shall be assessed a two minute minor penalty for unsportsmanlike conduct. Helmets that come off in the course of and resulting from the altercation will not result in a penalty to either player.

46.7 **Fighting After the Original Altercation** - A game misconduct penalty shall be imposed on any player who is assessed a major penalty for fighting after the original altercation has started.

Notwithstanding this rule, at the discretion of the Referee, the automatic game misconduct penalty may be waived for a player in the altercation if the opposing player was clearly the instigator of the altercation.

46.8 **Fighting Off the Playing Surface** - A misconduct or game misconduct penalty shall be imposed on any player involved in fighting off the playing surface or with another player who is off the playing surface. These penalties are in addition to any other time penalties assessed, including the major penalty for fighting.

Whenever a Coach or other non-playing Club personnel becomes involved in an altercation with an opposing player, Coach or other non-playing Club personnel on or off the ice, shall be automatically suspended from the game, ordered to the dressing room and the matter will be reported to the Commissioner for further disciplinary action.

46.9 **Fighting Other Than During the Periods of the Game** - Any teams whose players become involved in an altercation, other than during the periods of the game, shall be fined pursuant to **46.20,** in addition to any other appropriate penalties that may be imposed upon the participating players by supplementary discipline or otherwise.

Players involved in fighting other than during the periods of the game shall be assessed a major penalty and a game misconduct. Should one player be deemed the instigator of the fight, the game misconduct shall not be assessed to his opponent.

Any player who would be deemed to be an instigator pursuant to this rule at a time other than during the periods of the game shall be suspended pursuant to **46.20**.

In the case of altercations taking place after the period or game the fine under this rule shall be assessed only in the event that an altercation is commenced after the period or game has terminated.

Should players come onto the ice from their players' benches after the period ends and prior to the start of an altercation, they shall not be penalized if they remain in the vicinity of their players' bench and provided they do not get involved in any altercations.

46.10**Fighting Prior to the Drop of the Puck** – Unless this occurs prior to the start of the game or any period (see **46.9**), a fight that occurs prior to the drop of the puck during the course of normal face-off, the altercation shall be penalized as if it occurred during the regular playing time.

When, in the opinion of the Referee that, specific personnel changes have been made by one or both teams late in a game and ultimately an altercation ensues, the appropriate penalties are to be assessed and the incident reported to the Commissioner immediately following the game for review and possible supplementary discipline under Rule **28**.

46.11**Instigator** - An instigator of an altercation shall be a player who by his actions or demeanor demonstrates any/some of the following criteria: distance traveled; gloves off first; first punch thrown; menacing attitude or posture; verbal instigation or threats; conduct in retaliation to a prior game (or season) incident; obvious retribution for a previous incident in the game or season.

A player who is deemed to be the instigator of an altercation shall be assessed an instigating minor penalty, a major penalty for fighting and a ten-minute misconduct.

If the same player is deemed to be the instigator of a second altercation in the same game, he shall be assessed an instigating minor penalty, a major penalty for fighting and a game misconduct.

When a player receives his third instigator penalty in one Regular season, he is automatically given a game misconduct following that third violation.

A player who is deemed to be both the instigator and aggressor of an altercation shall be assessed an instigating minor penalty, a major penalty for fighting, a ten-minute misconduct (instigator) and a game misconduct penalty (aggressor).

Any request by a Club to have an instigator penalty reviewed and rescinded by the League must follow the same procedure for game misconduct penalties as outlined in **23.2**.

46.12**Instigator in Final Five Minutes of Regulation Time (or Anytime in Overtime)** - A player who is deemed to be the instigator of an altercation in the final five (5) minutes of regulation time or at any time in overtime shall be assessed an instigator minor penalty, a major penalty for fighting, and a game misconduct penalty, subject to the conditions outlined in **46.22**.

46.13**Jerseys** - A player who deliberately removes his jersey prior to participating in an altercation or who is clearly wearing a jersey that has been modified and does not conform to Rule **9** – Uniforms, shall be assessed a minor penalty for unsportsmanlike conduct and a game misconduct. This is in addition to other penalties to be assessed to the participants of an altercation. If the altercation never materializes, the player would receive a minor penalty for unsportsmanlike conduct and a ten-minute misconduct for deliberately removing his jersey.

A player who engages in a fight and whose jersey is removed (completely off his torso), other than through the actions of his opponent in the altercation or through the actions of the Linesman, shall be assessed a game misconduct penalty.

A player who engages in a fight and whose jersey is not properly "tied-down" (jersey properly fastened to pants), and who loses his jersey (completely off his torso) in that altercation, shall receive a game misconduct penalty. If the player loses his jersey despite the tie down remaining in tact and attached to the pants, the game misconduct is not applicable, however this must be reported to the League office so that the jersey and the tie down can be examined.

A player who is involved in an altercation, when the opponent has been identified as an instigator, shall not be assessed a game misconduct penalty if his jersey should be removed by an opponent or an official in the discharge of his duties, regardless as to whether or not he was properly "tied-down" (jersey properly fastened to pants).

46.14**Major Penalty** – A major penalty shall be imposed on any player who fights.

46.15**Match Penalty** - Any player wearing tape or any other material on his hands (below the wrist) who cuts or injures an opponent during an altercation will receive a match penalty in addition to any other penalties imposed including for fighting under this rule.

A match penalty shall be assessed to a player who punches an unsuspecting opponent and causes an injury.

46.16**Third Man In** - A game misconduct penalty, at the discretion of the Referee, shall be imposed on any player who is the first to intervene (third man in) in an altercation already in progress except when a match penalty is being imposed in the original altercation. This penalty is in addition to any other penalties incurred in the same incident.

This rule also applies to subsequent players who elect to intervene in the same or other altercations during the same stoppage of play.

Generally, this rule is applied when a fight occurs.

46.17**Fines and Suspensions – Aggressor** – (see **46.2**) A player who is deemed to be the aggressor for the third time in one Regular season shall be suspended for the next two regular season games of his team.

For the fourth aggressor penalty in the same Regular season, the player will be suspended for the next four games of his team. For the fifth aggressor penalty in the same Regular season, the player will be suspended for the next six games of his team.

During the Play-offs, any player who is deemed to be the aggressor for the second time shall be suspended automatically for the next Play-off game of his team. For each subsequent aggressor violation during the Play-offs, the automatic suspension shall be increased by one game.

Prior to the commencement of each Stanley Cup Final, a player will have his current aggressor violations removed from his current playoff record. They will remain part of his historical record.

46.18 **Fines and Suspensions – Clearing the Area of a Fight** - Failure by players (or goalkeepers as required) to clear the area of a fight shall, in addition to the other penalties that may be assessed, result in a fine to the team of $1,000 and the Coach of said team in the amount of $1,000.

46.19 **Fines and Suspensions – Failure to Proceed Directly to Penalty Bench** - Any player who, following a fight or other altercation in which he has been involved is broken up and for which he is penalized, fails to proceed directly and immediately to the penalty bench, or who causes any delay by retrieving his equipment (gloves, sticks, etc. shall be delivered to him at the penalty bench by teammates), shall incur an automatic fine of one hundred dollars ($100) in addition to all other penalties or fines incurred.

46.20 **Fines and Suspensions – Fighting Other Than During the Periods of the Game** - Any teams whose players become involved in an altercation, other than during the periods of the game (see **46.9**), shall be fined automatically twenty-five thousand dollars ($25,000) in addition to any other appropriate penalties that may be imposed upon the participating players by supplementary discipline or otherwise.

Any player who would be deemed to be an instigator pursuant to this rule at a time other than during the periods of the game shall be suspended automatically for ten (10) games. Such determination may be made by the Referee at the time of the incident or subsequently by the Commissioner or his designee based upon such reports and other information as he deems sufficient, including but not limited to television tapes.

46.21 **Fines and Suspensions – Instigator** - A player who is deemed to be the instigator of an altercation (see **46.11**) for the third time in one Regular season shall be suspended for the next two regular season games of his team.

For the fourth instigator penalty in the same Regular season, the player will be suspended for the next four games of his team. For the fifth instigator penalty in the same Regular season, the player will be suspended for the next six games of his team.

During the Play-offs, any player who is deemed to be the instigator of an altercation for the second time shall be suspended automatically for the next Play-off game of his team. For each subsequent instigator violation during the Play-offs, the automatic suspension shall be increased by one game.

Prior to the commencement of each Stanley Cup Final, a player will have his current instigator violations removed from his current playoff record. They will remain part of his historical record.

46.22 **Fines and Suspensions – Instigator in Final Five Minutes of Regulation Time (or Anytime in Overtime)** - A player who is deemed to be the instigator of an altercation in the final five (5) minutes of regulation time or at anytime in overtime (see **46.12**), shall be suspended for one game, pending a review of the incident.

When the one-game suspension is imposed, the Coach shall be fined $10,000 – a fine that will double for each subsequent incident.

The suspension shall be served unless, upon review of the incident, the Director of Hockey Operations, at his discretion, deems the incident is not related to the score, previous incidents in the game or prior games, retaliatory in nature, "message sending", etc. The length of suspension will double for each subsequent offense. This suspension shall be served in addition to any other automatic suspensions a player may incur for an accumulation of three or more instigator penalties.

No team appeals will be permitted either verbally or in writing regarding the assessment of this automatic suspension as all incidents are reviewed by the Director of Hockey Operations as outlined above.

## Rule 47 – Head-butting

47.1 **Head-butting** – The act of head-butting involves a player making intentional contact, or attempting to make contact, with an opponent by leading with his head and/or helmet.

47.2 **Double-minor Penalty** - A double-minor penalty shall be imposed on a player who attempts to head-butt an opponent.

47.3 **Major Penalty** - A major penalty shall be imposed on a player who head-butts an opponent (see **47.5**).

47.4 **Match Penalty** - A match penalty shall be imposed on a player who injures an opponent as a result of a head-butt.

47.5 **Game Misconduct Penalty** – When a major penalty is assessed under this rule, a game misconduct penalty must be imposed.

47.6 **Fines and Suspensions** – Refer to Rule 23.6 – Fines and Suspensions – Physical Fouls Category.

There are no specified fines or suspensions for head-butting, however, supplementary discipline can be applied by the Commissioner at his discretion (refer to Rule **28**).

## Rule 48 – Illegal Check to the Head

48.1 **Illegal Check to the Head** – A hit resulting in contact with an opponent's head where the head was the main point of contact and such contact to the head was avoidable is not permitted.

In determining whether contact with an opponent's head was avoidable, the circumstances of the hit including the following shall be considered:

*(i) Whether the player attempted to hit squarely through the opponent's body and the head was not "picked" as a result of poor timing, poor angle of approach, or unnecessary extension of the body upward or outward.*

(ii) *Whether the opponent put himself in a vulnerable position by assuming a posture that made head contact on an otherwise full body check unavoidable.*

(iii) *Whether the opponent materially changed the position of his body or head immediately prior to or simultaneously with the hit in a way that significantly contributed to the head contact.*

48.2 **Minor Penalty** – For violation of this rule, a minor penalty shall be assessed.

48.3 **Major Penalty** – There is no provision for a major penalty for this rule.

48.4 **Game Misconduct Penalty** – There is no provision for a game misconduct for this rule.

48.5 **Match Penalty** – The Referee, at his discretion, may assess a match penalty if, in his judgment, the player attempted to or deliberately injured his opponent with an illegal check to the head.

If deemed appropriate, supplementary discipline can be applied by the Commissioner at his discretion.

## Rule 49 - Kicking

49.1 **Kicking** – The action of a player deliberately using his skate(s) with a kicking motion to propel the puck or to contact an opponent.

49.2 **Goals** - Kicking the puck shall be permitted in all zones. A goal cannot be scored by an attacking player who uses a distinct kicking motion to propel the puck into the net with his skate/foot. A goal cannot be scored by an attacking player who kicks a puck that deflects into the net off any player, goalkeeper or official.

A puck that deflects into the net off an attacking player's skate who does not use a distinct kicking motion is a legitimate goal. A puck that is directed into the net by an attacking player's skate shall be a legitimate goal as long as no distinct kicking motion is evident. The following should clarify deflections following a kicked puck that enters the goal:

(i) *A kicked puck that deflects off the body of any player of either team (including the goalkeeper) shall be ruled no goal.*

(ii) *A kicked puck that deflects off the stick of any player (excluding the goalkeeper's stick) shall be ruled a good goal.*

(iii) *A goal will be allowed when an attacking player kicks the puck and the puck deflects off his own stick and then into the net.*

(iv) *A goal will be allowed when a puck enters the goal after deflecting off an attacking player's skate or deflects off his skate while he is in the process of stopping.*

A goal cannot be scored by an attacking player who kicks any equipment (stick, glove, helmet, etc.) at the puck, including kicking the blade of his own stick, causing the puck to cross the goal line.

49.3 **Match Penalty** – A match penalty shall be imposed on any player who kicks or attempts to kick another player.

Whether or not an injury occurs, the Referee will impose a five (5) minute time penalty under this rule.

49.4 **Fines and Suspensions** - There are no specified fines or suspensions for kicking and opponent, however, supplementary discipline can be applied by the Commissioner at his discretion (refer to Rule **28**).

## Rule 50 - Kneeing

50.1 **Kneeing** - Kneeing is the act of a player leading with his knee and in some cases extending his leg outwards to make contact with his opponent.

50.2 **Minor Penalty** - The Referee, at his discretion, may assess a minor penalty, based on the severity of the infraction, to a player guilty of kneeing an opponent.

50.3 **Major Penalty** - The Referee, at his discretion, may assess a major penalty, based on the severity of the infraction, to a player guilty of kneeing an opponent (see **50.5**).

50.4 **Match Penalty** – The Referee, at his discretion, may assess a match penalty if, in his judgment, the player attempted to or deliberately injured his opponent by kneeing.

50.5 **Game Misconduct Penalty** - When a player has been assessed a major penalty for kneeing he shall also be assessed a Game Misconduct.

50.6 **Fines and Suspensions** – Refer to Rule 23.6 – Fines and Suspenions – Physical Fouls Category.

There are no specified fines or suspensions for kneeing, however, supplementary discipline can be applied by the Commissioner at his discretion (refer to Rule **28**).

## Rule 51 - Roughing

51.1 **Roughing** – Roughing is a punching motion with the hand or fist, with or without the glove on the hand, normally directed at the head or face of an opponent.

Roughing is a minor altercation that is not worthy of a major penalty to either participant. (An altercation is a situation involving two players with at least one to be penalized).

51.2 **Minor Penalty** - A minor penalty shall be imposed on a player who strikes an opponent with his hand or fist.

51.3 **Match Penalty** - If, in the judgment of the Referee, a goalkeeper uses his blocking glove to punch an opponent in the head or face in an attempt to or to deliberately injure an opponent, a match penalty must be assessed.

51.4 **Fines and Suspensions** - There are no specified fines or suspensions for roughing, however, supplementary discipline can be applied by the Commissioner at his discretion (refer to Rule **28**).

## Rule 52 – Slew-footing

52.1 **Slew-footing** - Slew-footing is the act of a player using his leg or foot to knock or kick an opponent's feet from under him, or pushes an opponent's upper body backward with an arm or elbow, and at the same time with a forward motion of his leg, knocks or kicks the opponent's feet from under him, causing him to fall violently to the ice.

52.2 **Match Penalty** - Any player who is guilty of slew-footing shall be assessed a match penalty.

52.3 **Fines and Suspensions** - There are no specified fines or suspensions for slew-footing, however, supplementary discipline can be applied by the Commissioner at his discretion (refer to Rule **28**).

## Rule 53 – Throwing Equipment

53.1 **Throwing Equipment** – A player shall not throw a stick or any other object in any zone. A player who has lost or broken his stick may only receive a stick at his own players' bench or be handed one from a teammate on the ice (see **10.3**).

53.2 **Minor Penalty** - A minor penalty shall be imposed on any player on the ice who throws his stick or any part thereof or any other object in the direction of the puck or an opponent in any zone, except when such act has been penalized by the assessment of a penalty shot or the awarding of a goal.

When a defending player shoots or throws a stick or any other object at the puck or the puck carrier in the defending zone but does not interfere in any manner with the puck or puck carrier, a minor penalty shall be assessed.

When the player discards the broken portion of a stick or some other object by tossing it or shooting it to the side of the ice (and not over the boards) in such a way as will not interfere with play or opposing player, no penalty will be imposed for so doing. When moving a stick that is not broken, no penalty shall be assessed as long as it does not interfere with the play and the player who lost said stick is not attempting to retrieve it, otherwise an interference penalty must be assessed.

A minor penalty for unsportsmanlike conduct plus a game misconduct penalty shall be imposed on a player who throws his stick or any part thereof or any other object or piece of equipment outside the playing area in protest of an official's decision.

53.3 **Bench Minor Penalty** – Should any player, Coach, or non-playing person on the players' bench or penalty bench throw anything on the ice during the progress of the game or during a stoppage of play, a bench minor penalty for unsportsmanlike conduct shall be assessed. See **75.3**.

53.4 **Misconduct or Game Misconduct Penalty** - A misconduct penalty shall be imposed on a player who unintentionally or accidentally throws his stick or any part thereof or any other object or piece of equipment outside the playing area. If the offense is committed intentionally, a game misconduct penalty shall be assessed to the offending player. If the offense is committed in protest of an official's decision, a minor penalty for unsportsmanlike conduct plus a game misconduct penalty shall be assessed to the offending player.

53.5 **Match Penalty** – If a player attempts to or deliberately injures an opponent by throwing a stick or any other object or piece of equipment at an opposing player, Coach or non-playing club person, he shall be assessed a match penalty. If injury results from the thrown object, a match penalty must be assessed for deliberate injury of an opponent.

53.6 **Penalty Shot** - When any member of the defending team, including the Coach or any non-playing person, throws or shoots any part of a stick or any other object or piece of equipment at the puck or puck carrier in his defending zone, the Referee or Linesman shall allow the play to be completed and if a goal is not scored, a penalty shot shall be awarded to the non-offending team. This shot shall be taken by the player designated by the Referee as the player fouled.

If the officials are unable to determine the person against whom the offense was made, the non-offending team, through the Captain, shall designate a player on the ice at the time the offense was committed to take the shot.

If a player on a breakaway in the neutral or attacking zone is interfered with by a stick or any other object or piece of equipment that is thrown by any member of the defending team, including the Coach or any non-playing Club person, a penalty shot shall be awarded to the non-offending team. See also Rule **57.3** – Tripping for fouls from behind to a player on a breakaway.

If a player on a breakaway in the neutral or attacking zone is interfered with by an object thrown on the ice by a spectator that causes him to lose possession of the puck or to fall, the Referee shall award a penalty shot to the player who was fouled.

53.7 **Awarded Goal** - If, when the opposing goalkeeper has been removed, a member of the defending team, including the Coach or any non-playing person, throws or shoots any part of a stick or any other object or piece of equipment at the puck or puck carrier in the neutral or his own defending zone, thereby preventing the puck carrier from having a clear shot on an "open net", a goal shall be awarded to the attacking side.

For the purpose of this rule, an "open net" is defined as one from which a goalkeeper has been removed for an additional attacking player. The goalkeeper is considered off the ice once the replacement player has entered the playing surface.

53.8 **Fines and Suspensions** - There are no specified fines or suspensions for throwing equipment, however, supplementary discipline can be applied by the Commissioner at his discretion (refer to Rule **28**).

# SECTION 7 – RESTRAINING FOULS

## Rule 54 – Holding

54.1 **Holding** – Any action by a player that restrains or impedes the progress of an opposing player whether or not he is in possession of the puck.

54.2 **Minor Penalty** - A minor penalty shall be imposed on a player who holds an opponent by using his hands, arms or legs.

A player is permitted to use his arm in a strength move, by blocking his opponent, provided he has body position and is not using his hands in a holding manner, when doing so.

A player is not permitted to hold an opponent's stick. A minor penalty shall be assessed to a player who holds an opponent's stick (assessed and announced as "holding the stick").

A player is permitted to protect himself by defending against an opponent's stick. He must immediately release the stick and allow the player to resume normal play.

54.3 **Penalty Shot** – refer to Rule **57.3** – Tripping.

54.4 **Awarded Goal** – refer to Rule **57.4** – Tripping.

## Rule 55 – Hooking

55.1 **Hooking** - Hooking is the act of using the stick in a manner that enables a player to restrain an opponent.

When a player is checking another in such a way that there is only stick-to-stick contact, such action is not to be penalized as hooking.

55.2 **Minor Penalty** - A minor penalty shall be imposed on a player who impedes the progress of an opponent by "hooking" with his stick. A minor penalty for hooking shall be assessed to any player who uses the shaft of the stick above the upper hand to hold or hook an opponent.

55.3 **Major Penalty** - A major penalty shall be imposed on any player who injures an opponent by "hooking" (see **55.4**).

55.4 **Game Misconduct** – When a major penalty has been assessed for hooking as a result of an injury to an opponent, a game misconduct penalty must also be assessed.

55.5 **Penalty Shot** – refer to Rule **57.3** – Tripping.

55.6 **Awarded Goal** – refer to Rule **57.4** – Tripping.

55.7 **Fines and Suspensions** - A player who has been assessed a major penalty and a game misconduct under this rule shall be automatically fined one hundred dollars ($100).

If deemed appropriate, supplementary discipline can be applied by the Commissioner at his discretion (refer to Rule **28**).

## Rule 56 – Interference

56.1 **Interference** - A strict standard on acts of interference must be adhered to in all areas of the rink.

Body Position: Body position shall be determined as the player skating in front of or beside his opponent, traveling in the same direction. A player who is behind an opponent, who does not have the puck, may not use his stick, body or free hand in order to restrain his opponent, but must skate in order to gain or reestablish his proper position in order to make a check.

A player is allowed the ice he is standing on (body position) and is not required to move in order to let an opponent proceed. A player may "block" the path of an opponent provided he is in front of his opponent and moving in the same direction. Moving laterally and without establishing body position, then making contact with the non-puck carrier is not permitted and will be penalized as interference. A player is always entitled to use his body position to lengthen an opponent's path to the puck, provided his stick is not utilized (to make himself "bigger" and therefore considerably lengthening the distance his opponent must travel to get where he is going); his free hand is not used and he does not take advantage of his body position to deliver an otherwise illegal check.

Possession of the Puck:

The last player to touch the puck, other than the goalkeeper, shall be considered the player in possession. The player deemed in possession of the puck may be checked legally, provided the check is rendered immediately following his loss of possession.

Restrain: The actions of a player who does not have body position, but instead uses illegal means (e.g. hook with stick; hold with hands, trip with the stick or in any manner) to impede an opponent who is not in possession of the puck. Illegal means are acts which allow a player or goalkeeper to establish, maintain or restore body position other than by skating.

Pick: A "pick" is the action of a player who checks an opponent who is not in possession of the puck and is unaware of the impending check/hit. A player who is aware of an impending hit, not deemed to be a legal "battle for the puck," may not be interfered with by a player or goalkeeper delivering a "pick." A player delivering a "pick" is one who moves into an opponent's path without initially having body position, thereby taking him out of the play. When this is done, an interference penalty shall be assessed.

Free Hand: When a free hand is used to hold, pull, tug, grab or physically restrain an opponent from moving freely, this must be penalized as holding. The free hand may be used by a player to "fend off" an opponent or his stick, but may not be used to hold an opponent's stick or body.

Stick: A player who does not have body position on his opponent, who uses his stick (either the blade or the shaft, including the butt-end of the shaft) to impede or prevent his opponent from moving freely on the ice shall be assessed a hooking penalty.

56.2 **Minor Penalty** - A minor penalty shall be imposed on a player who interferes with or impedes the progress of an opponent who is not in possession of the puck.

A minor penalty shall be imposed on a player who restrains an opponent who is attempting to "fore-check."

A minor penalty shall be imposed on an attacking player who deliberately checks a defensive player, including the goalkeeper, who is not in possession of the puck.

A minor penalty shall be imposed on a player who shall cause an opponent who is not in possession of the puck to be forced off-side, causing a stoppage in play. If this action causes a delayed off-side (and not necessarily a stoppage in play), then the application of a penalty for interference is subject to the judgment of the Referee.

A minor penalty shall be imposed on a player who deliberately knocks a stick out of an opponent's hand, or who prevents a player who has dropped his stick or any other piece of equipment from regaining possession of it.

A minor penalty shall be imposed on a player who knocks or shoots any abandoned or broken stick or illegal puck or other debris towards an opposing puck carrier in a manner that could cause him to be distracted. (See also Rule **53** – Throwing Equipment.)

A minor penalty shall be imposed on any identifiable player on the players' bench or penalty bench who, by means of his stick or his body, interferes with the movements of the puck or any opponent on the ice during the progress of the play. In addition, should a player about to come onto the ice, play the puck while one or both skates are still on the players' or penalty bench, a minor penalty for interference shall be assessed.

The appropriate penalty according to the playing rules shall be assessed when a player on the players' or penalty bench gets involved with an opponent on the ice during a stoppage in play. The player(s) involved may be subject to additional sanctions as appropriate pursuant to Rule **28** – Supplementary Discipline.

56.3 **Bench Minor Penalty** - A bench minor penalty shall be imposed when an unidentifiable player on the players' bench or penalty bench or any Coach or non-playing Club personnel who, by means of his stick or his body, interferes with the movements of the puck or any opponent on the ice during the progress of the play.

56.4 **Major Penalty** - The Referee, at his discretion, may assess a major penalty, based on the degree of violence, to a player guilty of interfering with an opponent (see **56.5**).

56.5 **Game Misconduct Penalty** – When a major penalty is imposed under this rule for a foul resulting in an injury of an opponent, a game misconduct shall be imposed.

56.6 **Penalty Shot** - When a player in control of the puck in the neutral or attacking zone and having no other opponent to pass than the goalkeeper is interfered with by a stick or any part thereof or any other object or piece of equipment thrown or shot by any member of the defending team including the Coach or non-playing Club personnel, a penalty shot shall be awarded to the non-offending team. When a Coach or non-playing Club personnel is guilty of such an act, he shall be automatically suspended from the game, ordered to the dressing room and the matter will be reported to the Commissioner for possible further disciplinary action.

56.7 **Awarded Goal** - If, when the goalkeeper has been removed from the ice, any member of his team (including the goalkeeper) not legally on the ice, including the Coach or non-playing Club personnel, interferes by means of his body, stick or any other object or piece of equipment with the movements of the puck or an opposing player in the neutral or attacking zone, the Referee shall immediately award a goal to the non-offending team. When a Coach or non-playing Club personnel is guilty of such an act, he shall be automatically suspended from the game, ordered to the dressing room and the matter will be reported to the Commissioner for possible further disciplinary action.

56.8 **Fines and Suspensions** – Refer to Rule 23.6 – Fines and Suspensions – Physical Fouls Category.

There are no specified fines or suspensions for interference, however, supplementary discipline can be applied by the Commissioner at his discretion (refer to Rule 28).

## Rule 57 – Tripping

57.1 **Tripping** – A player shall not place the stick, knee, foot, arm, hand or elbow in such a manner that causes his opponent to trip or fall.

Accidental trips which occur simultaneously with a completed play will not be penalized. Accidental trips occurring simultaneously with or after a stoppage of play will not be penalized.

57.2 **Minor Penalty** - A minor penalty shall be imposed on any player who shall place his stick or any portion of his body in such a manner that it shall cause his opponent to trip and fall.

57.3 **Penalty Shot** - When a player, in the neutral or attacking zone, in control of the puck (or who could have obtained possession and control of the puck) and having no other opponent to pass than the goalkeeper, is tripped or otherwise fouled from behind, thus preventing a reasonable scoring opportunity, a penalty shot shall be awarded to the non-offending team. Nevertheless, the Referee shall not stop play until the attacking team has lost possession of the puck to the defending team.

The intention of this rule is to restore a reasonable scoring opportunity which has been lost. If, however, the player fouled is able to recover and obtain a reasonable scoring opportunity (or a teammate is able to gain a reasonable scoring opportunity), no penalty shot should be awarded but the appropriate penalty should be signaled and assessed if a goal is not scored on the play.

"Control of the puck" means the act of propelling the puck with the stick, hand or feet. If while it is being propelled, the puck is touched by another player or his equipment, or hits the goal or goes free, the player shall no longer be considered to be "in control of the puck".

In order for a penalty shot to be awarded for a player being fouled from behind, the following four (4) criteria must have been met:

(i) *The infraction must have taken place in the neutral or attacking zone (i.e. over the puck carrier's own blue line).*

(ii) *The infraction must have been committed from behind.*

(iii) *The player in possession and control (or, in the judgment of the Referee, the player clearly would have obtained possession and control of the puck) must have been denied a reasonable chance to score. The fact that the player got a shot off does not automatically eliminate this play from the penalty shot consideration criteria. If the foul was from behind and the player was denied a "more" reasonable scoring opportunity due to the foul, then the penalty shot should still be awarded.*

(iv) *The player in possession and control (or, in the judgment of the Referee, the player clearly would have obtained possession and control) must have had no opposing player between himself and the goalkeeper.*

If, in the opinion of the Referee, a player makes contact with the puck first and subsequently trips the opponent in so doing, no penalty shot will be awarded, but a minor penalty for tripping shall be assessed.

It should be noted that if the attacking player manages to get around the goalkeeper and has no defending player between him and the open goal, and he is fouled from behind by the goalkeeper or another defending player, no goal can be awarded since the goalkeeper is still on the ice. A penalty shot would be awarded.

57.4 **Awarded Goal** - If, when the opposing goalkeeper has been removed from the ice, a player in control of the puck (or who could have obtained possession and control of the puck) in the neutral or attacking zone is tripped or otherwise fouled with no opposition between him and the opposing goal, thus preventing a reasonable scoring opportunity, the Referee shall immediately stop play and award a goal to the attacking team.

# SECTION 8 – STICK FOULS

## Rule 58 – Butt-ending

58.1 **Butt-ending** – The action whereby a player uses the shaft of the stick, above the upper hand, to check an opposing player in any manner or jabs or attempts to jab an opposing player with this part of the stick.

58.2 **Double-minor Penalty** - A double-minor penalty will be imposed on a player who attempts to butt-end an opponent.

58.3 **Major Penalty** - A major penalty shall be imposed on a player who butt-ends an opponent (see section **58.5**).

58.4 **Match Penalty** - A match penalty shall be imposed on a player who injures an opponent as a result of a butt-end.

58.5 **Game Misconduct Penalty** – When a major penalty is imposed for butt-ending, a game misconduct penalty must also be assessed.

58.6 **Fines and Suspensions** - When a major penalty and game misconduct are imposed under this rule, an automatic fine of one hundred dollars ($100) will be imposed.

If deemed appropriate, supplementary discipline can be applied by the Commissioner at his discretion (refer to Rule **28**).

## Rule 59 – Cross-checking

59.1 **Cross-checking** - The action of using the shaft of the stick between the two hands to forcefully check an opponent.

59.2 **Minor Penalty** - A minor penalty, at the discretion of the Referee based on the severity of the contact, shall be imposed on a player who "cross checks" an opponent.

59.3 **Major Penalty** - A major penalty, at the discretion of the Referee based on the severity of the contact, shall be imposed on a player who "cross checks" an opponent (see **59.5**).

59.4 **Match Penalty** – The Referee, at his discretion, may assess a match penalty if, in his judgment, the player attempted to or deliberately injured his opponent by cross-checking.

59.5 **Game Misconduct Penalty** - When a major penalty is assessed for cross-checking, an automatic game misconduct penalty shall be imposed on the offending player.

59.6 **Fines and Suspensions** - When a major penalty is imposed under this rule, an automatic fine of one hundred dollars ($100) shall also be imposed.

If deemed appropriate, supplementary discipline can be applied by the Commissioner at his discretion (refer to Rule **28**).

## Rule 60 – High-sticking

60.1 **High-sticking** - A "high stick" is one which is carried above the height of the opponent's shoulders. Players must be in control and responsible for their stick. However, a player is permitted accidental contact on an opponent if the act is committed as a normal windup or follow through of a shooting motion, or accidental contact on the opposing center who is bent over during the course of a face-off. A wild swing at a bouncing puck would not be considered a normal windup or follow through and any contact to an opponent above the height of the shoulders shall be penalized accordingly.

60.2 **Minor Penalty** - Any contact made by a stick on an opponent above the shoulders is prohibited and a minor penalty shall be imposed.

60.3 **Double-minor Penalty** - When a player carries or holds any part of his stick above the shoulders of the opponent so that injury results, the Referee shall assess a double-minor penalty for all contact that causes an injury, whether accidental or careless, in the opinion of the Referee.

60.4 **Match Penalty** – When, in the opinion of the Referee, a player attempts to or deliberately injures an opponent while carrying or holding any part of his stick above the shoulders of the opponent, the Referee shall assess a match penalty to the offending player.

60.5 **Goals** - An apparent goal scored by an attacking player who strikes the puck with his stick carried above the height of the crossbar of the goal frame shall not be allowed. The determining factor is where the puck makes contact with the stick. If the puck makes contact with the stick at or below the level of the crossbar and enters the goal, this goal shall be allowed.

A goal scored by a defending player who strikes the puck with his stick carried above the height of the crossbar of the goal frame shall be allowed.

60.6 **Fines and Suspensions** - There are no specified fines or suspensions for high-sticking, however, supplementary discipline can be applied by the Commissioner at his discretion (refer to Rule **28**).

## Hooking

Although hooking can be classified as a stick-related foul, it has been placed in Section 7 – Restraining Fouls as Rule **55** as this tends to be the more prominent application of this rule.

## Rule 61 – Slashing

61.1 **Slashing** - Slashing is the act of a player swinging his stick at an opponent, whether contact is made or not. Non-aggressive stick contact to the pant or front of the shin pads, should not be penalized as slashing. Any forceful or powerful chop with the stick on an opponent's body, the opponent's stick, or on or near the opponent's hands that, in the judgment of the Referee, is not an attempt to play the puck, shall be penalized as slashing.

61.2 **Minor Penalty** - A minor penalty, at the discretion of the Referee based on the severity of the contact, shall be imposed on a player who slashes an opponent.

61.3 **Major Penalty** - A major penalty, at the discretion of the Referee based on the severity of the contact, shall be imposed on a player who slashes an opponent. When injury occurs, a major penalty must be assessed under this rule (see **61.5**).

61.4 **Match Penalty** – The Referee, at his discretion, may assess a match penalty if, in his judgment, the player attempted to or deliberately injured his opponent by slashing.

61.5 **Game Misconduct Penalty** – Whenever a major penalty is assessed for slashing, a game misconduct penalty must also be imposed.

61.6 **Penalty Shot** – refer to Rule **57.3** – Tripping.

61.7 **Awarded Goal** – refer to Rule **57.4** – Tripping.

61.8 **Fines and Suspensions** - There are no specified fines or suspensions for slashing, however, supplementary discipline can be applied by the Commissioner at his discretion (refer to Rule **28**).

## Rule 62 – Spearing

62.1 **Spearing** - Spearing shall mean stabbing an opponent with the point of the stick blade, whether contact is made or not.

62.2 **Double-minor Penalty** - A double-minor penalty will be imposed on a player who spears an opponent and does not make contact.

62.3 **Major Penalty** - A major penalty shall be imposed on a player who spears an opponent (see **62.5**).

62.4 **Match Penalty** - A match penalty shall be imposed on a player who injures an opponent as a result of a spear.

62.5 **Game Misconduct Penalty** - Whenever a major penalty is assessed for spearing, a game misconduct penalty must also be imposed.

62.6 **Fines and Suspensions** - There are no specified fines or suspensions for spearing, however, supplementary discipline can be applied by the Commissioner at his discretion (refer to Rule **28**).

# SECTION 9 – OTHER FOULS

## Rule 63 – Delaying the Game

63.1 **Delaying the Game** – A player or a team may be penalized when, in the opinion of the Referee, is delaying the game in any manner.

63.2 **Minor Penalty** - A minor penalty shall be imposed on any player, including the goalkeeper, who holds, freezes or plays the puck with his stick, skates or body in such a manner as to deliberately cause a stoppage of play. With regard to a goalkeeper, this rule applies outside of his goal crease area.

A minor penalty for delay of game shall be imposed on any player who deliberately shoots or bats (using his hand or his stick) the puck outside the playing area (from anywhere on the ice surface) during the play or after a stoppage of play.

When any player shoots or bats (using his hand or his stick) the puck directly (non-deflected) out of the playing surface from his defending zone, except where there is no glass, a penalty shall be assessed for delaying the game. The determining factor shall be the position of the puck when it was shot or batted by the offending player. If contact with the puck occurs while the puck is inside the defending zone, and subsequently goes out of play, the minor penalty shall be assessed. When the puck is shot into the players' bench, the penalty will not apply. When the puck is shot over the glass 'behind' the players' bench, the penalty will be assessed. When the puck goes out of the playing area directly off a face-off, no penalty shall be assessed.

A minor penalty shall be imposed on any player who delays the game by deliberately displacing a goal post from its normal position. The Referee shall stop play immediately when the offending team gains control of the puck.

In the event that a goalpost is deliberately displaced by a defending player, prior to the puck crossing the goal line between the normal position of the goalposts, the Referee shall assess a minor penalty for delaying the game if the attacking player has not yet taken the shot or in the act of taking the shot at the open net (see **63.6**).

When the net is accidentally displaced by an attacking player, and the defending side is in control of the puck and moving out of their zone, play shall be permitted to continue until such time as the non-offending team loses control of the puck. The resulting face-off will take place at a face-off spot in the zone nearest the location where the play was stopped, unless it is in the non-offending team's defending zone, and as such the ensuing face-off would be outside the blue line at one of the face-off spots in the neutral zone. It is possible for a goal to be scored at one end of the rink while the net at the other end has been dislodged, provided that the team being scored upon is the team responsible for dislodging the net at the other end of the rink.

A minor penalty shall be imposed on a player other than the goalkeeper who deliberately falls on or gathers the puck into his body. Any player who drops to his knees to block a shot should not be penalized if the puck is shot under him or becomes lodged in his clothing or equipment but any use of the hands to make the puck unplayable should be penalized promptly.

If a goalkeeper comes out of his crease to "cut down the angle" on a shot and after making the save covers the puck, this shall be legal. If the goalkeeper races out of his crease in an attempt to beat the attacking player to the puck and instead of playing the puck jumps on the puck causing a stoppage of play, this shall be a minor penalty for delay of game.

A minor penalty shall be imposed on a goalkeeper who, when he is in his own goal crease, deliberately falls on or gathers the puck into his body or who holds or places the puck against any part of the goal in such a manner as to cause a stoppage of play unless he is actually being checked by an opponent.

A goalkeeper shall not play the puck outside of the designated area behind the net. Should the goalkeeper play the puck outside of the designated area behind the goal line, a minor penalty for delay of game shall be imposed. The determining factor shall be the position of the puck. The minor penalty will not be assessed when a goalkeeper plays the puck while maintaining skate contact with his goal crease.

Play shall not be stopped nor the game delayed by reasons of adjustments to clothing, equipment, skates or sticks. For an infringement of this rule, a minor penalty shall be given. No penalty should be assessed when a water bottle is delivered to a goalkeeper, however, this should be conducted during time-outs and if, in the opinion of the Referee, it is being done to intentionally delay the game, a minor penalty may be assessed.

No delay shall be permitted for the repair or adjustment of goalkeeper's equipment. If adjustments are required, the goalkeeper shall leave the ice and his place shall be taken by the substitute goalkeeper immediately. For an infraction of this rule by a goalkeeper, a minor penalty shall be imposed.

63.3 **Bench Minor Penalty** - A bench minor penalty shall be imposed upon any Team which, after warning by the Referee to its Captain or Alternate Captain to place the correct number of players on the ice and commence play, fails to comply with the Referee's direction and thereby causes any delay by making additional substitutions (including, but not limited to, continually substituting goalkeepers for the purpose of stalling or delaying the game), by persisting in having its players off-side, or in any other manner.

63.4 **Objects Thrown on the Ice** – In the event that objects are thrown on the ice that interfere with the progress of the game, the Referee shall blow the whistle and stop the play and the puck shall be faced-off at a face-off spot in the zone nearest to the spot where play is stopped. When objects are thrown on the ice during a stoppage in play, including after the scoring of a goal, the Referee shall have announced over the public address system that any further occurrences will result in a bench minor penalty being assessed to the home Team. Articles thrown onto the ice following a special occasion (i.e. hat trick) will not result in a bench minor penalty being assessed. Refer also to Rule **53.6** when spectator interference occurs during a breakaway.

63.5 **Penalty Shot** - If the goal post is deliberately displaced by a goalkeeper or player during the course of a "breakaway," a penalty shot will be awarded to the non-offending team, which shot shall be taken by the player last in possession of the puck.

If by reason of insufficient time in the regular playing time or by reason of penalties already imposed, the minor penalty assessed to a player for deliberately displacing his own goal post cannot be served in its entirety within the regular playing time of the game or at any time in overtime, a penalty shot shall be awarded against the offending team.

No defending player, except the goalkeeper, will be permitted to fall on the puck, hold the puck, pick up the puck, or gather the puck into the body or hands when the puck is within the goal crease. For infringement of this rule, play shall immediately be stopped and a penalty shot shall be ordered against the offending team, but no other penalty shall be given. The rule shall be interpreted so that a penalty shot will be awarded only when the puck is in the crease at the instant the offense occurs. However, in cases where the puck is outside the crease, Rule **63** may still apply and a minor penalty may be imposed, even though no penalty shot is awarded. The significant factor when determining whether or not a penalty shot is warranted is the location of the puck at the time it was held, grabbed or gathered into the body. If the puck is in the crease, penalty shot. If the puck is outside the crease and gathered into the body of a player (other than the goalkeeper) who is inside the crease, minor penalty). See also Rule **67** – Handling Puck.

63.6 **Awarded Goal** - In the event that the goal post is displaced, either deliberately or accidentally, by a defending player, prior to the puck crossing the goal line between the normal position of the goalposts, the Referee may award a goal.

In order to award a goal in this situation, the goal post must have been displaced by the actions of a defending player, the puck must have been shot (or the player must be in the act of shooting) at the goal prior to the goal post being displaced, and it must be determined that the puck would have entered the net between the normal position of the goal posts.

When the goal post has been displaced deliberately by the defending team when their goalkeeper has been removed for an extra attacker thereby preventing an impending goal by the attacking team, the Referee shall award a goal to the attacking team.

The goal frame is considered to be displaced if either or both goal pegs are no longer in their respective holes in the ice, or the net has come completely off one or both pegs, prior to or as the puck enters the goal.

63.7 **Infractions** – The following list of infractions shall result in a penalty (minor, bench minor, penalty shot or awarded goal) being imposed by the Referee for delaying the game:

*(i) Deliberately shooting the puck out of play.*

*(ii) Deliberately throwing or batting the puck out of play.*

*(iii) Shooting or batting the puck (with the hand or with the stick) over the glass from the defending zone.*

*(iv) Deliberately displacing the goal from it's normal position (or accidentally by a defending player or goalkeeper in relation to the awarding of a goal).*

*(v) Refusing to place the correct number of players on the ice.*

*(vi) Persisting in having players in an off-side position.*

*(vii) Deliberately falling on the puck.*

*(viii) Adjustment of clothing or equipment.*

## Rule 64 – Diving / Embellishment

64.1 **Diving / Embellishment** – Any player who blatantly dives, embellishes a fall or a reaction, or who feigns an injury shall be penalized with a minor penalty under this rule.

A goalkeeper who deliberately initiates contact with an attacking player other than to establish position in the crease, or who otherwise acts to create the appearance of other than incidental contact with an attacking player, is subject to the assessment of a minor penalty for diving / embellishment.

64.2 **Minor Penalty** - A minor penalty shall be imposed on a player who attempts to draw a penalty by his actions ("diving / embellishment").

64.3 **Fines and Suspensions –** As outlined in League issued memorandum distributed to all teams prior to the 2015-2016 season.

## Rule 65 – Equipment

65.1 **Equipment** – The onus is on the player to maintain his equipment and uniform in playing condition as set forth in these rules.

65.2 **Minor Penalty** - All protective equipment, except gloves, headgear and goalkeepers' leg guards must be worn under the uniform. For violation of this rule, after warning by the Referee, a minor penalty shall be imposed. Players violating this rule shall not be permitted to participate in the game until such equipment has been corrected or removed.

Play shall not be stopped nor the game delayed by reasons of adjustments to clothing, equipment, skates or sticks. For an infringement of this rule, a minor penalty shall be given.

No delay shall be permitted for the repair or adjustment of goalkeeper's equipment. If adjustments are required, the goalkeeper shall leave the ice and his place shall be taken by the substitute goalkeeper immediately. For an infraction of this rule by a goalkeeper, a minor penalty shall be imposed.

## Rule 66 – Forfeit of Game

66.1 **Forfeit of Game** - In the event of failure by a Club to comply with a provision of the League constitution, by-laws, resolutions, rules or regulations affecting the playing of a game, the Referee shall, if so directed by the Commissioner or his designee, refuse to permit the game to proceed until the offending Club comes into compliance with such provision.

Should the offending club persist in its refusal to come into compliance, the Referee shall, with the prior approval of the Commissioner or his designee, declare the game forfeited and the non-offending Club the winner. Should the Referee declare the game forfeited because both Clubs have refused to comply with such a provision, the visiting Club shall be declared the winner.

If the game is declared forfeited prior to its having commenced, the score shall be recorded as 1-0 and no player shall be credited with any personal statistics.

If the game was in progress at the time it is declared forfeited, the score shall be recorded as zero for the loser and 1, or such greater number of goals that had been scored by it, for the winner; however, the players on both Clubs shall be credited with all personal statistics earned up to the time the forfeit was declared.

## Rule 67 – Handling Puck

67.1 **Handling Puck** - A player shall be permitted to stop or "bat" a puck in the air with his open hand, or push it along the ice with his hand, and the play shall not be stopped unless, in the opinion of the on-ice officials, he has deliberately directed the puck to a teammate, or has allowed his team to gain an advantage, in any zone other than the defending zone, in which case the play shall be stopped and a face-off conducted (see Rule **79** – Hand Pass). Play will not be stopped for any hand pass by players in their own defending zone.

67.2 **Minor Penalty – Player** - A player shall be permitted to catch the puck out of the air but must immediately place it or knock it down to the ice. If he catches it and skates with it, either to avoid a check or to gain a territorial advantage over his opponent, a minor penalty shall be assessed for "closing his hand on the puck".

Anytime a player places his hand over the puck while it is on the ice in order to conceal it from or prevent an opponent from playing the puck, a minor penalty shall be assessed for "closing his hand on the puck". When this is done in his team's goal crease area, a penalty shot shall be assessed (**67.4**) or a goal awarded (**67.5**).

A minor penalty shall be imposed on a player who, while play is in progress, picks up the puck off the ice with his hand.

67.3 **Minor Penalty – Goalkeeper** - A goalkeeper who holds the puck with his hands for longer than three seconds shall be given a minor penalty unless he is actually being checked by an opponent. The object of this entire rule is to keep the puck in play continuously and any action taken by the goalkeeper which causes an unnecessary stoppage must be penalized without warning.

A goalkeeper shall be assessed a minor penalty when he deliberately holds the puck in any manner which, in the opinion of the Referee, causes an unnecessary stoppage of play.

A goalkeeper shall be assessed a minor penalty when he throws the puck forward towards the opponent's net. In the case where the puck thrown forward by the goalkeeper being taken by an opponent, the Referee shall allow the resulting play to be completed, and if goal is scored by the non-offending team, it shall be allowed and no penalty given; but if a goal is not scored, play shall be stopped and a minor penalty shall be imposed against the goalkeeper.

A goalkeeper shall be assessed a minor penalty when he deliberately drops the puck into his pads or onto the goal net.

A goalkeeper shall be assessed a minor penalty when he deliberately piles up snow or obstacles at or near his net that, in the opinion of the Referee, would tend to prevent the scoring of a goal.

67.4 **Penalty Shot** - If a defending player, except a goalkeeper, while play is in progress, falls on the puck, holds the puck, picks up the puck, or gathers the puck into his body or hands from the ice in the goal crease area, the play shall be stopped immediately and a penalty shot shall be awarded to the non-offending team. See also Rule **63** – Delaying the Game.

67.5 **Awarded Goal** – When a goalkeeper, prior to proceeding to his players' bench to be replaced by an extra attacker, intentionally leaves his stick or other piece of equipment, piles snow or other obstacles at or near his net that, in the opinion of the Referee, would tend to prevent the puck from entering the net, a goal shall be awarded. In order to award a goal in this situation, the goalkeeper must have been replaced for an extra attacker, otherwise a minor penalty shall be assessed.

If a player, when the goalkeeper has been replaced for an extra attacker, falls on the puck, holds the puck, picks up the puck, or gathers the puck into his body or hands from the ice in the goal crease area, the play shall be stopped immediately and goal awarded to the non-offending team.

67.6 **Disallowed Goal** - A goal cannot be scored by an attacking player who bats or directs the puck with his hand into the net. A goal cannot be scored by an attacking player who bats or directs the puck and it is deflected into the net off any player, goalkeeper or official. When the puck enters the net on a clear deflection off a glove, the goal shall be allowed.

## Rule 68 – Illegal Substitution

68.1 **Illegal Substitution** – An illegal substitution shall be deemed to have occurred when a player enters the game illegally from either the players' bench (teammate not within the five (5) foot limit, refer to Rule **74** – Too Many Men on the Ice), from the penalty bench (penalty has not yet expired), when a major penalty is being served and the replacement player does not return to the ice from the penalty bench (see **68.2**), or when a player illegally enters the game for the sole purpose of preventing an opposing player from scoring on a breakaway (see **68.3** and **68.4**).

When an injured player is penalized and leaves the game, if he returns before the expiration of his penalty, he is not eligible to play. This includes coincidental penalties when his substitute is still in the penalty box awaiting a stoppage in play. The injured player must wait until his substitute has been released from the penalty box before he is eligible to play. See **8.1**.

68.2 **Bench Minor Penalty** – When a player receives a major penalty and a misconduct or game misconduct penalty at the same time, or when an injured player receives a major penalty and is unable to serve the penalty himself, the penalized team shall place a substitute player on the penalty bench before the major penalty expires and no replacement for the penalized player shall be permitted to enter the game except from the penalty bench. Any violation of this provision shall be treated as an illegal substitution under this rule calling for a bench minor penalty.

68.3 **Penalty Shot** – If a player of the attacking side in possession of the puck shall be in such a position as to have no opposition between him and the opposing goalkeeper, and while in such position he shall be interfered with by a player of the opposing side who shall have illegally entered the game, the Referee shall impose a penalty shot against the side to which the offending player belongs.

68.4 **Awarded Goal** - If, when the opposing goalkeeper has been removed from the ice, a player of the side attacking the unattended goal is interfered with in the neutral or attacking zone by a player who shall have entered the game illegally, the Referee shall immediately award a goal to the non-offending team.

68.5 **Disallowed Goal** – If a penalized player returns to the ice from the penalty bench before his penalty has expired by his own error or the error of the Penalty Timekeeper, any goal scored by his own team while he (or his substitute) is illegally on the ice shall be disallowed but all penalties imposed on either team shall be served as regular penalties. The penalized player must return to serve his unexpired time (and an additional minor penalty if he left the penalty bench on his own).

If a player shall illegally enter the game from his own players' bench or from any other location in the rink, any goal scored by his own team while he is illegally on the ice shall be disallowed but all penalties imposed on either team shall be served as regular penalties.

68.6 **Deliberate Illegal Substitution** – see Rule **74** – Too Many Men on the Ice.

## Rule 69 – Interference on the Goalkeeper

69.1 **Interference on the Goalkeeper** - This rule is based on the premise that an attacking player's position, whether inside or outside the crease, should not, by itself, determine whether a goal should be

allowed or disallowed. In other words, goals scored while attacking players are standing in the crease may, in appropriate circumstances be allowed. Goals should be disallowed only if: (1) an attacking player, either by his positioning or by contact, impairs the goalkeeper's ability to move freely within his crease or defend his goal; or (2) an attacking player initiates intentional or deliberate contact with a goalkeeper, inside or outside of his goal crease. Incidental contact with a goalkeeper will be permitted, and resulting goals allowed, when such contact is initiated outside of the goal crease, provided the attacking player has made a reasonable effort to avoid such contact. The rule will be enforced exclusively in accordance with the on-ice judgement of the Referee(s), but may be subject to a Coach's Challenge (see Rule 78.7).

For purposes of this rule, "contact," whether incidental or otherwise, shall mean any contact that is made between or among a goalkeeper and attacking player(s), whether by means of a stick or any part of the body.

The overriding rationale of this rule is that a goalkeeper should have the ability to move freely within his goal crease without being hindered by the actions of an attacking player. If an attacking player enters the goal crease and, by his actions, impairs the goalkeeper's ability to defend his goal, and a goal is scored, the goal will be disallowed.

If an attacking player has been pushed, shoved, or fouled by a defending player so as to cause him to come into contact with the goalkeeper, such contact will not be deemed contact initiated by the attacking player for purposes of this rule, provided the attacking player has made a reasonable effort to avoid such contact.

If a defending player has been pushed, shoved, or fouled by an attacking player so as to cause the defending player to come into contact with his own goalkeeper, such contact shall be deemed contact initiated by the attacking player for purposes of this rule, and if necessary a penalty assessed to the attacking player and if a goal is scored it would be disallowed.

69.2 **Penalty** - In all cases in which an attacking player initiates intentional or deliberate contact with a goalkeeper, whether or not the goalkeeper is inside or outside the goal crease, and whether or not a goal is scored, the attacking player will receive a penalty (minor or major, as the Referee deems appropriate). In all cases where the infraction being imposed is to the attacking player for hindering the goalkeeper's ability to move freely in his goal crease, the penalty to be assessed is for goalkeeper interference.

In exercising his judgment, the Referee should give more significant consideration to the degree and nature of the contact with the goalkeeper than to the exact location of the goalkeeper at the time of the contact.

69.3 **Contact Inside the Goal Crease** - If an attacking player initiates contact with a goalkeeper, incidental or otherwise, while the goalkeeper is in his goal crease, and a goal is scored, the goal will be disallowed.

If a goalkeeper, in the act of establishing his position within his goal crease, initiates contact with an attacking player who is in the goal crease, and this results in an impairment of the goalkeeper's ability to defend his goal, and a goal is scored, the goal will be disallowed.

If, after any contact by a goalkeeper who is attempting to establish position in his goal crease, the attacking player does not immediately vacate his current position in the goal crease (i.e. give ground to the goalkeeper), and a goal is scored, the goal will be disallowed. In all such cases, whether or not a goal is scored, the attacking player will receive a minor penalty for goalkeeper interference.

If an attacking player establishes a significant position within the goal crease, so as to obstruct the goalkeeper's vision and impair his ability to defend his goal, and a goal is scored, the goal will be disallowed.

For this purpose, a player "establishes a significant position within the crease" when, in the Referee's judgment, his body, or a substantial portion thereof, is within the goal crease for more than an instantaneous period of time.

Refer also to Reference Tables – Table 16 – Interference on the Goalkeeper Situations (page 151).

69.4 **Contact Outside the Goal Crease** - If an attacking player initiates any contact with a goalkeeper, other than incidental contact, while the goalkeeper is outside his goal crease, and a goal is scored, the goal will be disallowed.

A goalkeeper is not "fair game" just because he is outside the goal crease. The appropriate penalty should be assessed in every case where an attacking player makes unnecessary contact with the goalkeeper. However, incidental contact will be permitted when the goalkeeper is in the act of playing the puck outside his goal crease provided the attacking player has made a reasonable effort to avoid such unnecessary contact.

When a goalkeeper has played the puck outside of his crease and is then prevented from returning to his crease area due to the deliberate actions of an attacking player, such player may be penalized for goalkeeper interference. Similarly, the goalkeeper may be penalized, if by his actions outside of his crease he deliberately interferes with an attacking player who is attempting to play the puck or an opponent.

Refer also to Reference Tables – Table 16 – Interference on the Goalkeeper Situations (page 151).

69.5 **Coach's Challenge** – Refer to Rule 78.7.

69.6 **Face-off Location** – Whenever the Referee stops play to disallow a goal as a result of contact with the goalkeeper (incidental or otherwise), the resulting face-off shall take place at the nearest neutral zone face-off spot outside the attacking zone of the offending team.

69.7 **Rebounds and Loose Pucks** - In a rebound situation, or where a goalkeeper and attacking player(s) are simultaneously attempting to play a loose puck, whether inside or outside the crease, incidental

contact with the goalkeeper will be permitted, and any goal that is scored as a result thereof will be allowed.

In the event that a goalkeeper has been pushed into the net together with the puck by an attacking player after making a stop, the goal will be disallowed. If applicable, appropriate penalties will be assessed. If, however, in the opinion of the Referee, the attacking player was pushed or otherwise fouled by a defending player causing the goalkeeper to be pushed into the net together with the puck, the goal can be permitted.

In the event that the puck is under a player in or around the crease area (deliberately or otherwise), a goal cannot be scored by pushing this player together with the puck into the goal. If applicable, the appropriate penalties will be assessed, including a penalty shot if deemed to be covered in the crease deliberately (see Rule **63** – Delaying the Game).

69.8 **Fines and Suspensions** - An attacking player who, in the judgment of the Referee, initiates contact with the goalkeeper, whether inside or outside the crease, in a fashion that would otherwise warrant a penalty, will be assessed an appropriate penalty (minor or major and/or game misconduct) and will be subject to additional sanctions as appropriate pursuant to Rule **28** – Supplementary Discipline.

## Rule 70 – Leaving the Bench

70.1 **Leaving the Bench** - No player may leave the players' or penalty bench at any time during an altercation or for the purpose of starting an altercation.

70.2 **Legal Line Change** – A player who has entered the game while play is in progress from his own players' bench or legally from the penalty bench (penalty time has expired) who starts an altercation may be subject to discipline in accordance with Rule **28** – Supplementary Discipline.

A player or players who have entered the game on a legal line change during a stoppage of play, who line up in preparation for the ensuing face-off, and who participate in an altercation shall be penalized under the appropriate rule and will be subject to discipline in accordance with Rule **28** – Supplementary Discipline (a game misconduct is not automatic in this situation unless provided for as a result of his actions in the altercation).

70.3 **Leaving the Players' Bench** – Players shall not be permitted to come on the ice during a stoppage of play or at the end of the first and second periods for the purpose of warming-up. The Referee will report any violation of this rule to the Commissioner for disciplinary action.

Except at the end of each period or for entering the game legally, no player may, at any time, leave the players' bench. If it is necessary to proceed to the dressing room during the course of the game (and when it is required to proceed by way of the ice to access the dressing room), the player must wait for a stoppage of play and ensure there are not altercations in progress before proceeding.

The player who was the first or second player to leave the players' (or penalty bench) during an altercation or for the purpose of starting an altercation, from either or both teams shall be assessed a game misconduct penalty.

70.4 **Leaving the Penalty Bench** – Except at the end of each period or on expiration of his penalty, no player may, at any time, leave the penalty bench.

A player serving a penalty on the penalty bench, who is to be changed after the penalty has been served, must proceed at once by way of the ice and be at his own players' bench before any change can be made. For any violation of this rule, a bench minor penalty shall be imposed for too many men on the ice (see Rule **74** – Too Many Men on the Ice).

A penalized player who leaves the penalty bench before his penalty has expired, whether play is in progress or not, shall incur an additional minor penalty after serving his unexpired penalty.

Any player who, having entered the penalty bench, leaves the penalty bench prior to the expiration of his penalty for the purpose of challenging an official's ruling, shall be assessed a game misconduct penalty. He shall also be automatically suspended for the next three (3) regular League and/or playoff games of his Club. This rule does not replace any other more severe penalty that may be imposed for leaving the penalty bench for the purpose of starting or participating in an altercation as outlined in this rule.

Any penalized player leaving the penalty bench during a stoppage of play and during an altercation shall incur a minor penalty plus a game misconduct penalty. The minor penalty plus the unexpired time remaining in his original penalty must be served by a replacement player placed on the penalty bench by the Coach of the offending team.

If a player leaves the penalty bench before his penalty is fully served, the Penalty Timekeeper shall note the time and signal the officials who will stop play when the offending player's team obtains control of the puck. An additional minor penalty must be served by this player in addition to the time remaining in his original penalty (this unexpired time is calculated from the time he left the penalty bench illegally).

In the case of a player returning to the ice before his time has expired through an error of the Penalty Timekeeper, he is not to serve an additional penalty, but must serve his unexpired time this unexpired time is calculated from the time he left the penalty bench through the error of the Penalty Timekeeper).

At a stoppage of play following the expiration of their penalties, if a player or players exiting the penalty bench get involved in an altercation, those coming from the penalty bench shall be assessed the penalties they incur in the altercation in addition to a game misconduct and a ten (10) game suspension as outlined in **70.10**. Should a player coming from the penalty bench at a stoppage of play get involved with an opponent and the opponent is deemed to be the instigator of the altercation, then the player coming from the penalty bench would not be subject to the game misconduct and ten (10) game suspension.

70.5 **Bench Minor Penalty** – A bench minor penalty shall be imposed on a team whose player(s) leave the players' bench for any purpose other than a change of players and when no altercation is in progress.

If a Coach or non-playing Club personnel gets on the ice (unless directed to do so by an on-ice official, i.e. to attend to an injured player) after the start of a period and before that period is ended, the Referee shall impose a bench minor penalty against the team and report the incident to the Commissioner for disciplinary action.

70.6 **Game Misconduct Penalty** – A game misconduct penalty shall be imposed on the player who was the first or second player to leave the players' or penalty bench during an altercation or for the purpose of starting an altercation, from either or both teams.

Any penalized player leaving the penalty bench during a stoppage of play and during an altercation shall incur a minor penalty plus a game misconduct penalty. The minor penalty plus the unexpired time remaining in his original penalty must be served by a replacement player placed on the penalty bench by the Coach of the offending team.

Any player who has been ordered to the dressing room by the officials and returns to his bench or to the ice surface for any reason before the appropriate time shall be assessed a game misconduct and shall be suspended automatically without pay for the next ten (10) regular League and/or Play-off games.

Once a player enters the penalty bench, he must not leave until his penalty expires and his team is entitled to an additional player on the ice, or, at the end of a period to proceed to his dressing room, or, when he has received permission from an on-ice official. At any other time, he shall be assessed a game misconduct penalty under this rule.

70.7 **Penalty Shot** – If a player of the attacking side in possession of the puck shall be in such a position as to have no opposition between him and the opposing goalkeeper, and while in such position he shall be interfered with by a player of the opposing side who shall have illegally entered the game, the Referee shall impose a penalty shot against the side to which the offending player belongs.

70.8 **Awarded Goal** – If, when the opposing goalkeeper has been removed from the ice, a player of the side attacking the unattended goal is interfered with in the neutral or attacking zone by a player who shall have entered the game illegally, the Referee shall immediately award a goal to the non-offending team.

70.9 **Disallowed Goal** – If a penalized player returns to the ice from the penalty bench before his penalty has expired by his own error or the error of the Penalty Timekeeper, any goal scored by his own team while he is illegally on the ice shall be disallowed but all penalties imposed on either team shall be served as regular penalties.

If a player shall illegally enter the game from his own players' bench or from the penalty bench, any goal scored by his own team while he is illegally on the ice shall be disallowed but all penalties imposed on either team shall be served as regular penalties.

70.10 **Fines and Suspensions** – The first player to leave the players' or penalty bench illegally during an altercation or for the purpose of starting an altercation from either or both teams shall be suspended automatically without pay for the next ten (10) regular League and/or Play-off games of his team.

The second player to leave the players' or penalty bench illegally during an altercation or for the purpose of starting an altercation from either or both teams shall be suspended automatically without pay for the next five (5) regular League and/or Play-off games.

The determination as to which players shall be deemed the first or second players to have left their respective players' or penalty benches illegally shall be made by the Referees in consultation with the Linesmen and off-ice officials. In the event that they are unable to identify the offending players, the matter will be referred to the Commissioner or his designee and such determinations may be made subsequently based on reports and other information including but not limited to television tapes.

Any team that has a player penalized for being the first or second player to leave the players' or penalty bench illegally during an altercation or for the purpose of starting an altercation, shall be fined ten thousand dollars ($10,000) for the first instance. This fine shall be increased by five thousand dollars ($5,000) for each subsequent occurrence over the next following three-year period.

All players as well as the first and second players who leave the bench illegally during an altercation or for the purpose of starting an altercation shall be subject to an automatic fine in the amount equal to the maximum permitted under the collective bargaining agreement.

Any player who leaves the penalty bench illegally during an altercation and is not the first player to do so, shall be suspended automatically without pay for the next five (5) regular League and/or Play-off games.

Any Club executive or non-playing Club personnel not normally on the players' bench, who gets on the ice after the start of a period and before that period is ended, will be automatically fined two hundred dollars ($200) and the Referee will report the incident to the Commissioner for disciplinary action.

Any player who has been ordered to the dressing room by the officials and returns to his bench or to the ice surface for any reason before the appropriate time shall be assessed a game misconduct and shall be suspended automatically without pay for the next ten (10) regular League and/or Play-off games.

The Coach(es) of the team(s) whose player(s) left the players' bench(es) or penalty bench(es) illegally during an altercation shall be suspended, pending a review by the Commissioner. The Coach(es) also will be fined a maximum of ten thousand dollars ($10,000).

For all suspensions imposed on players under this rule, the Club of the player or goalkeeper shall pay to the League a sum equal to the pro-rata of that player's salary covered by the suspension. For purposes of computing amounts due for a player's suspension, the player's fixed salary shall be divided by the number of days in the regular season and then, said result shall be multiplied by the number of games suspended.

In addition, any Club that is deemed by the Commissioner to pay or reimburse to the player the amount of the fine or loss of salary assessed under this rule shall be fined automatically one hundred thousand dollars ($100,000).

In the event that suspensions imposed under this rule cannot be completed in regular League and/or Play-off games in any one season, the remainder of the suspension shall be served the following season.

## Rule 71 – Premature Substitution

71.1 **Premature Substitution** - When a goalkeeper leaves his goal area and proceeds to his players' bench for the purpose of substituting another player, the skater cannot enter the playing surface before the goalkeeper is within five feet (5') of the bench. If the substitution is made prematurely, the official shall stop play immediately unless the non-offending team has possession of the puck -- in which event the stoppage will be delayed until the puck changes possession.

There shall be no time penalty to the team making the premature substitution, but the resulting face-off will take place at the center ice face-off spot when play is stopped beyond the center red line. When play is stopped prior to the center red line, the resulting face-off shall be conducted at the nearest face-off spot in the zone where the play was stopped.

In all other situations not covered in the above, a minor penalty may result for "too many men on the ice" (see Rule **74**).

71.2 **Announcement** - The Referee shall request that the public address announcer make the following announcement: "Play has been stopped due to premature substitution for the goalkeeper."

## Rule 72 – Refusing to Play the Puck

72.1 **Refusing or Abstaining from Playing the Puck** - The purpose of this section is to enforce continuous action and both Referees and Linesmen should interpret and apply the rule to produce this result.

72.2 **Hand Pass** – When a hand pass has been initiated by one player to a teammate and the teammate elects not to play the puck to avoid the stoppage of play, and the opposing team also abstains from playing the puck (perhaps to allow time to expire on a penalty), the Referee shall stop the play and order the resulting face-off at the nearest face-off location to where the play was stopped for this violation.

72.3 **High Stick** – When a player contacts the puck with his stick above the normal height of the shoulders and a teammate elects not to play the puck to avoid the stoppage of play, and the opposing team also abstains from playing the puck (perhaps to allow time to expire on a penalty), the Referee shall stop the play and order the resulting face-off at the face-off spot in the zone to nearest to where the play was stopped for this violation. See also **76.2**.

72.4 **Icing** – If, in the opinion of the Referee, the defending side intentionally abstains from pursuing the puck beyond the face-off spots on an icing promptly when they are in a position to do so, he shall stop the play and order the resulting face-off on the adjacent corner face-off spot nearest the goal of the team at fault.

72.5 **Penalty** – When the Referee signals the delayed calling of a penalty to one team and a player of that team intentionally abstains from playing the puck in order to allow additional time to expire on the game or penalty time clocks, the Referee shall stop the play and order the resulting face-off at one of the face-off spots in the offending team's defending zone. See Rule **76.2**.

## Rule 73 – Refusing to Start Play

73.1 **Refusing to Start Play** – This rule applies to teams who refuse to play while both teams are on the ice or who withdraws from the ice and refuses to play or who refuses to come onto the ice at the start of the game or at the beginning of any period of the game, when ordered to do so by the Referee.

73.2 **Procedure – Team On Ice** - If, when both teams are on the ice, one team for any reason shall refuse to play when ordered to do so by the Referee, he shall warn the Captain and allow the team so refusing fifteen (15) seconds within which to begin the play or resume play. If at the end of that time, the team shall still refuse to play, the Referee shall impose a bench minor penalty for delay of game on a player of the offending team to be designated by the Coach of that team through the playing Captain. Should there be a repetition of the same incident, the Referee shall notify the Coach that he has been fined the sum of two hundred dollars ($200). The offending Coach shall be removed from the players' bench and assessed a game misconduct penalty.

Should the offending team still refuse to play, the Referee shall have no alternative but to declare that the game be forfeited to the non-offending Club and the case shall be reported to the Commissioner for further action (see Rule **66** – Forfeit of Game).

**First Violation**

(i) *Warn the Captain of the offending team and allow 15 seconds within which to resume play.*

(ii) *If at the end of the 15 seconds the team still refuses to resume play, assess a bench minor penalty to the offending team for delay of game.*

**Second Violation**

(i) *Warn the Captain of the offending team and allow 15 seconds within which to resume play.*

(ii) *If at the end of the 15 seconds the team still refuses to resume play, assess a bench minor penalty to the offending team for delay of game.*

(iii) *Referee is to notify the Coach of the offending team that he has* *been fined the sum of two hundred dollars ($200) and the Coach is to be assessed a game misconduct penalty.*

*(iv) If the team still refuses to play, the Referee shall declare the game be forfeited to the non-offending club (see Rule **66** – Forfeit of Game).*

73.3 **Procedure – Team Off Ice** - If a team, when ordered to do so by the Referee through its Club Executive, Manager or Coach, fails to go on the ice and start play within five (5) minutes, the Club Executive, Manager or Coach shall be fined five hundred dollars ($500), the game shall be forfeited and the case shall be reported to the Commissioner for further action (see Rule **66** – Forfeit of Game).

*(i) Once it is apparent to the Referee that the team is refusing to come onto the ice and begin play, a bench minor penalty is to be assessed to the offending team for delay of game.*

*(ii) Five (5) minutes will be provided for the offending team to return to the ice and begin play.*

*(iii) After the five (5) minutes has elapsed and the offending team still has not returned to the ice to resume play, the game shall be forfeited. The Commissioner of the League shall issue instructions pertaining to records, etc., of a forfeited game (see Rule **66** – Forfeit of Game).*

*(iv) Once the Club Executive, Manager or Coach has been notified of the five (5) minute warning, and the team returns to the ice to resume play within that time frame, a bench minor penalty for delay of game must be assessed to the offending team.*

*(v) A fine of five hundred dollars ($500) shall be applied to the Coach, Manager, or Club Executive responsible for the delay.*

## Rule 74 – Too Many Men on the Ice

74.1 **Too Many Men on the Ice** - Players may be changed at any time during the play from the players' bench provided that the player or players leaving the ice shall be within five feet (5') of his players' bench and out of the play before the change is made. Refer also to Rule **71** – Premature Substitution. At the discretion of the on-ice officials, should a substituting player come onto the ice before his teammate is within the five foot (5') limit of the players' bench (and therefore clearly causing his team to have too many players on the ice), then a bench minor penalty may be assessed.

When a player is retiring from the ice surface and is within the five foot (5') limit of his players' bench, and his substitute is on the ice, then the retiring player shall be considered off the ice for the purpose of Rule 70 – Leaving Bench.

If in the course of making a substitution, either the player entering the game or the player retiring from the ice surface plays the puck with his stick, skates or hands or who checks or makes any physical contact with an opposing player while either the player entering the game or the retiring player is actually on the ice, then the infraction of "too many men on the ice" will be called.

If in the course of a substitution either the player(s) entering the play or the player(s) retiring is struck by the puck accidentally, the play will not be stopped and no penalty will be called.

During the play, the player retiring from the ice must do so at the players' bench and not through any other exit leading from the rink. This is not a legal player change and therefore when a violation occurs, a bench minor penalty shall be imposed.

A player coming onto the ice as a substitute player is considered on the ice once both of his skates are on the ice. If he plays the puck or interferes with an opponent while still on the players' bench, he shall be penalized under Rule **56** – Interference.

74.2 **Bench Minor Penalty** – A bench minor penalty for too many men on the ice shall be assessed for a violation of this rule. This penalty can be assessed by the Referees or the Linesmen. Should a goal be scored by the offending team prior to the Referee or Linesman blowing his whistle to assess the bench minor penalty, the goal shall be disallowed and the penalty assessed for too many men on the ice.

74.3 **Penalty Bench** - A player serving a penalty on the penalty bench, who is to be changed after the penalty has been served, must proceed at once by way of the ice and be within five feet (5') of his own players' bench before any change can be made. For any violation of this rule, a bench minor penalty shall be imposed for too many men on the ice.

74.4 **Deliberate Illegal Substitution** - If by reason of insufficient playing time remaining, or by reason of penalties already imposed, a bench minor penalty is imposed for deliberate illegal substitution (too many men on the ice) which cannot be served in its entirety within the legal playing time, or at any time in overtime, a penalty shot shall be awarded against the offending team.

74.5 **Goalkeeper in Regular Season Overtime** - Once the goalkeeper has been removed for an extra attacker in overtime during the Regular season, he must wait for the next stoppage of play before returning to his position. Any attempt by the goalkeeper to return to his position prior to the next stoppage of play ("on the fly") shall be deemed to be an illegal substitution and a bench minor penalty shall be assessed for having an ineligible player would apply.

## Rule 75 – Unsportsmanlike Conduct

75.1 **Unsportsmanlike Conduct** – Players and non-playing Club personnel are responsible for their conduct at all times and must endeavor to prevent disorderly conduct before, during or after the game, on or off the ice and any place in the rink. The Referees may assess penalties to any of the above team personnel for failure to do so.

NOTE: When such conduct is directed at an official, Rule **39** – Abuse of Officials shall be applied.

75.2 **Minor Penalty** - A minor penalty for unsportsmanlike conduct shall be assessed under this rule for the following infractions:

(i) *Any identifiable player who uses obscene, profane or abusive language or gestures directed at any person.*

(ii) *Any player who is guilty of unsportsmanlike conduct including, but not limited to hair-pulling, biting, grabbing hold of a face mask, etc. If warranted, and specifically when injury results, the Referee may apply Rule* ***21*** *– Match Penalties.*

(iii) *Any player who throws any object onto the ice from the players' or penalty bench (or from any other off-ice location).*

(iv) *A player who deliberately removes his jersey prior to participating in an altercation or who is clearly wearing a jersey that has been modified and does not conform to Rule* ***9*** *– Uniforms, shall be assessed a minor penalty for unsportsmanlike conduct and a game misconduct. If the altercation never materializes, the player would receive a minor penalty for unsportsmanlike conduct and a ten-minute misconduct for deliberately removing his jersey.*

If a penalized player is assessed an additional unsportsmanlike conduct penalty either before or after he begins serving his original penalty(ies), the additional minor penalty is added to his unexpired time and served consecutively.

75.3 **Bench Minor Penalty** - A bench minor penalty for unsportsmanlike conduct shall be assessed under this rule for the following infractions:

(i) *When a player, Coach or non-playing Club personnel throws any object onto the ice from the players' or penalty bench (or from any other off-ice location) during the progress of the game or during a stoppage of play.*

(ii) *Any unidentifiable player or any Coach or non-playing Club personnel uses obscene, profane or abusive language or gesture directed towards any person.*

(iii) *Whenever Coaches and/or non-playing Club personnel uses obscene or profane language or gestures anywhere in the rink.*

75.4 **Misconduct Penalty** - Misconduct penalties shall be assessed under this rule for the following infractions:

(i) *Any player who persists in using obscene, profane or abusive language directed towards any person after being assessed a minor or bench minor penalty under this Rule.*

(ii) *Any player who deliberately throws any equipment out of the playing area. At the discretion of the Referee, a game misconduct may be imposed.*

(iii) *Any player who persists in any course of conduct (including threatening or abusive language or gestures or similar actions) designed to incite an opponent into incurring a penalty.*

(iv) *When a penalized player challenges or disputes the ruling of an official after he has already entered the penalty bench and play has resumed.*

(v) *In general, participants displaying this type of behavior are assessed a minor penalty, then a misconduct penalty and then a game misconduct penalty if they persist.*

75.5 **Game Misconduct Penalty** – Game misconduct penalties shall be assessed under this rule for the following infractions:

(i) *If a player persists in any course of conduct for which he was previously assessed a misconduct penalty.*

*(ii) Any player who uses obscene gestures on the ice or anywhere in the rink before, during or after the game. The Referee shall report the circumstances to the Commissioner of the League for further disciplinary action.*

*(iii) Coaches and non-playing Club personnel who have previously been assessed a bench minor penalty for the use obscene or profane language or gestures anywhere in the rink. A confidential report to the Commissioner shall be completed and filed with the League for possible further disciplinary action.*

*(iv) Any player who attempts to or deliberately injures a Manager, Coach or other non-playing Club personnel in any manner. Details of such incident must be reported immediately to the Commissioner and may be subject to additional sanctions as per Rule **28** – Supplementary Discipline.*

*(v) Any player or non-playing Club personnel who directs obscene, profane or abusive language or gestures to any person after the expiration of the game. This action may occur on or off the ice.*

*(vi) In general, participants displaying this type of behavior are assessed a minor penalty, then a misconduct penalty and then a game misconduct penalty if they persist.*

Any player or non-playing Club personnel penalized under this section may be subject to supplemental discipline under Rule **28**.

75.6 **Reports** - It is the responsibility of all game officials and all Club officials to send a confidential report to the Commissioner setting out the full details concerning the use of obscene gestures or language by any player, Coach or other team official. The Commissioner shall take such further disciplinary action as he shall deem appropriate.

# SECTION 10 – GAME FLOW

## Rule 76 – Face-offs

76.1 **Face-off** – The action of the Referee or Linesman in dropping the puck between the sticks of two opposing players to start or resume play. A face-off begins when the official indicates the location of the face-off and the officials and players take their appropriate positions. The face-off ends when the puck has been legally dropped.

A goalkeeper may not participate in a face-off.

76.2 **Face-off Locations** – All face-offs must be conducted on one of the nine (9) face-off spots located on the rink.

When a stoppage of play has been caused by any player of the attacking side in the attacking zone, the ensuing face-off shall be made in the neutral zone on the nearest face-off spot. If two rule violations are the reason for the stoppage of play (ie. high-sticking the puck and intentional off-side), the ensuing face-off location shall be determined as the spot that provides the least amount of territorial advantage to the offending team.

When the play is stopped for any reason not specifically attributable to either team while the puck is in the neutral zone, the ensuing face-off shall be conducted at the nearest face-off spot outside the blue line whenever possible. When it is unclear as to which of the four face-off spots is the nearest, the spot that gives the home team the greatest territorial advantage in the neutral zone will be selected for the ensuing face-off.

When players are penalized at a stoppage of play so as to result in penalties being placed on the penalty time clock to one team, the ensuing face-off shall be conducted at one of the two face-off spots in the offending team's end zone. There are only four exceptions to this application:

*(i) when a penalty is assessed after the scoring of a goal - face-off at center ice;*

*(ii) when a penalty is assessed at the end (or start) of a period - face-off at center ice;*

*(iii) when the defending team is penalized and the attacking players enter the attacking zone beyond the outer edge of the end zone face-off circle - face-off in the neutral zone (see paragraph 11 of this section);*

*(iv) when the team not being penalized ices the puck - face-off in the neutral zone outside the blue line of the team icing the puck.*

When an infringement of a rule has been committed by players of both sides in the play resulting in the stoppage, the ensuing face-off will be made at the nearest face-off spot in that zone.

When stoppage occurs between the end face-off spots and near end of the rink, the puck shall be faced-off at the end face-off spot on the side where the stoppage occurs unless otherwise expressly provided by these rules.

No face-off shall be made within fifteen feet (15') of the goal or side boards nor anywhere other than at a face-off spot.

When a goal is illegally scored as a result of a puck being

deflected directly off an official, the resulting face-off shall be made at the nearest face-off spot in the zone where the puck deflected off of the official.

When a goal is illegally scored by the attacking team by directing, batting, kicking or high-sticking the puck into the goal, the resulting face-off shall take place in the neutral zone at the nearest face-off spot.

When the game is stopped for any reason not specifically covered in the official rules, the puck must be faced-off at a face-off spot in the zone nearest to where it was last played.

Following a stoppage of play, should one or both defensemen who are the point players or any player coming from the bench of the attacking team, enter into the attacking zone beyond the outer edge of the end zone face-off circle during an altercation, gathering or "scrum," the ensuing face-off shall take place in the neutral zone near the blue line of the defending team. This rule also applies when an icing, an intentional off-side, or a high-sticking the puck violation (by the team of greater numerical strength of its opponent) has occurred, and the ensuing face-off is to be in the offending team's defending zone. Should any of the non-offending players enter into the attacking zone beyond the outer edge of the end zone face-off circle during an altercation, gathering or "scrum," the ensuing face-off shall take place in the neutral zone near the blue line of the defending team.

For a violation of Rule **71** – Premature Substitution, the resulting face-off will take place at the center ice face-off spot when play is stopped beyond the center red line. When play is stopped prior to the center red line, the resulting face-off shall be conducted at the nearest face-off spot in the zone where the play was stopped.

When play is stopped for an injured player, the ensuing face-off shall be conducted at the face-off spot in the zone nearest the location of the puck when the play was stopped. When the injured player's team has control of the puck in the attacking zone, the face-off shall be conducted at one of the face-off spots outside the blue line in the neutral zone. When the injured player is in his defending zone and the attacking team is in control of the puck in the attacking zone, the face-off shall be conducted at one of the defending team's end-zone face-off spots.

76.3 **Procedure –** As soon as the line change procedure has been completed by the Referee and he lowers his hand to indicate no further changes, the Linesman conducting the face-off shall blow his whistle. This will signal to both teams that they have no more than five (5) seconds to line up for the ensuing face-off. At the end of the five (5) seconds (or sooner if both centers are ready), the Linesman will conduct a proper face-off. If, however:

*(i)* *One or both centers are not positioned for the face-off,*

*(ii)* *One or both centers refrain from placing their stick on the ice,*

*(iii)* *Any player has encroached into the face-off circle,*

*(iv)* *Any player makes physical contact with an opponent, or*

*(v)* *Any player who lines up for the face-off in an off-side position,*

the Linesman shall have the offending center(s) replaced immediately prior to dropping the puck.

In the last two (2) minutes of regulation time or any time in overtime, the Linesman will still blow his whistle to initiate the face-off, but the five (5) second time limit will not be enforced. However, players must abide by the verbal directions given by the Linesman in his attempt to conduct a fast and fair face-off.

76.4 **Procedure – Centers** – The puck shall be faced-off by the Referee or the Linesman dropping the puck on the ice between the sticks of the players facing-off. Players facing-off will stand squarely facing their opponent's end of the rink approximately one stick length apart with the blade of their sticks on the ice.

When the face-off takes place at any of the nine face-off spots, the players taking part shall take their position so that they will stand squarely facing their opponent's end of the rink, and clear of the ice markings (where applicable). The sticks of both players facing-off shall have the blade on the ice, within the designated white area. At the eight face-off spots (excluding center ice face-off spot), the defending player shall place his stick within the designated white area first followed immediately by the attacking player. When the face-off is conducted at the center ice face-off spot, the visiting player shall place his stick on the ice first.

If a player facing-off fails to take his proper position immediately when directed by the official, the official may order him replaced for that face-off by any teammate then on the ice.

If a center is not at the designated face-off area once the five (5) second time limit has elapsed, the Linesman will drop the puck immediately. If the center is back from the face-off spot, is "quarterbacking" or refuses to come into the face-off area when instructed to do so by the Linesman, or the center is simply slow getting to the face-off spot when the five (5) seconds has elapsed, the puck shall be dropped. If the center attempts to arrive at the face-off spot just as the five seconds elapses in an attempt to gain an advantage to win the face-off, he is to be removed from the face-off and replaced, resulting in a face-off violation. If the face-off is a result of an icing infraction and the center attempts to arrive at the face-off spot just as the five seconds elapse to gain an advantage to win the face-off, he shall not be removed from the face-off. The center will be warned by the Linesman that he has committed a face-off violation. In the even the center then comits a second face-off violation or the action actually is the second face-off violation, a bench minor penalty shall be assessed.

If a player is ejected from the face-off, his replacement must come into position quickly or risk having the puck dropped by the Linesman without the player being set, or ejected from the face-off by the Linesman resulting in a bench minor penalty for delay of game for a second face-off violation during the same face-off.

When a team commits an icing infraction, any face-off violation will not result in the center being removed. The center will be warned by the Linesman that the team has committed their first face-off violation and any subsequent violation will result in a bench minor penalty for delay of game - face-off violation being assessed.

Both players facing-off are prohibited from batting the puck with their hand in an attempt to win the face-off. Any attempt by either center to win the face-off by batting the puck with their hand shall result in a minor penalty. This penalty shall be announced as "Minor Penalty for Delay of Game – Face-off Violation". The two players involved in the actual face-off (the centers) are not permitted to play the puck with their hand without incurring a penalty under this rule until such time as a third player (from either team) has at least touched the puck. Once the face-off is deemed complete (and a winner of the face-off is clear) hand passes shall be enforced as per Rule **79**.

76.5 **Procedure – Other Players** – No other player shall be allowed to enter the face-off circle or come within fifteen feet (15') of the players facing-off. All players must stand on-side on all face-offs.

During end-zone face-offs, all other players on the ice must position their bodies on their own side of the restraining lines marked on the outer edge of the face-off circles.

If a player other than the player taking the face-off moves into the face-off circle prior to the dropping of the puck, then the offending team's player taking the face-off shall be ejected from the face-off circle. This shall be considered a face-off violation.

Players on the attacking team (exclusive of the center) must establish their position first and then the defending team may counter and hold its position until the puck is dropped. A violation of this procedure shall be treated as face-off encroachment and the Linesman shall order the center of the offending team replaced. Should an attacking player attempt to establish a new position prior to the face-off, and the defending center steps back from the face-off spot in order to reposition his teammates, the face-off violation shall be charged to the attacking team as they must establish their position first.

76.6 **Violations** – If a center should move prematurely prior to the face-off, or if the Referee or Linesman shall have dropped the puck unfairly, the face-off shall be considered a face-off violation and it must be conducted again.

When a least two face-off violations have been committed by the same team during the same face-off, this team shall be penalized with a bench minor penalty to the offending team. This penalty shall be announced as a "Bench Minor Penalty for Delay of Game – Face-off Violation."

Face-off violations shall be summarized as follows (any of the four on-ice officials may identify a face-off violation):

(i) *Encroachment by any player other than the center into the face-off area prior to the puck being dropped. Players on the perimeter of the face-off circle must keep both skates outside the face-off circle (skate contact with the line is permitted). If a player's skate crosses the line into the face-off circle prior to the drop of the puck, this shall be deemed as a face-off violation. A player's stick may be inside the face-off circle provided there is no physical contact with his opponent or his opponent's stick.*

(ii) *Encroachment by any player into the area between the hash marks on the outer edges of the face-off circle prior to the puck being dropped. Players must also ensure that both of their skates do not cross their respective hash marks. Contact with the line with their skate is permitted. If a player's skate crosses the line into the area between the hash marks prior to the drop of the puck, this shall be deemed as a face-off violation. A player's stick may be inside the area between the hash marks provided there is no physical contact with his opponent or his opponent's stick.*

(iii) *Any physical contact with an opponent prior to the puck being dropped.*

(iv) *Failure by either center taking the face-off to properly position himself behind the restraining lines or place his stick on the ice (as outlined in Rule* ***76.4****). "Properly position himself behind the restraining lines" shall mean that the center must place his feet on either side of the restraining lines that are parallel to the side boards (contact with the lines is permissible), and the toe of the blade of his skates must not cross over the restraining lines that are perpendicular to the side boards as he approaches the face-off spot.*

*The blade of the stick must then be placed on the ice (at least the toe of the blade of the stick) in the designated white area of the face-off spot and must remain there until the puck is dropped.*

*Failure to comply with this positioning and face-off procedure will result in a face-off violation.*

Whenever a team has committed two face-off violations during the same face-off, the Referee shall immediately assess the offending team a bench minor penalty for delay of game. This penalty shall be announced as a "Bench Minor Penalty for Delay of Game – Face-off Violation."

Players who are late to the face-off location and therefore in an off-side position for the ensuing face-off will be warned once in the game by the Referee. This warning will also be given to the offending team's Coach. In this situation, the offending team's center is not ejected from the face-off. Any subsequent violation shall result in a bench minor penalty for delay of game being assessed to the offending team. This penalty shall be announced as a "Bench Minor Penalty for Delay of Game – Slow Proceeding to Face-off Location."

In the conduct of any face-off at any of the nine (9) face-off spots on the playing surface, no player facing-off shall make any physical contact with his opponent's body by means of his own body or by his stick except in the course of playing the puck after the face-off has been completed.

For violation of this rule, the Referee may, at his discretion impose a minor penalty or penalties on the player(s) whose action(s) caused the physical contact. Nonetheless, this physical contact prior to the dropping of the puck shall be deemed as a face-off violation and the Linesman shall order the center of the offending team replaced.

Face-off encroachment may be applied during face-offs at any of the nine (9) face-off spots on the playing surface. However, since no such lines are painted on the ice at the four (4) face-off spots adjacent to the blue lines, Linesmen shall use their judgment as to whether or not a violation has occurred. All players, other than the centers, shall be uniformly back from the face-off location similar to being outside the face-off circle for face-offs in the end zones.

76.7 **Line Changes** – No substitution of players shall be permitted until the face-off has been completed and play has resumed except when a penalty is imposed which affects the on-ice strength of either team.

Should an on-ice official notice that the defending team has not placed enough players on the ice for the ensuing face-off, the Referee in the neutral zone shall be notified and he will instruct the offending team to place another player(s) on the ice. If, in the opinion of the Referee that this is being done as a stalling tactic, he will issue a warning to the offending team's Coach and any subsequent violations shall result in the assessment of a bench minor penalty for delay of game.

Should an on-ice official notice that the attacking team has not placed enough players on the ice for the ensuing face-off, the Linesman will proceed with conducting the face-off in the normal manner. The attacking team must ensure they put the appropriate number of players on the ice at all times.

76.8 **Verification of Time** - Any loss of time on the game or penalty clocks due to a false face-off or face-off violation must be replaced. The Video Goal Judge may be consulted to ensure the time is accurately replaced.

The whistle will not be blown by the official to start play. Playing time will commence from the instant the puck is faced-off and will stop when the whistle is blown or a goal is scored.

## Rule 77 – Game and Intermission Timing

77.1 **Game Timing** – The time allowed for a game shall be three (3) twenty-minute periods of actual play with a rest intermission between periods.

77.2 **Intermission Timing** – Play shall be resumed promptly following each intermission upon the expiration of eighteen (18) minutes or a length of time designated by the League from the completion of play in the preceding period. Timing of the intermission commences immediately upon the conclusion of the period. (See Rule **34** – Game Timekeeper.)

For the purpose of keeping the spectators informed as to the time remaining during intermissions, the Game Timekeeper will use the electronic clock to record length of intermissions.

77.3 **Delays** - If any unusual delay occurs within five (5) minutes of the end of the first or second periods, the Referee may order the next regular intermission to be taken immediately. The balance of the period will be completed on the resumption of play with the teams defending the same goals after which the teams will change ends and resume play of the ensuing period without delay.

If a delay takes place with more than five (5) minutes remaining in the first or second period, the Referee will order the next regular intermission to be taken immediately only when requested to do so by the home Club.

## Rule 78 – Goals

78.1 **Goals and Assists** - It is the responsibility of the Official Scorer to award goals and assists, and his decision in this respect is final, notwithstanding the report of the Referee or any other game official. The use of video replay to verify the proper awarding of a goal or an assist is essential. Such awards shall be made or withheld strictly in accordance with the provisions of this rule. Therefore, it is essential that the Official Scorer be thoroughly familiar with every aspect of this rule; be alert to observe all actions which could affect the awarding of a goal or assist; and, above all, give or withhold awards with absolute impartiality.

In case of an obvious error in awarding a goal or an assist that has been announced, it should be corrected promptly, but changes should not be made in the official scoring summary after the Referee has signed the game report (except by the League's Chief Statistician).

The team scoring the greatest number of goals during the three (3) twenty-minute periods shall be the winner and shall be credited with two points in the League standings. In the event a winner during the regular season is determined in the overtime period or the shootout, the winning team shall be credited with two points in the League standings and the losing team will be credited with one point in the League standings.

78.2 **Crediting Goals** - A "goal" shall be credited in the scoring records to a player who shall have propelled the puck into the opponent's goal. Each "goal" shall count one point in the player's record. Only one point can be credited to any one player on a goal.

78.3 **Crediting Assists** - When a player scores a goal, an "assist" shall be credited to the player or players (maximum two) who touch the puck prior to the goal scorer provided no defender plays or has control of the puck subsequently. Each "assist" shall count one point in the player's record. Only one point can be credited to any one player on a goal.

78.4 **Scoring a Goal** - A goal shall be scored when the puck shall have been put between the goal posts by the stick of a player of the attacking side, from in front and below the crossbar, and entirely across a red line the width of the diameter of the goal posts drawn on the ice from one goal post to the other with the goal frame in its proper position. The goal frame shall be considered in its proper position when at least a portion of the flexible peg(s) are still inside both the goal post and the hole in the ice. The flexible pegs could be bent, but as long as at least a portion of the flexible peg(s) are still in the hole in the ice and the goal post, the goal frame shall be deemed to be in its proper position. The goal frame could be raised somewhat on one post (or both), but as long as the flexible pegs are still in contact with the holes in the ice and the goal posts, the goal frame shall not be deemed to be displaced.

A goal shall be scored if the puck is put into the goal in any way by a player of the defending side. The player of the attacking side who last touched the puck shall be credited with the goal but no assist shall be awarded.

If an attacking player has the puck deflect into the net, off his skate or body, in any manner, the goal shall be allowed. The player who deflected the puck shall be credited with the goal.

Should a player legally propel a puck into the goal crease of the opponent Club and the puck should become loose and available to another player of the attacking side, a goal scored on the play shall be legal.

78.5 **Disallowed Goals** – Apparent goals shall be disallowed by the Referee and the appropriate announcement made by the Public Address Announcer for the following reasons:

- *(i) When the puck has been directed, batted or thrown into the net by an attacking player other than with a stick.*
- *(ii) When the puck has been kicked using a distinct kicking motion.*
- *(iii) When the puck has deflected directly into the net off an official.*
- *(iv) When a goal has been scored and an ineligible player is on the ice.*
- *(v) When an attacking player has interfered with a goalkeeper in his goal crease.*
- *(vi) When the puck has entered the net after making contact with an attacking player's stick that is above the height of the crossbar. Where the puck makes contact with the stick is the determining factor. See **38.4(vi)**.*
- *(vii) When video review confirms the scoring of a goal at one end of the ice, any goal scored at the other end on the same play must be disallowed.*
- *(viii) When a Linesman reports a double-minor penalty for high-sticking, a major penalty or a match penalty to the Referee following the scoring of a goal by the offending team, the goal must be disallowed and the appropriate penalty assessed.*
- *(ix) When a goalkeeper has been pushed into the net together with the puck after making a save. See also **69.7**.*
- *(x) When the net becomes displaced accidentally. The goal frame is considered to be displaced if either or both goal pegs are no longer in their respective holes in the ice, or the net has come completely off one or both pegs, prior to or as the puck enters the goal.*
- *(xi) During the delayed calling of a penalty, the offending team cannot score unless the non-offending team shoots the puck into their own net. This shall mean that a deflection off an offending player or any physical action by an offending player that may cause the puck to enter the non-offending team's goal, shall not be considered a legal goal. Play shall be stopped before the puck enters the net (whenever possible) and the signaled penalty assessed to the offending team.*
- *(xii) When the Referee deems the play has been stopped, even if he had not physically had the opportunity to stop play by blowing his whistle.*
- *(xiii) Any goal scored, other than as covered by the official rules, shall not be allowed.*

78.6 **Video Review** – Any potential goal requiring video review must be reviewed prior to or during the next stoppage of play. No goal may be awarded (or disallowed) as a result of video review once the puck has been dropped and play has resumed. See Rule **38**.

When a team scores an apparent goal that is not seen by the on-ice officials and play continues, the play shall be reviewed by the Video Goal Judge at the next stoppage of play. If the goal is confirmed by video review, the clock (including penalty time clocks, if applicable) is re-set to the time the goal was scored. If the goal is not confirmed by video review, no adjustment is required to the clock time.

Only one goal can be awarded at any stoppage of play. If the apparent goal was scored by Team A, and is subsequently confirmed as a goal by the Video Goal Judge, any goal scored by Team B during the period of time between the apparent goal By Team A and the stoppage of play (Team B's goal), the Team B goal would not be awarded. However, if the apparent goal by Team A is deemed to have entered the goal, albeit illegally (i.e. distinct kicking motion), the goal shall be disallowed by the Video Goal Judge and since the play should have stopped for this disallowed goal, no goal can be awarded to Team B on the same play. The clock (including penalty time clocks, if applicable) must be re-set to the time of the disallowed Team A goal and play resumed.

Any penalties signaled during the period of time between the apparent goal and the next stoppage of play shall be assessed in the normal manner, except when a minor penalty is to be assessed to the team scored upon, and is therefore nullified by the scoring of the goal. Refer to Rules **16.2** and **18.2**. If an infraction happens after the first stoppage of play following an apparent goal (infraction after the whistle) by either team, it is assessed and served in the normal manner regardless as to the decision rendered by the Video Goal Judge.

78.7 **Coach's Challenge** – This expanded video review is intended to be extremely narrow in scope and the original call on the ice is to be overturned if, and only if, a determination is made by the On-Ice Official(s) (in consultation with the Toronto Video Room) that the original call on the ice was not correct. If a review is not conclusive and/or there is any doubt whatsoever as to whether the call on the ice was correct, the On-Ice Official(s) will be instructed to confirm their original call.

A team may only request a Coach's Challenge to review the following scenarios:

*(i)* ***"Off-side" Play Leading to a Goal*** *– A play that results in a "GOAL" call on the ice where the defending team asserts that the play should have been stopped by reason of an "Off-side" infraction by the attacking team.*

*NOTE 1: The standard for overturning the call in the event of a "GOAL" call on the ice is that the Toronto Video Room, after reviewing any and all available replays and consulting with the Linesman, determines that one or more Players on the attacking team preceded the puck into the attacking zone prior to the goal being scored and that, as a result, the play should have been stopped for an "Off-side" infraction; where this standard is met, the goal will be disallowed.*

*NOTE 2: Goals will only be reviewed for a potential "Off-side" infraction if: (a) the puck does not come out of the attacking zone again; or (b) all members of the attacking team do not clear the attacking zone again, between the time of the "Off-side" play and the time the goal is scored.*

*NOTE 3: In the event a goal is reversed due to the Toronto Video Room (after consulting with the Linesman) determining that the play was "Off-side" prior to the goal being scored, the clock (including penalty time clocks, if applicable) will be re-set to the time at which the play should have been stopped for the "Off-side" infraction.*

*NOTE 4: If one or more penalties (major or minor) are assessed between the time of the "Off-side" play and the video review that disallows the apparent goal, the offending team(s) (and responsible Player(s)) will still be required to serve the penalty(ies) identified and assessed, and the time of the penalty(ies) will be recorded as the time at which the play should have been stopped for the "Off-side" infraction.*

*(ii)* ***Scoring Plays Involving Potential "Interference on the Goalkeeper"***

*(a) A play that results in a "GOAL" call on the ice where the defending team asserts that the goal should have been disallowed due to "Interference on the Goalkeeper", as described in Rules 69.1, 69.3 and 69.4; or*

*(b) A play that results in a "NO GOAL" call on the ice despite the puck having entered the net, where the On-Ice Officials have determined that the attacking team was guilty of "Interference on the Goalkeeper" but where the attacking team asserts: (i) there was no actual contact of any kind initiated by an attacking Player with the goalkeeper; or (ii) the attacking Player was pushed, shoved, or fouled by a defending Player causing the attacking Player to come into contact with the goalkeeper; or (iii) the attacking Player's positioning within the goal crease did not impair the goalkeeper's ability to defend his goal and, in fact, had no discernible impact on the play.*

*NOTE 1: The standard for overturning the call in the event of a "GOAL" call on the ice is that the Referee, after reviewing any and all available replays and consulting with the Toronto Video Room, determines that the goal should have been disallowed due to "Interference on the Goalkeeper," as described in Rules 69.1, 69.3 and 69.4.*

*NOTE 2: The standard for overturning the call in the event of a "NO GOAL" call on the ice is that the Referee, after reviewing any and all replays and consulting with the Toronto Video Room, determines that the goal on the ice should have been allowed because either: (i) there was no actual contact of any kind initiated by the attacking Player with the goalkeeper; or (ii) the attacking Player was pushed, shoved or fouled by a defending Player causing the attacking Player to come into contact with the goalkeeper; or (iii) the attacking Player's positioning within the crease did not impair the goalkeeper's ability to defend his goal and, in fact, had no discernible impact on the play.*

*NOTE 3: The Video Review process on these plays (whether initiated by way of a Coach's Challenge or by Hockey Operations in the final minute of play or in Overtime) will be utilized exclusively for purposes of confirming or overturning a "GOAL" or "NO GOAL" call on the ice on scoring plays potentially involving "Interference on the Goalkeeper." The Video Review process on these plays -- regardless of its outcome -- will not be utilized for any other purpose, including, specifically, for assessing minor or major penalties for Goalkeeper Interference.*

A team may only request a Coach's Challenge if they have their time-out available and the Coach's Challenge must be effectively initiated prior to the resumption of play.

If the Coach's Challenge does not result in the original call on the ice being overturned, the team exercising such challenge will forfeit its time-out.

If the Coach's Challenge does result in the call on the ice being overturned, the team successfully exercising such challenge will retain its time-out.

78.8 **League Initiated Review** - In the final minute of play in the 3rd period and at any point in Overtime (Regular Season and Playoffs), Hockey Operations will initiate the review of any scenario that would otherwise be subject to a Coach's Challenge.

Hockey Operations will continue to initiate and be responsible for the review of all goals subject to Video Review under Rule 38.4. Where a Coach's Challenge is available on a scoring play potentially involving "Interference on the Goalkeeper" or "Off-side," Hockey Operations will, as an initial and threshold matter, determine that the puck entered the net and is a good hockey goal before the play will be subject to further review by means of a Coach's Challenge (or, in the final minute of play or in Overtime, a review initiated by Hockey Operations). If a team requests a Coach's Challenge but Video Review under Rule 38.4 renders such Challenge unnecessary, then the Challenge will be deemed not to have been made and the timeout will be preserved.

## Rule 79 – Hand Pass

79.1 **Hand Pass** - A player shall be permitted to stop or "bat" a puck in the air with his open hand, or push it along the ice with his hand, and the play shall not be stopped unless, in the opinion of the on-ice officials, he has directed the puck to a teammate, or has allowed his team to gain an advantage, and subsequently possession and control of the puck is obtained by a player of the offending team, either directly or deflected off any player or official.

A player shall be permitted to catch the puck out of the air but must immediately place it or knock it down to the ice. If he catches it and skates with it, either to avoid a check or to gain a territorial advantage over his opponent, a minor penalty shall be assessed for "closing his hand on the puck" under Rule **67** – Handling Puck.

79.2 **Defending Zone** - Play will not be stopped for any hand pass by players in their own defending zone. A hand pass in the defending zone is considered to have occurred when both the player making the pass and the player receiving the pass have both of their skates inside their defending zone.

79.3 **Face-Off Location** – When a hand pass violation has occurred, the ensuing face-off shall take place at the nearest face-off spot in the zone where the offense occurred, unless the offending team gains a territorial advantage, then the face-off shall be at the nearest face-ff spot in the zone where the stoppage of play occurred, unless otherwise covered in the rules. When a hand pass violation occurs by a team in their attacking zone, the ensuing face-off shall be conducted at one of the face-off spots outside the defending team's blue line in the neutral zone.

## Rule 80 – High-sticking the Puck

80.1 **High-sticking the Puck** – Batting the puck above the normal height of the shoulders with a stick is prohibited. When a puck is struck with a high stick and subsequently comes into the possession and control of a player from the offending team (including the player who made contact with the puck), either directly or deflected off any player or official, there shall be a whistle.

When a puck has been contacted by a high stick, the play shall be permitted to continue, provided that:

*(i) the puck has been batted to an opponent (when a player bats the puck to an opponent, the Referee shall give the "washout" signal immediately. Otherwise, he will stop the play).*

*(ii) a player of the defending side shall bat the puck into his own goal in which case the goal shall be allowed.*

Cradling the puck on the blade of the stick (like lacrosse) above the normal height of the shoulders shall be prohibited and a stoppage of play shall result. If this is done by a player on a penalty shot or shootout attempt, the shot shall be stopped immediately and considered complete.

80.2 **Face-Off Location** - When the play is stopped for the high-sticking the puck violation, the ensuing face-off must take place at the spot that provides the least amount of territorial advantage to the team striking the puck, either where the puck was contacted illegally, or where it was last played by the offending team. If the attacking team is at fault and the play is stopped while the puck is in the attacking zone, the ensuing face-off must be moved to the nearest face-off spot in the neutral zone (except when **80.4** is applicable).

80.3 **Disallowed Goal** – When an attacking player causes the puck to enter the opponent's goal by contacting the puck above the height of the crossbar, either directly or deflected off any player or official, the goal shall not be allowed. The determining factor is where the puck makes contact with the stick. If the puck makes contact with the stick at or below the level of the crossbar and enters the goal, this goal shall be allowed.

A goal scored as a result of a defending player striking the puck with his stick carried above the height of the crossbar of the goal frame into his own goal shall be allowed.

80.4 **Numerical Advantage** - When either team is below the numerical strength (short-handed) of its opponent and a player of the team of greater numerical strength (power-play) causes a stoppage of play by striking the puck with his stick above the height of his shoulder, the resulting face-off shall be made at one of the end zone face-off spots adjacent to the goal of the team causing the stoppage. The numerical strength is determined at the time the play is stopped (not necessarily when the puck was struck with the high stick).

Should a player of the team of greater numerical strength (power-play) cause a stoppage of play by striking the puck with his stick above the height of his shoulder, and in so doing causes the puck to go out of play, the resulting face-off shall still be made at one of the end zone face-off spots adjacent to the goal of the team causing the stoppage.

Should a player of the team of greater numerical strength (power-play) cause a stoppage of play by striking the puck with his stick above the height of the crossbar, and in so doing causes the puck to enter the goal, the goal shall be disallowed and the resulting face-off shall still be made at one of the end zone face-off spots adjacent to the goal of the team causing the stoppage.

## Rule 81 – Icing

81.1 **Icing** – For the purpose of this rule, the center red line will divide the ice into halves. Should any player of a team, equal or superior in numerical strength (power-play) to the opposing team, shoot, bat or deflect the puck from his own half of the ice beyond the goal line of the opposing team, play shall be stopped. For the purpose of deflected pucks, this only applies when the puck was originally propelled down the ice by the offending team.

For the purpose of this rule, the point of last contact with the puck by the team in possession shall be used to determine whether icing has occurred or not. As such, the team in possession must "gain the line" in order for the icing to be nullified. "Gaining the line" shall mean that the puck, while on the player's stick (not the player's skate) must make contact with the center red line in order to nullify a potential icing.

For the purpose of interpretation of the rule, there are two judgments required for "icing the puck". The Linesman must first determine that the puck will cross the goal line. Once the Linesman determines that the puck will cross the goal line, icing is completed upon the determination as to which player (attacking or defending) would first touch the puck. This decision by the Linesman will be made by no later than the instant the first player reaches the end zone face-off dots with the player's skate being the determining factor. Should the puck be shot down the ice in such a manner that it travels around the boards and/or back towards the end zone face-off dots, the same procedure shall be in effect in that the Linesman shall determine within a similar distance as to who will have touched the puck first.

For clarification, the determining factor is which player would first touch the puck, not which player would first reach the end zone face-off dots.

If the race for the puck is too close to determine by the time the first player reaches the end zone face-off dots, icing shall be called.

The puck striking or deflecting off an official does not automatically nullify a potential icing.

81.2 **Face-Off Location** – The resulting face-off following an icing call shall be at the end face-off spot of the offending team, unless on the play, the puck shall have entered the net of the opposing team, in which case the goal shall be allowed.

If during the period of a delayed whistle due to a foul by a player of the side not in possession, the side in possession "ices" the puck, then the face-off following the stoppage of play shall take place in the neutral zone near the defending blue line of the team icing the puck.

If, in the opinion of the Referee, the defending side intentionally abstains from playing the puck promptly when they are in a position to do so, he shall stop the play and order the resulting face-off on the adjacent corner face-off spot nearest the goal of the team at fault.

If the Linesman shall have erred in calling an "icing the puck" infraction (regardless of whether either team is short-handed), the puck shall be faced-off on the center ice face-off spot.

81.3 **Goalkeeper** - If, in the opinion of the Linesman, the goalkeeper feigns playing the puck, attempts to play the puck, or skates in the direction of the puck on an icing at any time, the potential icing shall not be called and play shall continue.

If, however, a goalkeeper is legitimately out of the crease in an attempt to go to the players' bench to be substituted for an extra attacker and in no way makes an attempt to play the puck, the icing should not be nullified under this section.

If the goalkeeper is out of his crease prior to the shot being taken, and simply retreats to his crease making no attempt to play the puck or feign playing the puck, the potential icing shall remain in effect.

81.4 **Line Change on Icing** - A team that is in violation of this rule shall not be permitted to make any player substitutions prior to the ensuing face-off. Should the offending team elect to utilize their team time-out at this stoppage of play, they are still not permitted to make any player substitutions. However, a team shall be permitted to make a player substitution to replace a goalkeeper who had been substituted for an extra attacker, to replace an injured player, or when a penalty has been assessed which affects the on-ice strength of either team. The determination of players on ice will be made when the puck leaves the offending player's stick.

81.5 **No Icing** – When the puck is shot and rebounds from the body or stick of an opponent in his own half of the ice so as to cross the goal line of the player shooting, it shall not be considered "icing."

When a puck is shot by a team from their own half of the ice and is deflected several times before crossing the center red line, icing shall be nullified if at least one of these deflections was off an opposing player.

If a player of the side shooting the puck down the ice who is on-side and eligible to play the puck does so before it is touched by an opposing player, the play shall continue and it shall not be considered a violation of this rule.

If the puck shall go beyond the goal line in the opposite half of the ice directly from either of the players while facing-off, it shall not be considered a violation of this rule.

If, in the opinion of the Linesman, any player (other than the goalkeeper) of the opposing team is able to play the puck before it passes his goal line, but has not done so, play shall continue and the icing violation shall not be called. This includes the situation whereby the opposing team, while in the process of making player substitutions during the play, are able to play the puck, but choose not to do so to avoid being called for too many men on the ice. Icing should not be called.

If the puck touches any part of a player of the opposing side, including his skates or his stick, or if it touches any part of the opposing team's goalkeeper, including his skates or his stick, at any time before or after crossing the goal line, it shall not be considered icing.

If a goalkeeper takes any action to dislodge the puck from the back of the net, icing shall not be called.

81.6 **Numerical Strength** – If the puck was so shot by a player of a side below the numerical strength of the opposing team, play shall continue and the icing violation shall not be called.

When a team is "short-handed" as the result of a penalty and the penalty is about to expire, the decision as to whether there has been an "icing" shall be determined at the instant the penalty expires. Should the puck be released from the stick of the player shooting the puck down the ice prior to the penalty expiring, the icing infraction shall not apply. The action of the penalized player remaining in the penalty box will not alter the ruling.

When a team is "short-handed" by reason of a major penalty, and they have neglected to ensure there is a player on the penalty bench to exit upon the expiry of the penalty, they will continue to play short-handed but are not permitted to ice the puck. Icing will be called. They may substitute for this penalized player at the next stoppage of play. See Rule **20.3** – Major Penalties.

## Rule 82 – Line Changes

82.1 **Line Change** - Following the stoppage of play, the visiting team shall promptly place a line-up on the ice ready for play and no substitution shall be made from that time until play has been resumed. The home team may then make any desired substitution, except in cases following an icing, which does not result in the delay of the game.

"Placing a line-up on the ice" shall mean that both teams shall place the full complement of players (and not exceed) to which they are entitled within the line change time frame.

If there is any undue delay by either team in changing players, the Referee shall order the offending team or teams to take their positions immediately and not permit any further player changes.

When a substitution has been made under the above rule, no additional substitution may be made until play commences.

Once the line change procedure has been completed (**82.2**), no additional player substitutions shall be permitted until the face-off has been completed legally and play has resumed, except when a penalty or penalties are imposed that affect the on-ice strength of either or both teams. This may include penalties imposed following the completion of the line change and prior to the face-off, or due to a penalty assessed for a face-off violation.

A team that is in violation of Rule **81** – Icing shall not be permitted to make any player substitutions prior to the ensuing face-off. However, a team shall be permitted to make a player substitution to replace a goalkeeper who had been substituted for an extra attacker, to replace an injured player, or when a penalty has been assessed which affects the on-ice strength of either team. The determination of players on ice will be made when the puck leaves the offending player's stick.

Goalkeepers' substitution during a game will be conducted within the same time frame as a regular line change. No extra time will be allotted to the goalkeeper coming off the bench, except in the case where an injury to a goalkeeper occurs.

82.2 **Procedure** - Following a stoppage of play, the Referee will enforce the following line change procedure once he has determined that this procedure may begin:

*(i)* *The Referee shall give the visiting team up to five (5) seconds to make its line change.*

*(ii)* *The Referee shall raise his hand to indicate no further changes by the visiting team and to commence the home team's line change.*

*(iii)* *The Referee shall give the home team up to eight (8) seconds to make its line change.*

*(iv)* *The Referee shall lower his hand to indicate no further changes by the home team.*

*(v)* *Any attempt by the either team to make a change after the Referee's signal, attempt to place too many men on the ice for the subsequent line change, or attempt to make additional personnel changes, shall not be permitted and the Referee will send the players who have attempted to change back to their players' bench. The Referee will then issue a warning to the offending team (through the Coach) indicating that any subsequent violations during the rest of the game (including overtime), shall result in a bench minor penalty for delaying the game. This penalty shall be announced as a "Bench Minor Penalty for Delay of Game – Improper Line Change."*

*(vi)* *The Linesman conducting the face-off will blow his whistle (once the Referee has lowered his hand for the line changes) to indicate that all players must be in position and on-side for the face-off within five (5) seconds. The face-off will then be conducted in accordance with Rule*

*76 – Face-offs.*

(vii) *Players who are slow (after the five-second warning whistle given by the Linesman) getting to the face-off location or who are in an off-side position for the ensuing face-off will be warned once in the game by the Referee. This warning will also be given to the offending team's Coach. In this situation, the offending team's center is not ejected from the face-off. Any subsequent violation shall result in a bench minor penalty for delay of game being assessed to the offending team.*

(viii) *In the last two (2) minutes of regulation time and any time in the overtime period(s), points (vi) and (vii) above are not applicable. The Linesman shall give the teams a reasonable amount of time to set up for the ensuing face-off after points (1) through (5) above have been enforced.*

82.3 **Bench Minor Penalty** - Any attempt by the visiting team to make a change after the Referee's signal shall result in the assessment of a bench minor penalty for delay of game.

Players must proceed directly to the location of the face-off to participate in the ensuing face-off. Any attempts to delay the game by stalling or otherwise unnecessary actions by either team shall result in the assessment of a bench minor penalty for delaying the game. This penalty shall be announced as a "Bench Minor Penalty for Delay of Game – Slow Proceeding to Face-off Location (or, Slow Proceeding to Players' Bench)."

During the play, if a player wishes to retire from the ice and be replaced by a substitute, he must do so at the players' bench and not through any other exit leading from the rink. This is not a legal player change and therefore when a violation occurs, a bench minor penalty shall be imposed.

## Rule 83 – Off-side

83.1 **Off-side** - Players of the attacking team must not precede the puck into the attacking zone.

The position of the player's skates and not that of his stick shall be the determining factor in all instances in deciding an off-side. A player is off-side when both skates are completely over the leading edge of the blue line involved in the play.

A player is on-side when either of his skates are in contact with, or on his own side of the line, at the instant the puck completely crosses the leading edge of the blue line regardless of the position of his stick. However, a player actually controlling the puck who shall cross the line ahead of the puck shall not be considered "off-side," provided he had possession and control of the puck prior to his skates crossing the blue line.

It should be noted that while the position of the player's skates is what determines whether a player is "off-side," nevertheless the question of an "off-side" never arises until the puck has completely crossed the leading edge of the blue line at which time the decision is to be made.

If a player legally carries or passes the puck back into his own defending zone while a player of the opposing team is in such defending zone, the off-side shall be ignored and play permitted to continue.

83.2 **Deflections / Rebounds** – When a defending player propels the puck out of his defending zone and the puck clearly rebounds off a defending player in the neutral zone back into the defending zone, all attacking players are eligible to play the puck. However, any action by an attacking player that causes a deflection/rebound off a defending player in the neutral zone back into the defending zone (i.e. stick check, body check, physical contact), a delayed off-side shall be signaled by the Linesman.

A puck that deflects back into the defending zone off an official who is in the neutral zone will be off-side (or delayed off-side, as appropriate).

83.3 **Delayed Off-side** – A situation where an attacking player (or players) has preceded the puck across the attacking blue line, but the defending team is in a position to bring the puck back out of its defending zone without any delay or contact with an attacking player, or, the attacking players are in the process of clearing the attacking zone.

If an off-side call is delayed, the Linesman shall drop his arm to nullify the off-side violation and allow play to continue if:

*(i) All players of the offending team clear the zone at the same instant (skate contact with the blue line) permitting the attacking players to re-enter the attacking zone, or*

*(ii) The defending team passes or carries the puck into the neutral zone.*

If, during the course of the delayed off-side, any member of the attacking team touches the puck, attempts to gain possession of a loose puck, forces the defending puck carrier further back into his own zone, or who is about to make physical contact with the defending puck carrier, the Linesman shall stop play for the off-side violation.

If, during a delayed off-side, an attacking player in the attacking zone elects to proceed to his players' bench (which extends into the attacking zone) to be replaced by a teammate, he shall be considered to have cleared the zone provided he is completely off the ice and his replacement comes onto the ice in the neutral zone. If his replacement comes onto the ice in the attacking zone, if the delayed off-side is still in effect, he too must clear the attacking zone. If the remaining attacking players have cleared the attacking zone and the Linesman has lowered his arm for the delayed off-side, he shall be considered on-side.

83.4 **Disallowed Goal** – If the puck is shot into the attacking zone creating a delayed off-side, the play shall be allowed to continue under the normal clearing-the-zone rules. Should the puck, as a result of this shot, enter the defending team's goal, either directly or off the goalkeeper, a player, the boards, the glass, a piece of equipment or an official on the ice, the goal shall be disallowed as the original shot was off-side. The fact that the attacking team may have cleared the zone prior to the puck entering the goal has no bearing on this ruling.

The face-off will be conducted at the face-off spot in the zone closest to the point of origin of the shot that gives the offending team the least amount of territorial advantage.

The only way an attacking team can score a goal on a delayed off-side situation is if the defending team shoots or puts the puck into their own net without action or contact by the offending team.

Other than in situations involving a delayed off-side and the puck entering the goal or a successful Coach's Challenge (see Rule 78.7), no goal can be disallowed after the fact for an off-side violation, except for the human factor involved in blowing the whistle.

83.5 **Coach's Challenge** – Refer to Rule 78.7.

83.6 **Face-Off Location** - For violation of this rule, the play is stopped and the puck shall be faced-off in the neutral zone at the face-off spot nearest the attacking zone of the offending team when the violation occurs as a result of the attacking team carrying the puck over the attacking blue line, or from the face-off spot in the zone closest to the point of origin of the shot or pass (even if deflected off an attacking or defending player or an official).

For every delayed off-side situation, including an intentional off-side, the Linesman will raise his non-whistle arm. He will allow play to continue and, if a stoppage of play occurs, there will be three possible face-off locations:

*(i) If carried over the blue line – face-off outside the blue line.*

*(ii) If shot into the zone (or errant pass) – nearest face-off spot in the zone from which the pass or shot originated that gives the offending team the least amount of territorial advantage (even if deflected off an attacking or defending player or an official).*

*(iii) If the defending player is pressured or about to be checked by an attacking player – nearest face-off spot in the zone from which the pass or shot originated that gives the offending team the least amount of territorial advantage (even if deflected off an attacking or defending player or an official).*

*(iv) If deemed to be an intentional off-side – face-off spot in the offending team's end zone.*

When the Linesman signals a delayed off-side and a defending player shoots the puck which goes over the glass and out of play, the ensuing face-off shall be conducted at one of the defending zone end zone face-off spots (and the defending player would be assessed a minor penalty under Rule **63** – Delaying the Game).

When the Linesman signals a delayed off-side and the original shot deflects off a defending player and out of play, the ensuing face-off shall take place at the nearest face-off spot in the zone from where the puck was shot.

When the defending team is about to be penalized in the defending zone and the Linesman has a delayed off-side signaled against the attacking team on the same play, the ensuing face-off shall be conducted at one of the defending zone end zone face-off spots.

83.7 **Intentional Off-side** - An intentional off-side is one which is made for the purpose of securing a stoppage of play regardless of the reason, whether either team is short-handed.

If in the opinion of the Linesman, an intentional off-side play has been made, the puck shall be faced-off at the end face-off spot in the defending zone of the offending team.

If, while an off-side call is delayed, a player of the offending team deliberately touches the puck to create a stoppage of play, the Linesman will signal an intentional off-side.

If, in the judgement of the Linesman, the attacking player(s) are making an effort to exit the attacking zone and are in close proximity to the blue line at the time the puck is shot into the zone, the play will not be deemed to be an intentional off-side.

## Rule 84 – Overtime

84.1 **Overtime – Regular-season** - During regular-season games, if at the end of the three (3) regular twenty (20) minute periods, the score shall be tied, each team shall be awarded one point in the League standings.

The teams will then play an additional overtime period of not more than five (5) minutes with the team scoring first declared the winner and being awarded an additional point. The overtime period shall be played with each team at a numerical strength of three (3) skaters and one (1) goalkeeper.

The overtime period will commence following a shoveling of the entire ice surface by arena personnel utilizing the same procedures as are utilized during TV time-outs.

*NOTE: No intermission time shall be put on the clock between the end of regulation and the start of overtime, but the expectation is that the overtime period should commence approximately two (2) minutes after the end of regulation. Once the shoveling has been completed, the clock will be reset to 5:00 minutes and the overtime period will begin immediately.*

The players will remain at their respective benches during the period in which the shoveling of the entire ice surface takes place.

*NOTE: Teams are not permitted to return to the dressing room during this time.*

The teams must change ends for the overtime period.

*NOTE: For the entire overtime period, teams will defend the same end-zone as they do in the second period.*

Goalkeepers must go to their respective players' benches during this rest period, however, penalized players must remain on the penalty bench. Should a penalized player exit the penalty bench, he shall be returned immediately by the officials with no additional penalty being assessed, unless he commits an infraction of any other rule.

84.2 **Overtime – Regular-season – Extra Attacker** - A team shall be allowed to pull its goalkeeper in favor of an additional skater in the overtime period. However, should that team lose the game during the time in which the goalkeeper has been removed, it would forfeit the automatic point gained in the tie at the end of regulation play, except if the goalkeeper has been removed at the call of a delayed penalty against the other team. Should the goalkeeper proceed to his bench for an extra attacker due to a delayed penalty call against the opposing team, and should the non-offending team shoot the puck directly into their own goal, the game shall be over and the team that was to be penalized declared the winner.

Once the goalkeeper has been removed for an extra attacker in overtime during the regular-season, he must wait for the next stoppage of play before returning to his position. He cannot change "on the fly." If he does, a bench minor penalty shall be assessed for having an ineligible player.

84.3 **Overtime – Regular-season – Penalties** – When regulation time ends and the teams are 5 on 3, teams will start overtime 5 on 3. Once player strength reaches 5 on 4 or 5 on 5, at the next stoppage of play, player strength is adjusted to 4 on 3 or 3 on 3, as appropriate.

When regulation ends and teams are 4 on 4 teams will start overtime 3 on 3.

If at the end of regulation time teams are 3 on 3, overtime starts 3 on 3. Once player strength reaches 4 on 4, 5 on 4 or 5 on 5, at the next stoppage player strength is adjusted to 3 on 3 or 4 on 3 as appropriate.

At no time will a team have less than three players on the ice. This may require a fourth and/or fifth skater to be added in the event penalties are assessed.

Refer to Reference Tables – Table 17 – Penalties In Effect Prior to the Start of Overtime – Regular Season on page 157.

If a team is penalized in overtime, teams play 4 on 3. If both teams are penalized with minor penalties at the same stoppage of play (with no other penalties in effect), teams will continue to play 3 on 3.

In overtime, if a team is penalized such that a two-man advantage is called for, then the offending team will remain at three (3) skaters while the non-offending team will be permitted five (5) skaters.

At the first stoppage of play after the two-man advantage is no longer in effect, the numerical strength of the teams will revert back to 4 on 3 or 3 on 3, as appropriate.

Refer to Reference Tables – Table 18 – Penalties Assessed in Overtime – Regular Season on page 158.

84.4 **Shootout** - During regular-season games, if the game remains tied at the end of the five (5) minute overtime period, the teams will proceed to a shootout. The rules governing the shootout shall be the same as those listed under Rule **24** - Penalty Shot.

The shootout will commence following a shoveling of the entire ice surface by arena personnel using the same procedures as are utilized during TV time-outs.

Goalkeepers shall occupy the goal closest to their Team's players' bench. The home team shall have the choice of shooting first or second. The teams shall alternate shots.

*NOTE: For the shootout, teams will defend the same end-zone as they do in the first and third periods.*

Eligible players from each team shall participate in the shootout and they shall proceed in such order as the Coach selects. All players are eligible to participate in the shootout unless they are serving a ten-minute misconduct or have been assessed a game misconduct or match penalty. When a goalkeeper has been assessed a misconduct, the player designated to serve the misconduct penalty becomes ineligible for the shootout. If the misconduct is assessed to the goalkeeper during the course of the shootout, the player designated to serve the misconduct must be a player who has yet to shoot and thus becomes ineligible to shoot.

Guidelines related to stick measurement requests during the shootout are outlined in **10.7** – Stick Measurements – Prior to Shootout Attempt.

Once the shootout begins, the goalkeeper cannot be replaced unless he is injured. No warm up shall be permitted for a substitute goalkeeper.

Each team will be given three shots, unless the outcome is determined earlier in the shootout. After each team has taken three shots, if the score remains tied, the shootout will proceed to a "sudden death" format. No player may shoot twice until everyone who is eligible has shot. If, however, because of injury or penalty, one team has fewer players eligible for the shootout than its opponent, both teams may select from among the players who have already shot. This procedure would continue until the team with fewer players has again used all eligible shooters.

Regardless of the number of goals scored during the shootout portion of overtime, the final score recorded for the game will give the winning team one more goal than its opponent, based on the score at the end of overtime.

The losing goalkeeper will not be charged with the extra goal against. The player scoring the game-winning goal in the shootout will not be credited with a goal scored in his personal statistics.

If a team declines to participate in the shootout procedure, the game will be declared as a shootout loss for that Team. If a team declines to take a shot it will be declared as "no goal."

84.5 **Overtime – Playoffs –** In the Stanley Cup Playoffs, when a game is tied after three (3) twenty (20) minute regular periods of play, the teams shall take a fifteen (15) minute intermission and resume playing twenty (20) minute periods, changing ends for the start of each overtime period. The team scoring the first goal in overtime shall be declared the winner of the game.

## Rule 85 – Puck Out of Bounds

85.1 **Puck Out of Bounds** - When a puck goes outside the playing area at either end or either side of the rink, strikes any obstacles above the playing surface other than the boards or glass, causes the glass, lighting, timing device or the supports to break, it shall be faced-off at the nearest face-off spot in the zone from where it was shot or deflected out of play that gives the team at fault the least amount of

territorial advantage, except when the attacking team in the attacking zone is responsible for causing the puck to go out of play, the ensuing face-off shall take place at the nearest face-off spot in the neutral zone outside the offending team's attacking zone. With respect to when the attacking team is responsible for the puck going out of play in the attacking zone, the following exceptions apply and as a result, the face-off shall be conducted at one of the face-off spots in the attacking zone:

*(i) Shot at the net that deflects off the goal post or crossbar*

*(ii) Shot at the net that breaks the glass*

*(iii) Shot at the net that goes off the side of the net and out of play*

*(iv) Shot at the net that goes off the dasher boards or glass and out of play*

*(v) Shot at the net that is tipped or deflected by a teammate out of play*

*(vi) Shot or shoot-in that becomes wedged in or on the goal net*

If the puck comes to rest on top of the boards surrounding the playing area, it shall be considered to be in play and may be played legally by hand or stick.

When the puck goes outside the playing area directly off the face-off, regardless as to which player may have last contacted the puck, the face-off shall remain in the same spot and no penalty will be assessed to either team for delaying the game.

When the puck is shot and it makes contact with the gloves or the body of a player hanging over the players' bench, or if the puck enters the players' bench through an open bench door, the face-off shall take place at the nearest face-off spot in the zone from where the puck was shot, however, if the puck hits an opposing player's glove or body that is hanging over the opposing team's players' bench or enters the opposing team's players' bench through an open bench door, the face-off shall take place in the neutral zone adjacent to the opponent's players' bench.

Should the puck strike the curved glass located at the end of either players' bench, play shall be stopped when observed by any of the on-ice officials. The ensuing face-off shall be determined as if the puck went outside the playing area.

Should the puck strike the spectator netting at the ends and the corners of the arena, play shall be stopped and the ensuing face-off shall be determined as if the puck went outside the playing area. However, if the puck striking the spectator netting goes unnoticed by the on-ice officials, play shall continue as normal and resulting play with the puck shall be deemed a legitimate play. Players must not stop playing the game until they hear the whistle to do so.

85.2 **Puck Unplayable** - When the puck becomes lodged in the netting on the outside of either goal so as to make it unplayable, or if it is "frozen" between opposing players intentionally or otherwise, the Referee shall stop the play.

The puck may be played off the goal netting by either team. However, should the puck remain on the goal netting for more than three (3) seconds, play shall be stopped. Should the goalkeeper use his stick or glove to freeze the puck on the back of the net or should a defending player shield an attacking player from playing the puck off the back of the net, the face-off shall take place at one of the face-off spots in the defending zone.

Should the puck go under the goal either from behind or the side, or through the mesh from behind or the side, if this is witnessed by an on-ice official, play should be stopped immediately and the ensuing face-off should take place at the nearest face-off spot in the zone nearest to the location where the play was stopped.

85.3 **Puck Out of Sight** - Should a scramble take place or a player accidentally fall on the puck and the puck be out of sight of the Referee, he shall immediately blow his whistle and stop the play. The puck shall then be faced-off at the nearest face-off spot in the zone where the play was stopped unless otherwise provided for in the rules.

85.4 **Puck Striking Official** - Play shall not be stopped if the puck touches an official anywhere on the rink, regardless of whether a team is short-handed or not.

A puck that deflects back into the defending zone off an official who is in the neutral zone, will be deemed to be off-side as per Rule **83** – Off-side.

The puck striking or deflecting off an official does not automatically nullify a potential icing.

When a puck deflects off an official and goes out of play, the ensuing face-off will take place at the face-off spot in the zone nearest to where the puck deflected off the official.

If a goal is scored as a result of being deflected directly into the net off an official, the goal shall not be allowed.

85.5 **Face-Off Location** - Notwithstanding this rule, should an attacking player cause the puck to go out of play or become unplayable in the attacking zone, the face-off shall take place at a neutral zone face-off spot or at a face-off spot in the zone from which the puck left the ice, whichever is less advantageous to the attacking team.

For a puck that is unplayable due to being lodged in the netting or as a result of it being frozen between opposing players, the resulting face-off shall be at either of the adjacent face-off spots unless in the opinion of the Referee, the stoppage was caused by the attacking team, in which case the resulting face-off shall be conducted in the neutral zone or at the nearest face-off spot in the zone from which the puck was shot, whichever gives the offending team the least amount of territorial advantage, unless otherwise covered in these rules.

When the puck hits the goal post or crossbar and goes out of play, regardless which team shot the puck, the ensuing face-off shall take place at one of the end zone face-off spots in the zone where the puck went out of play. If, however, the attacking team shoots the puck into the zone and a delayed off-side is indicated, or if the attacking team contacts the puck with a high-stick or bats the puck with a glove and it then deflects off the goal post or crossbar and goes out of play, the ensuing face-off shall be in the neutral zone outside the offending team's attacking zone.

85.6 **Minor Penalty** – A minor penalty for delay of game shall be imposed on a goalkeeper who deliberately drops the puck on the goal netting to cause a stoppage of play.

85.7 **Verification of Time** - Any loss of time on the game or penalty clocks due to the puck going out of play must be replaced. The Video Goal Judge may be consulted to ensure the time is accurately replaced.

## Rule 86 – Start of Game and Periods

86.1 **Start of Game and Periods** - The game shall be commenced at the time scheduled by a "face-off" in the center of the rink and shall be renewed promptly at the conclusion of each intermission in the same manner.

86.2 **Bench Minor Penalty** – A bench minor penalty shall be imposed on either or both teams if they are not on the ice or can be seen proceeding to the ice to start the second, third or any overtime period when the intermission time on the clock has expired.

At the start of the second, third and any overtime period, all players with the exception of the starting players must proceed directly to their respective players' benches. Skating, warm-ups or on-ice activities by non-starters will result in a bench minor penalty for delay of game to the offending team.

When the visiting team must proceed by the way of the ice to their dressing room at the end of a period, they must wait for a signal from one of the officials before proceeding. Failure to wait for the official's signal shall result in the assessment of a bench minor penalty for delay of game.

86.3 **Choice of Ends** - Home clubs shall have the choice of goals to defend at the start of the game except where both players' benches are on the same side of the rink, in which case the home club shall start the game defending the goal nearest to its own bench. The teams shall change ends for each period of regulation time and, in the playoffs, for each period of overtime. (See Rule **84** – Overtime)

86.4 **Delays** - No delay shall be permitted by reason of any ceremony, exhibition, demonstration or presentation unless consented to reasonably in advance by the visiting team.

86.5 **End of Periods** - At the end of each period, the home team players must proceed directly to their dressing room while the visiting team players must wait for a signal from the official to proceed only if they have to go on the ice to reach their dressing room. Failure to comply with this regulation will result in a bench minor penalty for delay of game.

Players shall not be permitted to come on the ice during a stoppage of play or at the end of the first and second periods for the purpose of warming-up. The Referee will report any violation of this rule to the Commissioner for disciplinary action.

86.6 **Pre-Game Warm-Up** - During the pre-game warm-up (which shall not exceed sixteen (16) minutes in duration) and before the commencement of play in any period, each team shall confine its activity to its own end of the rink. Refer to Rule **46.9** - Fighting.

The Game Timekeeper shall be responsible for signaling the commencement and termination of the pre-game warm-up and any violation of this rule by the players shall be reported to the Commissioner.

Twenty (20) minutes before the time scheduled for the start of the game, both teams shall vacate the ice and proceed to their dressing rooms while the ice is being flooded. Both teams shall be signaled by the Game Timekeeper to return to the ice together in time for the scheduled start of the game.

86.7 **Start of Game** - At the beginning of the game, if a team fails to appear on the ice promptly without proper justification, a fine shall be assessed against the offending team, the amount of the fine to be decided by the Commissioner.

86.8 **Start of Periods** - At the beginning of the second and third periods, and overtime periods in playoffs (0:00 on the clock), clubs must be on the ice or be observed to be proceeding to the ice. Failure to comply with this regulation will result in a bench minor penalty for delay of game.

Before the start of the second and third periods (and overtime periods in the playoffs), the teams will proceed directly to their respective players' benches. Only the starting line-up will be allowed on the ice. The visiting team will immediately place its starting line-up at the face-off circle, then the home team will follow, with the Referee allowing the home team to make a line change if so desired prior to the face-off. Skating, warm-ups or on-ice activities by non-starters will result in a bench minor penalty for delay of game to the offending team.

No warm-up involving pucks on the ice shall be permitted for a goalkeeper at the start of any period. If, after one warning, this continues, the Referee shall assess a delay of game penalty to the offending team.

## Rule 87 – Time-outs

87.1 **Time-out** - Each team shall be permitted to take one thirty-second time-out during the course of any game, regular season or playoffs. All players including goalkeepers on the ice at the time of the time-out will be allowed to go to their respective benches.

This time-out must be taken during a normal stoppage of play. Only one time-out, commercial or team, shall be permitted at any one stoppage of play. For the purpose of this rule, a commercial time-out is deemed an "official time-out" and not charged to either team.

Any player designated by the Coach will indicate to the Referee (prior to the drop of the puck) that his team is exercising its option and the Referee will report the time-out to the Game Timekeeper who shall be responsible for signaling the termination of the time-out.

No time-out shall be granted following a face-off violation.

When a penalty shot has been awarded to either team by the Referee, no time-out will be granted once instructions have been given to the player taking the shot and the goalkeeper defending the shot. No time-out will be granted during the shootout.

No warm-up involving pucks on the ice shall be permitted for a goalkeeper or replacement goalkeeper during a time-out. If, after one warning, this continues, the Referee shall assess a delay of game penalty to the offending team.

Television commercial time-out guidelines are established by the League. However, no commercial time-out is permitted after the scoring of a goal. No commercial time-out is permitted after the calling of an icing infraction, except when a penalty or penalties are assessed that affect the on-ice strength of either team.

## TABLE 1
## (Rule 15 – Calling of Penalties)
## SUMMARY OF PENALTIES TO COACHES AND NON-PLAYING CLUB PERSONNEL

| | Description | Rule | |
|---|---|---|---|
| (i) | Hitting the boards with a stick | Rule 39.3 | |
| (ii) | Interference with an opponent on a breakaway | Rule 56.6 | |
| (iii) | Interference with an opponent or the puck while play is in progress | Rule 56.3 | |
| (iv) | Interference with an opponent or the puck while the goalkeeper has been removed | Rule 56.7 | |
| (v) | Interfering with an official | Rule 39.3 | |
| (vi) | Leaving the bench by stepping onto the ice before the end of the period | Rule 70.5 | |
| (vii) | Obscene language or gestures | Rule 39.3<br>Rule 39.5 | Rule 75.3<br>Rule 75.5 |
| (viii) | Physically abusing an official | Rule 40.7 | |
| (ix) | Refusing to start play (teams in their dressing room) | Rule 73.3 | |
| (x) | Refusing to start play (teams on the ice) | Rule 73.2 | |
| (xi) | Throwing a stick on the ice to a player who has lost or broken a stick | Rule 39.3 | |
| (xii) | Throwing any object onto the ice | Rule 75.3 | |
| (xiii) | Throwing stick (breakaway on an open net) | Rule 53.7 | |
| (xiv) | Throwing stick (defending zone) | Rule 53.6 | |

## TABLE 2
## (Rule 16 – Minor Penalties)
## SUMMARY OF MINOR PENALTIES

| | Description | Rule |
|---|---|---|
| (i) | Boarding | Rule 41 |
| (ii) | Broken stick | Rule 10 |
| (iii) | Charging | Rule 42 |
| (iv) | Clipping | Rule 44 |
| (v) | Closing hand on puck | Rule 67 |
| (vi) | Concealing puck with hand | Rule 67 |
| (vii) | Cross-checking | Rule 59 |
| (viii) | Delay of game | Rule 63 |
| (ix) | Elbowing | Rule 45 |
| (x) | Goalkeeper interference | Rule 69 |
| (xi) | High-sticking | Rule 60 |
| (xii) | Holding | Rule 54 |
| (xiii) | Holding the stick | Rule 54 |
| (xiv) | Hooking | Rule 55 |
| (xv) | Illegal Check to the Head | Rule 48 |

## TABLE 2
## (Rule 16 – Minor Penalties)
## SUMMARY OF MINOR PENALTIES

| Description | | Rule |
|---|---|---|
| (xvi) | Illegal equipment | Rule 12 |
| (xvii) | Illegal stick | Rule 10 |
| (xviii) | Instigator | Rule 46 |
| (xix) | Interference | Rule 56 |
| (xx) | Kneeing | Rule 50 |
| (xxi) | Leaving penalty bench too early | Rule 70 |
| (xxii) | Leaving the crease (goalkeeper) | Rule 27 |
| (xxiii) | Participating in the play beyond the center red line (goalkeeper) | Rule 27 |
| (xxiv) | Roughing | Rule 51 |
| (xxv) | Slashing | Rule 61 |
| (xxvi) | Throwing puck towards opponent's goal (goalkeeper) | Rule 67 |
| (xxvii) | Throwing stick | Rule 53 |
| (xxviii) | Tripping | Rule 57 |
| (xxix) | Use of hand on face-off | Rule 76 |
| (xxx) | Unsportsmanlike conduct | Rule 75 |

## TABLE 3
## (Rule 17 – Bench Minor Penalties)
## SUMMARY OF BENCH MINOR PENALTIES

| Description | | Rule |
|---|---|---|
| (i) | Abuse of officials | Rule 39 |
| (ii) | Delay of game | Rule 63 |
| (iii) | Deliberate illegal substitution | Rule 74 |
| (iv) | Face-off violation | Rule 76 |
| (v) | Illegal substitution | Rule 68 |
| (vi) | Improper starting line-up | Rule 7 |
| (vii) | Interference from players' or penalty bench | Rule 56 |
| (viii) | Interference with an official | Rule 39 |
| (ix) | Leaving bench at end of period | Rule 86 |
| (x) | Refusing to start play | Rule 73 |
| (xi) | Stepping onto ice during period (Coach) | Rule 70 |
| (xii) | Throwing objects onto ice | Rule 63 |
| (xiii) | Too many men on the ice | Rule 74 |
| (xiv) | Unsportsmanlike conduct | Rule 75 |
| (xv) | Unsustained request for measurement | Rule 10 |

## TABLE 4
### (Rule 18 – Double-minor Penalties)
### SUMMARY OF DOUBLE-MINOR PENALTIES

| Description | Rule |
|---|---|
| (i) Butt-ending | Rule 58 |
| (ii) Head-butting | Rule 47 |
| (iii) High-sticking | Rule 60 |
| (iv) Spearing | Rule 62 |

## TABLE 5
### (Rule 20 – Major Penalties)
### SUMMARY OF MAJOR PENALTIES

| Description | Rule |
|---|---|
| (i) Boarding | Rule 41 |
| (ii) Butt-ending | Rule 58 |
| (iii) Charging | Rule 42 |
| (iv) Checking from behind | Rule 43 |
| (v) Clipping | Rule 44 |
| (vi) Cross-checking | Rule 59 |
| (vii) Elbowing | Rule 45 |
| (viii) Fighting | Rule 46 |
| (ix) Head-butting | Rule 47 |
| (x) Hooking | Rule 55 |
| (xi) Interference | Rule 56 |
| (xii) Kneeing | Rule 50 |
| (xiii) Slashing | Rule 61 |
| (xiv) Spearing | Rule 62 |

## TABLE 6
### (Rule 20 – Major Penalties)
### SUMMARY OF MAJOR PENALTIES THAT RESULT IN AN AUTOMATIC GAME MISCONDUCT

| Description | Rule |
|---|---|
| (i) Butt-ending | Rule 58 |
| (ii) Checking from behind | Rule 43 |
| (iii) Clipping | Rule 44 |
| (iv) Cross-checking | Rule 59 |
| (v) Fighting (after original altercation) | Rule 46 |
| (vi) Fighting (when aggressor) | Rule 46 |

## TABLE 6
### (Rule 20 – Major Penalties)
### SUMMARY OF MAJOR PENALTIES THAT RESULT IN AN AUTOMATIC GAME MISCONDUCT

| Description | Rule |
|---|---|
| (vii) Fighting (second instigator in game) | Rule 46 |
| (viii) Fighting (instigator in final 5 minutes) | Rule 46 |
| (ix) Fighting (third instigator in season) | Rule 46 |
| (x) Head-butting | Rule 47 |
| (xi) Hooking | Rule 55 |
| (xii) Kneeing | Rule 50 |
| (xiii) Slashing | Rule 61 |
| (xiv) Spearing | Rule 62 |

## TABLE 7
### (Rule 20 – Major Penalties)
### SUMMARY OF MAJOR PENALTIES THAT RESULT IN AN AUTOMATIC GAME MISCONDUCT WHEN THERE IS AN INJURY TO THE FACE OR HEAD

| Description | Rule |
|---|---|
| (i) Boarding | Rule 41 |
| (ii) Charging | Rule 42 |
| (iii) Elbowing | Rule 45 |

## TABLE 8
### (Rule 21 – Match Penalties)
### SUMMARY OF MATCH PENALTIES

| Description | Rule |
|---|---|
| (i) Attempt to injure (in any manner) | Rule 21 |
| (ii) Biting | Rule 21 |
| (iii) Boarding | Rule 41 |
| (iv) Butt-ending * | Rule 58 |
| (v) Charging | Rule 42 |
| (vi) Checking from behind | Rule 43 |
| (vii) Clipping | Rule 44 |
| (viii) Cross-checking | Rule 59 |
| (ix) Deliberate injury (in any manner) | Rule 21 |
| (x) Elbowing | Rule 45 |
| (xi) Goalkeeper who uses his blocking glove to the head or face of an opponent* | Rule 51 |
| (xii) Grabbing of the face mask | Rule 21 |

## TABLE 8
## (Rule 21 – Match Penalties)
## SUMMARY OF MATCH PENALTIES

| Description | Rule |
|---|---|
| (xiii) Hair pulling | Rule 21 |
| (xiv) Head-butting * | Rule 47 |
| (xv) High-sticking | Rule 60 |
| (xvi) Illegal Check to the Head | Rule 48 |
| (xvii) Kicking a player (or goalkeeper) | Rule 49 |
| (xviii) Kneeing | Rule 50 |
| (xix) Punching and injuring an unsuspecting opponent * | Rule 46 |
| (xx) Slashing | Rule 61 |
| (xxi) Slew-footing | Rule 52 |
| (xxii) Spearing * | Rule 62 |
| (xxiii) Throwing stick or any object | Rule 53 |
| (xxiv) Wearing tape on hands in altercation * | Rule 46 |

* NOTE - match penalty must be assessed when injury results

## TABLE 9
## (Rule 22 – Misconduct Penalties)
## SUMMARY OF MISCONDUCT PENALTIES

| Description | Rule | |
|---|---|---|
| (i) Banging boards with stick in protest of an official's ruling | Rule 39 | |
| (ii) Continuing or attempting to continue a fight | Rule 46 | |
| (iii) Deliberately breaking stick or refusing to surrender stick for measurement | Rule 10 | |
| (iv) Deliberately throwing any equipment (including stick) out of playing area | Rule 39 | Rule 53 |
| (v) Entering or remaining in the Referee's crease | Rule 39 | |
| (vi) Fighting off the playing surface (or with another player who is off the playing surface) | Rule 46 | |
| (vii) Inciting an opponent | Rule 75 | |
| (viii) Instigating a fight | Rule 46 | |
| (ix) Interfering or distracting opponent taking a penalty shot | Rule 24 | |
| (x) Knocking or shooting puck out of reach of an official | Rule 39 | |
| (xi) Leaving bench to speak to official | Rule 6 | |
| (xii) Refusing to change non-regulation piece of protective equipment (second violation) | Rule 9 | |
| (xiii) Use of profane or abusive language | Rule 75 | |
| (xiv) Verbal abuse of an official | Rule 39 | |

## TABLE 10
## (Rule 23 – Game Misconduct Penalties)
## SUMMARY OF GAME MISCONDUCT PENALTIES

| Description | | Rule | |
|---|---|---|---|
| (i) | Butt-ending | Rule 58 | |
| (ii) | Charging | Rule 42 | |
| (iii) | Clipping | Rule 44 | |
| (iv) | Continues or attempts to continue a fight | Rule 46 | |
| (v) | Cross-checking | Rule 59 | |
| (vi) | Deliberately attempts to injure a Manager, Coach or other non-playing personnel | Rule 75 | |
| (vii) | Elbowing | Rule 45 | |
| (viii) | Fighting off the playing surface | Rule 46 | |
| (ix) | First or second player to leave the players' bench during or to start an altercation | Rule 70 | |
| (x) | First to intervene in an altercation (third man in) | Rule 46 | |
| (xi) | Head-butting | Rule 47 | |
| (xii) | Hooking | Rule 55 | |
| (xiii) | Inciting an opponent into incurring a penalty | Rule 75 | |
| (xiv) | Interference | Rule 56 | |
| (xv) | Interferes with a game official in the performance of their duties | Rule 39 | |
| (xvi) | Intervening in an altercation | Rule 46 | |
| (xvii) | Kneeing | Rule 50 | |
| (xviii) | Leaving the penalty bench during an altercation | Rule 70 | |
| (xix) | Not properly tied down during an altercation | Rule 46 | |
| (xx) | Obscene language or gestures | Rule 39 | Rule 75 |
| (xxi) | Ordered to dressing room but returns | Rule 70 | |
| (xxii) | Persists to challenge or dispurte official's ruling | Rule 39 | |
| (xxiii) | Persists in continuing an altercation | Rule 46 | |
| (xxiv) | Physically abuses an official | Rule 40 | |
| (xxv) | Removing jersey prior to an altercation | Rule 46 | |
| (xxvi) | Resisting a Linesman in the discharge of his duties | Rule 39 | |
| (xxvii) | Secondary altercation | Rule 46 | |
| (xxviii) | Slashing | Rule 61 | |
| (xxix) | Spearing | Rule 62 | |
| (xxx) | Third major penalty in a game | Rule 20 | |
| (xxxi) | Throwing stick outside the playing area | Rule 53 | |

## TABLE 11
## (Rule 25 – Penalty Shot)
## SUMMARY OF PENALTY SHOTS

| | Description | Rule | |
|---|---|---|---|
| (i) | Deliberate illegal substitution | Rule 68 | |
| (ii) | Intentionally dislodging the net from its moorings during the course of a breakaway | Rule 63 | |
| (iii) | Intentionally dislodging the net from its moorings when the penalty cannot be served in its entirety within regulation time | Rule 63 | |
| (iv) | Falling on the puck in the goal crease | Rule 63 | |
| (v) | Picking up the puck with the hand in the goal crease | Rule 63 | |
| (vi) | Player on a breakaway who is interfered with by an object thrown or shot by a defending team player | Rule 53 | Rule 56 |
| (vii) | Player on a breakaway who is interfered with by a player who has illegally entered the game | Rule 70 | |
| (viii) | Player throws or shoots an object at the puck in his defending zone | Rule 53 | |
| (ix) | Player on a breakaway who is fouled from behind. | Rule 24<br>Rule 54<br>Rule 55 | Rule 57<br>Rule 61 |

## TABLE 12
## (Rule 26 – Awarded Goals)
## SUMMARY OF AWARDED GOALS (WHEN GOALKEEPER HAS BEEN REMOVED FOR AN EXTRA ATTACKER)

| | Description | Rule |
|---|---|---|
| (i) | Delaying the game | Rule 63 |
| (ii) | Handling the puck | Rule 67 |
| (iii) | Illegal substitution | Rule 68 |
| (iv) | Interference | Rule 56 |
| (v) | Leaving the players' or penalty bench | Rule 70 |
| (vi) | Throwing stick | Rule 53 |
| (vii) | Tripping (fouling from behind – including hooking, holding, slashing, etc.) | Rule 57 |

## TABLE 13
## (Rule 28 – Goalkeeper's Penalties)
## SUMMARY OF GOALKEEPER PENALTIES

| | Description | Rule | |
|---|---|---|---|
| (i) | Illegal stick | Rule 10 | |
| (ii) | Illegal equipment | Rule 9 | Rule 12 |
| (iii) | Leaving crease during an altercation | Rule 27 | |
| (iv) | Proceeding to players' bench | Rule 27 | |
| (v) | Participates in the play beyond the center red line | Rule 27 | |
| (vi) | Playing puck in restricted area | Rule 1<br>Rule 27 | Rule 63 |
| (vii) | Proceeds to players' bench to replace stick | Rule 10 | |
| (viii) | Deliberately shoots or bats puck out of play | Rule 63 | |
| (ix) | Deliberately falls on the puck inside or outside the goal crease | Rule 63 | |
| (x) | Deliberately drops the puck in his pads or on the goal net | Rule 67 | |
| (xi) | Piling snow or other obstacles | Rule 67 | |
| (xii) | Throwing the puck towards opponent's goal | Rule 67 | |
| (xiii) | Using blocking glove to punch an opponent in the head or face | Rule 51 | |

## TABLE 14
## (Rule 16 – Minor Penalties)
## GOALS SCORED AGAINST A SHORT-HANDED TEAM

| Ex | Time | Team A | Team B | Answer | Remarks |
|---|---|---|---|---|---|
| Minor penalty expiration criteria:<br><br>a. Is the team scored against, short-handed?<br>b. Are they serving a minor penalty on the clock?<br>c. If the answer is yes to a) and b), delete the minor penalty with the least amount of time on the clock, except when coincidental penalties are being served. | | | | | |
| **One player with a double minor penalty:** | | | | | |
| A1 | 3:00<br>4:30 | A15 – 2+2 | <br>Goal | No player returns | First penalty ends, the second begins at 4:30. |
| A2 | 3:00<br>5:30 | A15 – 2+2 | <br>Goal | A15 returns. | The first penalty has expired, the second ends with the scoring of the goal. |
| **One player with a minor and a major penalty:** | | | | | |
| B1 | 3:00<br>4:30 | A15 – 5+2 | <br>Goal | No penalty terminates. | The major penalty must be served first. |
| B2 | 3:00<br>8:30 | A15 – 5+2 | <br>Goal | A15 returns. | The major penalty has expired, the minor penalty ends with the scoring of the goal. |

## TABLE 14
### (Rule 16 – Minor Penalties)
### GOALS SCORED AGAINST A SHORT-HANDED TEAM

| Ex | Time | Team A | Team B | Answer | Remarks |
|---|---|---|---|---|---|
| **Two players of the same team – combination of minor and major penalties:** | | | | | |
| C1 | 3:00<br>4:00<br>4:30 | A15 – 2<br>A23 – 2 | <br><br>Goal | A15 returns. | |
| C2 | 3:00<br>4:00<br>4:30 | A15 – 2<br>A23 – 5 | <br><br>Goal | A15 returns. | |
| C3 | 3:00<br>4:00<br>4:30 | A15 – 5<br>A23 – 2 | <br><br>Goal | A23 returns. | |
| C4 | 3:00<br>4:00<br>4:30<br><br>5:30 | A15 – 2+2<br>A23 – 2 | <br><br>Goal<br><br>Goal | <br><br>No player returns.<br>A23 returns. | <br><br>The first minor to A15 ends.<br>A23 returns because he has the least amount of time to serve in his minor penalty. |
| C5 | 3:00<br>(S*)<br>4:30 | A15 – 2<br>A23 – 2+2 | <br><br>Goal | A15 returns.<br><br>* S = signaled | The signaled double-minor penalty to A23 is assessed at 4:30. |
| C6 | 3:00<br>4:00<br>4:30 | A15 – 5+2<br>A23 – 2 | <br><br>Goal | A23 returns. | A15 must first serve his major penalty. A23 returns as he is serving a minor penalty. |
| C7 | 3:00<br>7:30<br>8:30 | A15 – 5+2<br>A23 – 2 | <br><br>Goal | A23 returns. | Least amount of time to serve. |
| C8 | 3:00<br>6:00<br>8:00 | A15 – 5+2<br>A23 – 2 | <br><br>Goal | Both A15 and A23 return. | The major penalty to A15 has expired. His minor penalty ends with the goal. A23's minor penalty has expired. |
| C9 | 3:00<br>8:00<br>9:00 | A15 – 5+2<br>A23 – 2 | <br><br>Goal | Captain's choice. | The major penalty to A15 has expired. Both minors terminate at the same time. |
| **Three players of the same team – Delayed (D) or Signaled (S) penalty (no stoppage of play):** | | | | | |
| D1 | 3:00<br>3:30<br>4:00<br>4:30<br>5:00<br>5:30 | A15 – 2<br>A23 – 2<br>A6 – 2(D) | <br><br><br>Goal<br>Goal<br>Goal | <br><br><br>A15 returns.<br>A23 returns.<br>A6 returns. | <br><br><br>Delayed penalty to A6 begins at 4:30 |
| D2 | 3:00<br>3:30<br>(S)<br>4:30 | A15 – 2<br>A23 – 2<br>A6 – 2 | <br><br><br>Goal | <br><br><br>A15 returns and the penalty to A6 starts. | |

## TABLE 14
## (Rule 16 – Minor Penalties)
## GOALS SCORED AGAINST A SHORT-HANDED TEAM

| Ex | Time | Team A | Team B | Answer | Remarks |
|---|---|---|---|---|---|
| | 5:00 | | Goal | A23 returns and A6 remains in the box. | |
| D3 | 3:00<br>3:30<br>(S)<br>4:30 | A15 – 5<br>A23 – 2<br>A6 – 2 | <br><br><br>Goal | A23 returns and the penalty to A6 starts. | |
| D4 | 3:00<br>7:30<br>(S)<br>8:00 | A15 – 5<br>A23 – 2<br>A6 – 2 | <br><br><br>Goal | A15 and A23 return and the penalty to A6 starts. | The major penalty to A15 is completed. The minor penalty to A23 ends on the scoring of the goal. |
| **One player from each team – combination of minors and majors:** | | | | | |
| E1 | 3:00<br>3:30<br>4:30<br>5:00 | A15 - 2 | <br>B12 – 2<br>Goal<br>Goal | <br><br>No player returns.<br>A15 returns. | <br><br>Teams are at equal strength.<br>His minor penalty has been completed. |
| E2 | 3:00<br>3:30<br>4:30 | A15 – 5+2 | <br>B12 – 2<br>Goal | No player returns. | Teams are at equal strength. |
| E3 | 3:00<br>7:30<br>8:00 | A15 – 5+2 | <br>B12 – 2<br>Goal | No player returns. | The major penalty to A15 is complete but the teams remain at equal strength. |
| E4 | 3:00<br>3:30<br>4:30<br>5:00<br>5:30 | A15 – 2+2 | <br>B12 – 2<br>Goal<br>Goal<br>Goal | <br><br>No player returns.<br>No player returns.<br>A15 returns. | <br><br>Teams are at equal strength.<br>The first minor to A15 is competed but teams remain at equal strength.<br>The first minor penalty to A15 and that of B12 are complete. The second minor penalty to A15 ends with the goal. |
| E5 | 3:00<br>6:00<br>8:00 | A15 – 5+2 | <br>B12 – 2<br>Goal | A15 returns. | The major penalty to A15 and the minor penalty to B12 have expired. The minor penalty to A15 ends on the scoring of the goal. |
| E6 | 3:00<br>3:30<br>(S)<br>4:10 | A15 – 2<br><br>A23 – 2 | <br>B12 – 2<br><br>Goal | No player returns. | The goal nullifies the signaled penalty to A23 (Reason: Team A was not short-handed). |

## TABLE 14
## (Rule 16 – Minor Penalties)
## GOALS SCORED AGAINST A SHORT-HANDED TEAM

| Ex | Time | Team A | Team B | Answer | Remarks |
|---|---|---|---|---|---|
| **Unequal number of players – combination of minors and majors:** | | | | | |
| F1 | 3:00<br>3:30<br>4:00<br>4:30 | A15 – 2<br><br>A23 – 2<br> | <br>B12 – 2<br><br>Goal | A15 returns. | He had the least amount of time to serve in his minor penalty. |
| F2 | 3:00<br>3:30<br>4:00<br>5:00 | A15 – 2<br><br>A23 – 2<br> | <br>B12 – 2<br><br>Goal | A15 returns. | His minor penalty is completed. Teams are at equal strength at the time of the goal. |
| F3 | 3:00<br>3:30<br>4:00<br>4:30 | A15 – 2<br>A23 – 2<br><br> | <br><br>B12 – 2<br>Goal | A15 returns. | |
| F4 | 3:00<br>3:30<br>4:00<br>4:30 | <br>A15 – 2<br>A23 – 5<br> | B12 – 2<br><br><br>Goal | A15 returns. | Least amount of time to serve in his minor penalty. |
| F5 | 3:00<br>3:30<br>4:00<br>4:30<br>5:00 | <br>A15 – 2<br>A23 – 2<br><br> | B12 – 2<br><br><br>Goal<br>Goal | <br><br><br>A15 returns.<br>A23 returns | <br><br><br>Least amount of time to serve in his minor penalty.<br> |
| F6 | 3:00<br>3:30<br>4:00<br>4:30 | A15 – 5<br><br>A23 – 2<br> | <br>B12 – 5<br><br>Goal | A23 returns. | Least amount of time (and Team A is short-handed by reason of a minor penalty). |
| F7 | 3:00<br>3:30<br>4:00<br>4:30 | A15 – 2<br><br>A23 – 5<br> | <br>B12 – 5<br><br>Goal | A15 returns. | Least amount of time (and Team A is short-handed by reason of a minor penalty). |
| F8 | 3:00<br>3:30<br>4:00<br>4:30 | A15 – 5<br>A23 – 2<br><br> | <br><br>B12 – 2<br>Goal | A23 returns. | Short-handed by reason of a minor penalty. |
| F9 | 3:00<br>3:30<br>4:00<br>4:30 | A15 – 5<br><br>A23 – 2<br> | <br>B12 – 2<br><br>Goal | A23 returns. | Short-handed by reason of a minor penalty. |
| F10 | 3:00<br>3:30<br>4:00<br>4:30 | A15 – 2<br>A23 – 5<br><br> | <br><br>B12 – 2<br>Goal | A15 returns. | Short-handed by reason of a minor penalty. |
| F11 | 3:00<br>3:30<br>4:00<br>4:30 | <br>A15 – 2<br>A23 – 2<br> | B12 – 5<br><br><br>Goal | A15 returns. | Least amount of time. |
| F12 | 3:00<br>3:30<br>4:00<br>4:30 | A15 – 2+2<br><br>A23 – 2<br> | <br>B12 – 2<br><br>Goal | No player returns. | First minor penalty to A15 ends. |

## TABLE 14
## (Rule 16 – Minor Penalties)
## GOALS SCORED AGAINST A SHORT-HANDED TEAM

| Ex | Time | Team A | Team B | Answer | Remarks |
|---|---|---|---|---|---|
| F13 | 3:00 | A15 – 2 | | | |
| | 3:15 | A23 – 2 | | | |
| | 3:30 | | B12 – 2 | | |
| | 3:45 | A6 – 2(D) | | | |
| | 4:00 | | Goal | A15 returns. | The penalty to A6 begins at 4:00 |
| | 4:30 | | Goal | A23 returns. | Least amount of time. |
| F14 | 3:00 | A15 – 2 | B12 – 2 | A23 returns. | Penalties to A6 and B3 are not on the clock. |
| | 3:15 | A23 – 2 | | | |
| | 3:30 | A6 – 2 | B3 – 2 | | |
| | 5:10 | | Goal | | |
| F15 | 3:00 | A15 – 2 | | Signaled penalty to B3 is not assessed. | The penalty to B12 does not make Team B short-handed. |
| | 3:30 | | B12 – 2 | | |
| | 4:00 | A23 – 2 | | | |
| | (S) | | B3 - 2 | | |
| | 4:30 | Goal | | | |
| F16 | 3:00 | A15 – 2 | | A15 returns. | The minor penalty to A6 begins at 4:30. |
| | 3:30 | | B12 – 2 | | |
| | 4:00 | A23 – 2 | | | |
| | (S) | A6 – 2 | | | |
| | 4:30 | | Goal | | |
| **Coincidental penalties – equal number of players on each team:** | | | | | |
| G1 | 3:00 | A15 – 5+2 | B12 – 2+2 | No player returns. | Teams are at equal strength. |
| | 4:30 | | Goal | | |
| G2 | 3:00 | A15 – 2+5 | B12 – 5 | The substitute for A15 returns. | Coincidental major penalties. |
| | 4:30 | | Goal | | |
| G3 | 3:00 | A15 – 2 | | A15 returns. | Coincidental penalties are not put on the clock. |
| | 3:30 | A23 – 2 | B12 – 2 | | |
| | 4:30 | | Goal | | |
| G4 | 3:00 | A15 – 2 | B12 – 2 | A23 returns. | |
| | 3:30 | A23 – 2 | | | |
| | 4:30 | | Goal | | |
| G5 | 3:00 | A15 – 2 | B12 – 2 | No player returns. | Team A is short-handed, however, it is with a major penalty. |
| | 3:30 | A23 – 5 | | | |
| | 4:30 | | Goal | | |
| G6 | 3:00 | A15 – 2 | B12 – 5 | A15 returns. | Team A is below the numerical strength of it's opponent. Minor penalty to A15 expires on the scoring of the goal. |
| | 3:30 | A23 – 5 | | | |
| | 4:30 | | Goal | | |
| G7 | 3:00 | A15 – 2 | | A15 returns. | |
| | 3:30 | A23 – 2 | | | |
| | 4:30 | | Goal | | |
| G8 | 3:00 | A15 – 2 | | A15 returns. | Penalties to A23 and B12 are not on the clock. |
| | 3:30 | A23 – 5 | B12 – 5 | | |
| | 4:30 | | Goal | | |
| G9 | 3:00 | A15 – 5 | | No player returns. | A15 is serving a major penalty. Penalties to A23 and B12 are not on the clock. |
| | 3:30 | A23 – 2 | B12 – 2 | | |
| | 4:30 | | Goal | | |

## TABLE 14
## (Rule 16 – Minor Penalties)
## GOALS SCORED AGAINST A SHORT-HANDED TEAM

| Ex | Time | Team A | Team B | Answer | Remarks |
|---|---|---|---|---|---|
| G10 | 3:00<br>3:30<br>4:30 | A15 – 5<br>A23 – 2 | <br>B12 – 5<br>Goal | A23 returns. | Short-handed by reason of a minor penalty. |
| G11 | 3:00<br>3:30<br>4:30 | A15 – 2+2<br>A23 – 2 | B12 – 5<br><br>Goal | No player returns. | First minor penalty to A15 is eliminated. |
| G12 | 3:00<br>3:30<br>(S)<br>4:30 | A15 – 2<br>A23 – 5<br>A6 – 2 | B12 – 2<br><br><br>Goal | The penalty to A6 is not assessed (unless it is a major or match penalty). | |
| G13 | 3:00<br>3:30<br>4:00<br>4:30<br>4:45 | A15 – 2<br>A23 – 2<br>A6 – 2 | <br>B12 – 2<br><br>Goal<br>Goal | <br><br><br>A15 returns.<br>A6 returns. | Penalties to A23 and B12 are not on the clock. |
| G14 | 3:00<br>3:30<br>(S)<br>4:30 | A15 – 2<br>A23 – 2<br>A6 – 2 | <br>B12 – 2<br><br>Goal | A15 returns. | The minor penalty to A6 begins at 4:30. The penalties to A23 and B12 are not on the clock. |
| G15 | 3:00<br>3:30 | A15 – 2+2 | B12 – 2<br>Goal | Minor penalty to A15 is eliminated. | Team A would have placed an additional player in the penalty box to serve the extra minor penalty to A15. NOTE: A15's additional minor penalty begins at 3:30 due to the scoring of the goal by Team B, but does not affect the on-ice strength. |
| **Ex** | **Time** | **Team A** | **Team B** | **Answer** | **Remarks** |
| **Coincident penalties – unequal number of players on each team:** | | | | | |
| H1 | 3:00<br><br>4:30 | A15 – 2<br>A23 – 2 | B12 – 2<br><br>Goal | Captain's choice. | This choice must be made at the time of assessment of the penalties. |
| H2 | 3:00<br><br>4:30 | A15 – 2<br>A23 – 5 | B12 – 2<br><br>Goal | No player returns. | The major penalty makes the team short-handed. The penalties to A15 and B12 do not go on the clock. |
| H3 | 3:00<br><br>4:30 | A15 – 2<br>A23 – 2 | B12 – 5<br><br>Goal | Captain's choice. | The minor penalties end at the same time. |
| H4 | 3:00<br><br>4:30 | A15 – 2<br>A23 – 5 | B12 – 5<br><br>Goal | A15 returns. | Major penalties are coincidental and do not go on the clock. |

## TABLE 14
## (Rule 16 – Minor Penalties)
## GOALS SCORED AGAINST A SHORT-HANDED TEAM

| Ex | Time | Team A | Team B | Answer | Remarks |
|---|---|---|---|---|---|
| H5 | 3:00<br><br>4:30 | A15 – 5<br>A23 – 2 | B12 – 2<br><br>Goal | No player returns. | Coincidental minor penalties. Team A is short-handed by reason of the major penalty. Penalties to A23 and B12 do not go on the clock. |
| H6 | 3:00<br><br>4:30 | A15 – 2+2<br>A23 – 2 | B12 – 2<br><br>Goal | Captain's choice. The minor penalty to B12 can cancel off with any one of the minor penalties assessed to the two players on Team A. | Depending on the choice made by Team A, A23 may return or the first minor penalty to A15 will end with the scoring of the goal, or the replacement player serving the extra minor to A15 will return. |
| H7 | 3:00<br><br>4:30 | A15 – 2<br>A23 – 2+2 | B12 – 2<br><br>Goal | Captain's choice. The minor penalty to B12 can cancel off with any one of the minor penalties assessed to the two players on Team A. | Depending on the choice made by Team A, A15 may return or the first minor penalty to A23 will end with the scoring of the goal, or the replacement player serving the extra minor to A23 will return. |
| H8 | 3:00<br><br><br>4:00<br><br>4:30 | A15 – 2<br>A23 – 2<br>A6 – 2 | B12 – 2<br><br><br>Goal<br><br>Goal | <br><br><br>Captain's choice.<br><br>Remaining player returns. | <br><br><br>B12 and one of the minor penalties to Team A (depending on choice) will not go on the clock.<br><br>According to the choice made by Team A when the penalties were assessed. |
| H9 | 3:00<br><br><br>4:30 | A15 – 5<br>A23 – 2<br>A6 – 2 | B12 – 2<br><br><br>Goal | Captain's choice. | Coincidental penalty rule applies to B12 and either A23 or A6 (and these penalties would not go on the clock). |
| H10 | 4:00<br>4:30<br>5:00 | A15 – 2<br>A23 – 2+2 | B12 – 2<br><br>Goal | No player returns. | A23's first penalty terminates. A23's second penalty starts. |

**NOTE: Coincident penalties must always be served in their entirety**

## TABLE 15
### (Rule 19 – Coincidental Penalties)
### COINCIDENTAL PENALTIES
### (all penalties assessed at the same stoppage)

| | Team A | Penalties | Team B | Penalties | On-ice Strength |
|---|---|---|---|---|---|
| Example 1 | A3 | 2 | B10 | 2+2 | Team B will play one player short-handed for two minutes. Team B must place an additional player to serve the extra minor penalty to B10. |
| Example 2 | A3<br>A5 | 2<br>2+2 | B10<br>B12 | 2+2<br>2 | Teams play at full strength. |
| Example 3 | A3<br>A5 | 2+2<br>5 | B10<br>B12 | 2+2<br>5 | Teams play at full strength. |
| Example 4 | A3 | 2+5 | B10<br>B12 | 2<br>5 | Teams play at full strength |
| Example 5 | A3<br>A5 | 2+5<br>2 | B10<br>B12 | 2<br>5 | Team A will play one player short-handed for two minutes. Team A Captain's choice to determine which penalty would go on the penalty time clock. Should A3 be chosen, then an additional team A player must be placed on the penalty bench to serve the minor penalty for A3. |
| Example 6 | A3<br>A5 | 2+2<br>5 | B10 | 2+2 | Team A one player short-handed for five minutes. |
| Example 7 | A3<br>A5 | 2+2<br>2 | B10 | 2 | Team A Captain's choice to play one player short-handed for four minutes or two players short-handed for two minutes. Should he choose the latter, an additional team A player must be placed on the penalty bench to serve the minor penalty for A3. |
| Example 8 | A9<br>A24 | 2<br>2 | B2<br>B18 | 2+2<br>2 | Team B will be one player short-handed for two minutes. Team B Captain's choice of which player's time will go on the penalty time clock. If he chooses B2, then team B must place an additional player on the penalty bench to serve B2's minor penalty. |
| Example 9 | A3 | 5 | B5 | 5 | Teams play at full strength. |

## TABLE 15
## (Rule 19 – Coincidental Penalties)
## COINCIDENTAL PENALTIES
## (all penalties assessed at the same stoppage)

| | Team A | Penalties | Team B | Penalties | On-ice Strength |
|---|---|---|---|---|---|
| Example 10 | A3 | 5 | B5<br>B7 | 5<br>5 | Team B short-handed for five minutes (Captain's choice). |
| Example 11 | A3<br>A4 | 5<br>5 | B5<br>B7 | 5<br>5 | Teams play at full strength. |
| Example 12 | A3 | 5+5 | B5 | 5 | Team A short-handed for five minutes. Team A must place an additional player on the penalty bench to serve the extra major penalty. |
| Example 13 | A3 | 5+5 | B5<br>B7 | 5<br>5 | Teams play at full strength. |
| Example 14 | A3<br>A4 | 5+5<br>5 | B7 | 5 | Team A has the choice to cancel one of the two major penalties assessed to A3 or to simply cancel the one to A4. Should they choose A3, they will require an additional player in the penalty box. |
| Example 15 | A3<br>A4 | 5+5<br>5 | B5<br>B7 | 5<br>5 | Team A will be short-handed for five minutes. Team choice to cancel majors assessed. Should they choose A3, they will require an additional player in the penalty box. |
| Example 16 | A3 | 2+5 | B7 | 5 | Team A must place another player in the penalty box to serve the additional minor penalty to A3 immediately. |
| Example 17 | A3 | 2+5 | B7 | 2+5 | Teams play at full strength. |
| Example 18 | A3 | 2+5 | B5<br>B7 | 5<br>5 | Team A short-handed for two minutes. Team B shorthanded for five minutes (Captain's choice). Team A must place another player in the penalty box to serve the minor penalty. |
| Example 19 | A3 | 2 | B5 | 5 | In the last five minutes of the game or anytime in overtime, the three minute differential will be posted on the penalty clock. Team B will play short-handed for three minutes and it will be served in the same manner as a major penalty. |
| Example 20 | A3 | 2+2 | B5 | 5 | In the last five minutes of the game or anytime in overtime, the one minute differential will be posted on the penalty clock. Team B will play |

## TABLE 15
## (Rule 19 – Coincidental Penalties)
## COINCIDENTAL PENALTIES
## (all penalties assessed at the same stoppage)

| | Team A | Penalties | Team B | Penalties | On-ice Strength |
|---|---|---|---|---|---|
| | | | | | short-handed for one minute and it will be served in the same manner as a major penalty. |
| Example 21 | A3 | 5 | B5<br>B7 | 2<br>2 | In the last five minutes of the game or anytime in overtime, this example does NOT adhere to the requirements of Rule 19.4. Teams play 4 on 3. |
| Example 22 | A3<br>A4 | 5<br>2 | B5<br>B7 | 2+2<br>2 | In the last five minutes of the game or anytime in overtime, this example does meet the requirements of Rule 19.4 and the one minute differential will be posted on the penalty clock. Team A will play short-handed for one minute and it will be served in the same manner as a major penalty. |
| Example 23 | A3 | 2+5 | B5 | 2+2+5 | Team B will play short-handed for two minutes. Team B will require an additional player in the penalty box to serve the minor penalty. |
| Example 24 | A3<br>A4 | 2+5<br>5 | B5<br>B7 | 5<br>5 | Team A will play short-handed for two minutes. Team A will require an additional player in the penalty box to serve the minor penalty. |
| Example 25 | A3<br>A4 | 2+5<br>2+2+5 | B5<br>B7 | 2+5<br>5+5 | Team A will be short-handed either one player for four minutes, or two players for two minutes (Captain's choice). Team B will be short-handed for five minutes (Captain's choice). |
| Example 26 | A3<br>A4 | 2+5<br>5 | B5<br>B7 | 2+2+5<br>5+5 | Team B will be short-handed either one player for seven minutes or two players, one for two minutes and one for five minutes (Captain's choice). |
| Example 27 | A3<br>A4 | 2+5<br>5 | B5 | 5 | Team A will be short-handed, either one player for seven minutes, or two players, one for two minutes and one for five minutes (Captain's choice). |
| Example 28 | A3 | 2+5+5 | B5<br>B7 | 2+5<br>5 | Teams play at full strength. |
| Example 29 | A5<br>A6<br>A7 | 2<br>5+5<br>5 | B12<br>B13<br>B14 | 5+5<br>2<br>5 | Teams play at full strength. |

## TABLE 15
### (Rule 19 – Coincidental Penalties)
### COINCIDENTAL PENALTIES
### (all penalties assessed at the same stoppage)

| | Team A | Penalties | Team B | Penalties | On-ice Strength |
|---|---|---|---|---|---|
| Example 30 | A3 | 2+10 | B5 | 2 | Teams play 4 on 4. |
| Example 31 | A3 | 2+10 | B5 | 2+10 | Teams play 4 on 4. |
| Example 32 | A3<br>A4 | 2<br>10 | B5<br>B7 | 2<br>10 | Teams play 4 on 4. |

## TABLE 16
### (Rule 69 – Interference on the Goalkeeper)
### INTERFERENCE ON THE GOALKEEPER SITUATIONS

| Situation | Result |
|---|---|
| **1. THE GOALKEEPER IS IN THE GOAL CREASE.** | |
| A. An attacking player is standing in the goal crease when the puck enters the crease then crosses the goal line. In no way does he affect the goalkeeper's ability to defend his goal. | Goal is allowed. This is a good goal. |
| B. An attacking player makes incidental contact with the goalkeeper, however, no goal is scored on the play. | Play continues, no whistle. |
| C. An attacking player makes incidental contact with the goalkeeper at the same time a goal is scored. | Goal is disallowed. The official in his judgment may call a minor penalty on the attacking player. The announcement should be, "No goal due to interference with the goalkeeper." |
| D. An attacking player makes other than incidental contact with the goalkeeper, however, no goal is scored on the play. | A minor penalty, plus assessment of whatever other penalties may be appropriate up to and including supplementary discipline. |

## TABLE 16
### (Rule 69 – Interference on the Goalkeeper)
### INTERFERENCE ON THE GOALKEEPER SITUATIONS

| Situation | Result |
|---|---|
| E. An attacking player makes other than incidental contact with the goalkeeper at the time a goal is scored. | Goal is disallowed, and a minor and/or major penalty, plus assessment of whatever penalties may be appropriate up to and including supplementary discipline. |
| **2. THE GOALKEEPER IS OUT OF THE GOAL CREASE.** | |
| A. An attacking player makes incidental contact with the goalkeeper, however, no goal is scored on the play. | Play continues, no whistle. |
| B. An attacking player makes incidental contact with the goalkeeper at the time a goal is scored. | Goal is allowed. |
| C. An attacking player makes other than incidental contact with the goalkeeper, however, no goal is scored on the play. | A minor and/or major penalty, plus assessment of whatever other penalties may be appropriate up to and including supplementary discipline. |
| D. An attacking player makes other than incidental contact with the goalkeeper at the time a goal is scored. | A minor and/or major penalty, plus assessment of whatever other penalties may be appropriate up to and including supplementary discipline and the goal is disallowed. |
| **3. A PLAYER PUSHES, SHOVES, OR FOULS ANOTHER PLAYER INTO THE GOALKEEPER, WHO IS IN OR OUT OF THE CREASE.** | |
| A. The attacking player, after having made a reasonable effort to avoid contact, makes contact with the goalkeeper at the time a goal is scored. | Goal is allowed. |
| B. The contact by the attacking player with the goalkeeper is other than incidental and the attacking player, in the judgment of the Referee, did not make a reasonable effort to avoid such contact. However, no goal is scored on the play. | A minor and/or major penalty, plus assessment of whatever other penalties may be appropriate up to and including supplementary discipline. |

## TABLE 16
## (Rule 69 – Interference on the Goalkeeper)
## INTERFERENCE ON THE GOALKEEPER SITUATIONS

| Situation | Result |
|---|---|
| C. The contact by the attacking player with the goalkeeper is other than incidental and the attacking player, in the judgment of the Referee, did not make a reasonable effort to avoid such contact at the time a goal is scored. | A minor and/or major penalty may be called at the discretion of the Referee plus assessment of whatever other penalties may be appropriate up to and including supplementary discipline and the goal is disallowed. |
| D. An attacking player, through his actions pushes, shoves or fouls a defending player into the goalkeeper at the time a goal is scored. | A penalty may be called at the discretion of the Referee for the actions of the attacking player and the goal is disallowed. |
| **4. BATTLE FOR LOOSE PUCK WITH THE GOALKEEPER WHILE THE GOALKEEPER IS IN OR OUT OF THE GOAL CREASE.** | |
| A. An attacking player makes incidental contact with the goalkeeper while both are attempting to play a loose puck at the time a goal is scored. | Goal is allowed. |
| B. An attacking player makes other than incidental contact with the goalkeeper while both are attempting to play a loose puck at the time a goal is scored. | A minor and/or major penalty, plus assessment of whatever other penalties may be appropriate up to and including supplementary discipline and the goal is disallowed. |
| **5. SCREENING SITUATIONS.** | |
| A. An attacking player skates in front of the goalkeeper at the top of the goal crease, at the same time a goal is being scored. The attacking player remains in motion and does not maintain a significant position in the crease in front of the goalkeeper. | Goal is allowed. This is a good goal. |
| B. An attacking player skates in front of the goalkeeper, well inside the crease, at the same time a goal is being scored. The attacking player remains in motion and, in the judgment of the Referee, maintains a significant | Goal is disallowed. The announcement should be, "No goal due to interference with the goalkeeper." |

## TABLE 16
### (Rule 69 – Interference on the Goalkeeper)
### INTERFERENCE ON THE GOALKEEPER SITUATIONS

| Situation | Result |
|---|---|
| position in the crease impairing the goalkeeper's ability to defend his goal. | |
| C. An attacking player skates in front of the goalkeeper, outside the crease, at the same time a goal is being scored. The attacking player remains in motion and impairs the goalkeeper's ability to defend his goal. | Goal is allowed. |
| D. An attacking player plants himself within the goal crease, as to obstruct the goalkeeper's vision and impair his ability to defend his goal, and a goal is scored. | Goal is disallowed. The announcement should be, "No goal due to interference with the goalkeeper." |
| E. An attacking player plants himself on the crease line or outside the goal crease, as to obstruct the goalkeeper's vision and impair his ability to defend his goal, and a goal is scored. | Goal is allowed. |
| **6. CROWDING THE GOALKEEPER.** | |
| A. A goalkeeper initiates contact with an attacking player to establish position in the crease and the attacking player vacates the position immediately. No goal is scored on the play. | Play continues, no whistle. |
| B. A goalkeeper initiates contact with an attacking player to establish position in the crease and the attacking player does not vacate the position, however, no goal is scored on the play. A possible penalty depends on the Referee's judgment as to the degree of contact and degree of resistance with the attacking player and whether the goalkeeper was truly trying to establish a position. | Minor penalty. This player runs the risk of "bad things" happening by being in the crease. In this example it is a minor penalty. |

## TABLE 16
## (Rule 69 – Interference on the Goalkeeper)
## INTERFERENCE ON THE GOALKEEPER SITUATIONS

| Situation | Result |
|---|---|
| C. A goalkeeper initiates contact with an attacking player in the crease to establish position and the attacking player vacates the position immediately at the time a goal is scored. Even though the attacking player vacates his position immediately, the contact impairs the goalkeeper's ability to defend his goal. | Goal is disallowed. The announcement should be, "No goal due to interference with the goalkeeper." |
| D. A goalkeeper initiates contact with an attacking player to establish position in the crease and the attacking player refuses to give ground at the time a goal is scored. | Goal is disallowed. A minor penalty is not assessed (loss of goal only). The announcement should be, "No goal due to interference with the goalkeeper." |
| E. A goalkeeper deliberately initiates contact with an attacking player other than to establish position in the crease, or otherwise acts to make unnecessary contact with the attacking player. | Minor penalty to the goalkeeper (slashing, etc.). |
| F. A goalkeeper initiates contact with an attacking player to establish position in the crease by using excessive force or acting in a manner which would otherwise warrant a penalty, and the attacking player refuses to give ground at the time a goal is scored. | Coincidental minors (goalkeeper/attacking player) [In this situation, the Referee would emphatically display to players and the fans that he was calling penalties before the puck entered the net, and thus the play was dead at the time the infractions occurred and thus stated there is no goal.] |
| G. A goalkeeper initiates contact with an attacking player to establish position in the crease by using excessive force or acting in a manner which would otherwise warrant a penalty, and the attacking player vacates the crease at the time a goal is scored. | A minor penalty to the goalkeeper and the goal is disallowed. This is an example where the attacking player has prevented the goalkeeper from doing his job by being in the crease. The announcement should be, "No goal due to interference with the goalkeeper (plus the announcement of the goalkeeper's penalty)." |
| H. A goalkeeper initiates contact with an attacking player to establish position in the crease by using excessive force or | Minor penalty to goalkeeper. |

## TABLE 16
### (Rule 69 – Interference on the Goalkeeper)
### INTERFERENCE ON THE GOALKEEPER SITUATIONS

| Situation | Result |
|---|---|
| acting in a manner which would otherwise warrant a penalty and the attacking player vacates the crease, but no goal is scored. | |
| **7. CONTACT WITH THE GOALKEEPER.** | |
| A. An attacking player initiates contact with the goalkeeper, inside or outside the goal crease, in a fashion that would otherwise warrant a penalty (e.g. "runs" the goalkeeper). | Appropriate penalty (minor and/or major and a game misconduct) and subject to additional sanctions as appropriate, pursuant to Rule 33A – Supplementary Discipline. |
| B. An attacking player is in the crease and makes every effort to vacate the crease and the goalkeeper initiates contact to embellish and draw a penalty. No goal is scored on the play. | This is a dive and a minor penalty to the goalkeeper (diving). |
| C. A defensive player directs the puck into his own net while an attacking player initiates contact with the goalkeeper. | Goal is disallowed and a minor and/or major penalty, plus assessment of whatever other penalties may be appropriate up to and including supplementary discipline to the attacking player. |
| D. A defensive player directs the puck into his own net while an attacking player is standing in the goal crease. The attacking player does not affect the goalkeeper's ability to make the save. | Goal is allowed. |

## TABLE 17
## (Rule 84 – Overtime)
## PENALTIES IN EFFECT PRIOR TO THE START OF OVERTIME – REGULAR SEASON

| Ex | Time in 3rd Period | Team A | Team B | Resolve |
|---|---|---|---|---|
| 1 | 19:10 | A5 - 2 | B17 – 2 | The penalty times remain on the penalty time clock and the teams begin overtime playing three (3) on three (3). At first whistle following the expiration of the penalties, the on-ice strength reverts back to three (3) on three (3). |
| 2 | 19:10<br>19:50 | A5 – 2<br>A7 – 2 | B17 – 2 | The teams would begin the overtime period playing four (4) on three (3). At the first stoppage of play following the expiration of the penalties to A5 and B17, the on-ice strength would be adjusted from five (5) on four (4) down to four (4) on three (3). |
| 3 | 19:10<br>19:25<br>19:40 | A5 – 2<br><br>A7 – 2 | <br>B17 – 2<br> | Overtime will begin with the player strength of three (3) skaters for team A and four (4) skaters for team B. Through the normal expiration of penalty times, the penalized players will return to the ice. With continuous play, the potential of reaching an on-ice strength of five (5) on five (5) is a possibility. However, the on-ice strength would be adjusted accordingly at the next stoppage of play. |
| 4 | 19:10<br>19:30<br>19:40 | A5 – 2<br>A7 – 2<br> | B17 – 2<br><br>B36 – 2 | Overtime will begin with the player strength of three (3) on three (3). Should there be a stoppage of play following the expiration of A5 and B17's penalties, the on-ice strength shall be adjusted to three (3) on three (3) skaters. As the penalties to A7 and B36 expire, the on ice strength could get to four (4) on four (4). At stoppages, the strength would be adjusted to four (4) on three (3) or three (3) on three (3) as appropriate. With continuous play, the potential of reaching an on-ice strength of five (5) on five (5) is a possibility. However, the on-ice strength would be adjusted accordingly at the next stoppage of play. |

## TABLE 17
## (Rule 84 – Overtime)
## PENALTIES IN EFFECT PRIOR TO THE START OF OVERTIME – REGULAR SEASON

| Ex | Time in 3rd Period | Team A | Team B | Resolve |
|---|---|---|---|---|
| 5 | 19:10<br>19:20<br>19:30<br>19:40 | A5 – 2<br><br>A7 – 2 | <br>B17 – 2<br><br>B36 – 2 | Overtime on-ice strength will begin at three (3) on three (3). Through the normal expiration of penalty times, the penalized players will return to the ice. With continuous play, the potential of reaching an on-ice strength of five (5) on five (5) is a possibility. However, the on-ice strength would be adjusted accordingly at the next stoppage of play to either four (4) on three (3) or three (3) on three (3), as the situation dictates at that particular stoppage of play. |

## TABLE 18
## (Rule 84 – Overtime)
## PENALTIES ASSESSED IN OVERTIME – REGULAR SEASON

| Time in OT | Team A | Team B | On-ice Strength |
|---|---|---|---|
| 0:30 | A23 – 2 | | Team A – 3 skaters<br>Team B – 4 skaters |
| 1:00 | | B17 – 2 | Team A – 3 skaters<br>Team B – 3 skaters |
| 1:30 | A7 – 2 | | Team A – 3 skaters<br>Team B – 4 skaters |

Once team A has received their second minor penalty, each team must add one player to their on-ice strength. Should the penalty to A23 expire bringing the on-ice strength back to four (4) on four (4) and there is a subsequent stoppage of play, the on-ice strength must be adjusted down to three (3) on three (3) at this point. However, if there is a stoppage of play once the penalty to B17 has expired (and before A7's expires), the on-ice strength would be adjusted to four (4) on three (3). If there is no stoppage in play until both teams have returned to five skaters each, at the next stoppage of play the on-ice strength would be adjusted back down to three (3) on three (3).

**Rule Number**

# A

**Rule Number**

**Rule Number**



## B

**Rule Number**

**Rule Number**



## C

**Rule Number**

**Rule Number**

**Rule Number**

**Rule Number**

**Rule Number**

**Rule Number**

**Rule Number**

**Rule Number**

**Rule Number**

## E

**Rule Number**



# F

**Rule Number**

**Rule Number**

**Rule Number**

# G

**Rule Number**

**Rule Number**

**Rule Number**

**Rule Number**

# H

**Rule Number**



## I

**Rule Number**

Rule Number

**Rule Number**

**Rule Number**



## J

**Rule Number**

# K



# L

**Rule Number**

**Rule Number**

**Rule Number**

**Rule Number**

**Rule Number**



## N

**Rule Number**



## O

**Rule Number**

**Rule Number**



## P

**Rule Number**

**Rule Number**

**Rule Number**

**Rule Number**

**Rule Number**

**Rule Number**

## R

Rule Number

**Rule Number**

# S

**Rule Number**

**Rule Number**

**Rule Number**



## T

**Rule Number**

**Rule Number**



## U



## V

**Rule Number**



## W



## Z

# *NOTES*

# NOTES

# 2016-2017 NHL Schedule

### Wed. Oct. 12, 2016

| Game | Visitor | Home |
|---|---|---|
| 1 | TOR | OTT |
| 2 | STL | CHI |
| 3 | CGY | EDM |
| 4 | LAK | SJS |

### Thu. Oct. 13, 2016

| Game | Visitor | Home |
|---|---|---|
| 5 | MTL | BUF |
| 6 | NYI | NYR |
| 7 | WSH | PIT |
| 8 | BOS | CBJ |
| 9 | DET | TBL |
| 10 | NJD | FLA |
| 11 | MIN | STL |
| 12 | CAR | WPG |
| 13 | ANA | DAL |

### Fri. Oct. 14, 2016

| Game | Visitor | Home |
|---|---|---|
| 14 | CHI | NSH |
| 15 | EDM | CGY |
| 16 | PHI | LAK |

### Sat. Oct. 15, 2016

| Game | Visitor | Home |
|---|---|---|
| 17 | BOS | TOR |
| 18 | MTL | OTT |
| 19 | NJD | TBL |
| 20 | DET | FLA |
| 21 | ANA | PIT |
| 22 | NYI | WSH |
| 23 | SJS | CBJ |
| 24 | WPG | MIN |
| 25 | NYR | STL |
| 26 | NSH | CHI |
| 27 | DAL | COL |
| 28 | PHI | ARI |
| 29 | CGY | VAN |

### Sun. Oct. 16, 2016

| Game | Visitor | Home |
|---|---|---|
| 30 | ANA | NYI |
| 31 • | BUF | EDM |
| 32 | CAR | VAN |

### Mon. Oct. 17, 2016

| Game | Visitor | Home |
|---|---|---|
| 33 | SJS | NYR |
| 34 | COL | PIT |
| 35 | OTT | DET |
| 36 | BOS | WPG |

### Tue. Oct. 18, 2016

| Game | Visitor | Home |
|---|---|---|
| 37 | ANA | NJD |
| 38 | SJS | NYI |
| 39 | COL | WSH |
| 40 | PIT | MTL |
| 41 | ARI | OTT |
| 42 | FLA | TBL |
| 43 | DAL | NSH |
| 44 | LAK | MIN |
| 45 | PHI | CHI |
| 46 | BUF | CGY |
| 47 | CAR | EDM |
| 48 | STL | VAN |

### Wed. Oct. 19, 2016

| Game | Visitor | Home |
|---|---|---|
| 49 | DET | NYR |
| 50 | TOR | WPG |

### Thu. Oct. 20, 2016

| Game | Visitor | Home |
|---|---|---|
| 51 | NJD | BOS |
| 52 | ANA | PHI |
| 53 | SJS | PIT |
| 54 | ARI | MTL |
| 55 | COL | TBL |
| 56 | WSH | FLA |
| 57 | TOR | MIN |
| 58 | LAK | DAL |
| 59 | CAR | CGY |
| 60 | STL | EDM |
| 61 | BUF | VAN |

### Fri. Oct. 21, 2016

| Game | Visitor | Home |
|---|---|---|
| 62 | ARI | NYI |
| 63 | CHI | CBJ |
| 64 | NSH | DET |

### Sat. Oct. 22, 2016

| Game | Visitor | Home |
|---|---|---|
| 65 | MTL | BOS |
| 66 | TBL | OTT |
| 67 | SJS | DET |
| 68 | COL | FLA |
| 69 | MIN | NJD |
| 70 | CAR | PHI |
| 71 | NYR | WSH |
| 72 | TOR | CHI |
| 73 | PIT | NSH |
| 74 | CBJ | DAL |
| 75 | STL | CGY |
| 76 | VAN | LAK |

### Sun. Oct. 23, 2016

| Game | Visitor | Home |
|---|---|---|
| *77 •* | *EDM* | *WPG* |
| ***2016 Tim Hortons NHL Heritage Classic™*** *(Investors Group Field, Winnipeg, Man.)* | | |
| 78 | MIN | NYI |
| 79 | ARI | NYR |
| 80 • | VAN | ANA |

### Mon. Oct. 24, 2016

| Game | Visitor | Home |
|---|---|---|
| 81 | PHI | MTL |
| 82 | CGY | CHI |

### Tue. Oct. 25, 2016

| Game | Visitor | Home |
|---|---|---|
| 83 | MIN | BOS |
| 84 | ARI | NJD |
| 85 | BUF | PHI |
| 86 | FLA | PIT |
| 87 | TBL | TOR |
| 88 | CAR | DET |
| 89 | CGY | STL |
| 90 | WPG | DAL |
| 91 | OTT | VAN |
| 92 | CBJ | LAK |
| 93 | ANA | SJS |

### Wed. Oct. 26, 2016

| Game | Visitor | Home |
|---|---|---|
| 94 | MTL | NYI |
| 95 | BOS | NYR |
| 96 | WSH | EDM |
| 97 | NSH | ANA |

### Thu. Oct. 27, 2016

| Game | Visitor | Home |
|---|---|---|
| 98 | MIN | BUF |
| 99 | ARI | PHI |
| 100 | NYI | PIT |
| 101 | FLA | TOR |
| 102 | TBL | MTL |
| 103 | DET | STL |
| 104 | DAL | WPG |
| 105 | NSH | LAK |
| 106 | CBJ | SJS |

### Fri. Oct. 28, 2016

| Game | Visitor | Home |
|---|---|---|
| 107 | CHI | NJD |
| 108 | NYR | CAR |
| 109 | WPG | COL |
| 110 | OTT | CGY |
| 111 | EDM | VAN |
| 112 | CBJ | ANA |

### Sat. Oct. 29, 2016

| Game | Visitor | Home |
|---|---|---|
| 113 • | FLA | BUF |
| 114 | TOR | MTL |
| 115 | BOS | DET |
| 116 | TBL | NJD |
| 117 | PIT | PHI |
| 118 | LAK | STL |
| 119 | DAL | MIN |
| 120 | COL | ARI |
| 121 | WSH | VAN |
| 122 | NSH | SJS |

### Sun. Oct. 30, 2016

| Game | Visitor | Home |
|---|---|---|
| 123 • | BUF | WPG |
| 124 • | FLA | DET |
| 125 • | PHI | CAR |
| 126 | TOR | NYI |
| 127 | TBL | NYR |
| 128 | LAK | CHI |
| 129 | OTT | EDM |
| 130 | WSH | CGY |

### Tue. Nov. 1, 2016

| Game | Visitor | Home |
|---|---|---|
| 131 | TBL | NYI |
| 132 | STL | NYR |
| 133 | DAL | CBJ |
| 134 | EDM | TOR |
| 135 | CAR | OTT |
| 136 | BOS | FLA |
| 137 | BUF | MIN |
| 138 | WSH | WPG |
| 139 | CGY | CHI |
| 140 | NSH | COL |
| 141 | SJS | ARI |
| 142 | ANA | LAK |

### Wed. Nov. 2, 2016

| Game | Visitor | Home |
|---|---|---|
| 143 | VAN | MTL |
| 144 | DET | PHI |
| 145 | PIT | ANA |

• *AFTERNOON GAME*



SUBJECT TO CHANGE

### Thu. Nov. 3, 2016

| Game | Visitor | Home |
|---|---|---|
| 146 | TOR | BUF |
| 147 | PHI | NYI |
| 148 | EDM | NYR |
| 149 | WPG | WSH |
| 150 | VAN | OTT |
| 151 | BOS | TBL |
| 152 | NJD | FLA |
| 153 | COL | CHI |
| 154 | STL | DAL |
| 155 | NSH | ARI |
| 156 | PIT | LAK |
| 157 | CGY | SJS |

### Fri. Nov. 4, 2016

| Game | Visitor | Home |
|---|---|---|
| 158 | MTL | CBJ |
| 159 | WPG | DET |
| 160 | ARI | ANA |

### Sat. Nov. 5, 2016

| Game | Visitor | Home |
|---|---|---|
| 161 • | MIN | COL |
| 162 | NYR | BOS |
| 163 | VAN | TOR |
| 164 | PHI | MTL |
| 165 | BUF | OTT |
| 166 | NJD | TBL |
| 167 | EDM | NYI |
| 168 | FLA | WSH |
| 169 | CBJ | STL |
| 170 | CAR | NSH |
| 171 | CHI | DAL |
| 172 | CGY | LAK |
| 173 | PIT | SJS |

### Sun. Nov. 6, 2016

| Game | Visitor | Home |
|---|---|---|
| 174 • | EDM | DET |
| 175 • | COL | STL |
| 176 | NJD | CAR |
| 177 | WPG | NYR |
| 178 | DAL | CHI |
| 179 | CGY | ANA |

### Mon. Nov. 7, 2016

| Game | Visitor | Home |
|---|---|---|
| 180 | BUF | BOS |
| 181 | VAN | NYI |
| 182 | TBL | FLA |

### Tue. Nov. 8, 2016

| Game | Visitor | Home |
|---|---|---|
| 183 | CAR | NJD |
| 184 | VAN | NYR |
| 185 | DET | PHI |
| 186 | EDM | PIT |
| 187 | SJS | WSH |
| 188 | LAK | TOR |
| 189 | BOS | MTL |
| 190 | OTT | NSH |
| 191 | DAL | WPG |
| 192 | ARI | COL |

### Wed. Nov. 9, 2016

| Game | Visitor | Home |
|---|---|---|
| 193 | ANA | CBJ |
| 194 | OTT | BUF |
| 195 | CHI | STL |

### Thu. Nov. 10, 2016

| Game | Visitor | Home |
|---|---|---|
| 196 | CBJ | BOS |
| 197 | MIN | PIT |
| 198 | ANA | CAR |
| 199 | LAK | MTL |
| 200 | VAN | DET |
| 201 | NYI | TBL |
| 202 | SJS | FLA |
| 203 | STL | NSH |
| 204 | DAL | CGY |
| 205 | WPG | ARI |

### Fri. Nov. 11, 2016

| Game | Visitor | Home |
|---|---|---|
| 206 | NJD | BUF |
| 207 | PHI | TOR |
| 208 | LAK | OTT |
| 209 | WSH | CHI |
| 210 | WPG | COL |
| 211 | DAL | EDM |

### Sat. Nov. 12, 2016

| Game | Visitor | Home |
|---|---|---|
| 212 | DET | MTL |
| 213 | SJS | TBL |
| 214 | NYI | FLA |
| 215 | BUF | NJD |
| 216 | MIN | PHI |
| 217 | TOR | PIT |
| 218 | WSH | CAR |
| 219 | STL | CBJ |
| 220 | ANA | NSH |
| 221 | BOS | ARI |
| 222 | NYR | CGY |

### Sun. Nov. 13, 2016

| Game | Visitor | Home |
|---|---|---|
| 223 • | LAK | WPG |
| 224 • | DAL | VAN |
| 225 • | MIN | OTT |
| 226 | MTL | CHI |
| 227 • | BOS | COL |
| 228 | NYR | EDM |

### Mon. Nov. 14, 2016

| Game | Visitor | Home |
|---|---|---|
| 229 | TBL | NYI |

### Tue. Nov. 15, 2016

| Game | Visitor | Home |
|---|---|---|
| 230 | OTT | PHI |
| 231 | SJS | CAR |
| 232 | WSH | CBJ |
| 233 | NSH | TOR |
| 234 | FLA | MTL |
| 235 | TBL | DET |
| 236 | BUF | STL |
| 237 | CGY | MIN |
| 238 | CHI | WPG |
| 239 | NJD | DAL |
| 240 | LAK | COL |
| 241 | NYR | VAN |
| 242 | EDM | ANA |

### Wed. Nov. 16, 2016

| Game | Visitor | Home |
|---|---|---|
| 243 | PIT | WSH |
| 244 | ARI | CGY |

### Thu. Nov. 17, 2016

| Game | Visitor | Home |
|---|---|---|
| 245 | TBL | BUF |
| 246 | WPG | PHI |
| 247 | FLA | TOR |
| 248 | NSH | OTT |
| 249 | SJS | STL |
| 250 | BOS | MIN |
| 251 | COL | DAL |
| 252 | ARI | VAN |
| 253 | NJD | ANA |
| 254 | EDM | LAK |

### Fri. Nov. 18, 2016

| Game | Visitor | Home |
|---|---|---|
| 255 | PIT | NYI |
| 256 | DET | WSH |
| 257 | NYR | CBJ |
| 258 | MTL | CAR |
| 259 | CHI | CGY |

### Sat. Nov. 19, 2016

| Game | Visitor | Home |
|---|---|---|
| 260 • | TBL | PHI |
| 261 • | NJD | LAK |
| 262 | WPG | BOS |
| 263 | PIT | BUF |
| 264 | TOR | MTL |
| 265 | FLA | OTT |
| 266 | EDM | DAL |
| 267 | NSH | STL |
| 268 | COL | MIN |
| 269 | SJS | ARI |
| 270 | CHI | VAN |

### Sun. Nov. 20, 2016

| Game | Visitor | Home |
|---|---|---|
| 271 • | CBJ | WSH |
| 272 | FLA | NYR |
| 273 • | WPG | CAR |
| 274 | CGY | DET |
| 275 • | LAK | ANA |

### Mon. Nov. 21, 2016

| Game | Visitor | Home |
|---|---|---|
| 276 | CGY | BUF |
| 277 | NYR | PIT |
| 278 | COL | CBJ |
| 279 | TBL | NSH |
| 280 | MIN | DAL |
| 281 | CHI | EDM |
| 282 | NJD | SJS |

### Tue. Nov. 22, 2016

| Game | Visitor | Home |
|---|---|---|
| 283 | STL | BOS |
| 284 | CAR | TOR |
| 285 | OTT | MTL |
| 286 | PHI | FLA |
| 287 | NYI | ANA |

### Wed. Nov. 23, 2016

| Game | Visitor | Home |
|---|---|---|
| 288 | DET | BUF |
| 289 | TOR | NJD |
| 290 | PIT | NYR |
| 291 | STL | WSH |
| 292 | CGY | CBJ |
| 293 | WPG | MIN |
| 294 | PHI | TBL |
| 295 | DAL | NSH |
| 296 | EDM | COL |
| 297 | VAN | ARI |
| 298 | NYI | LAK |
| 299 | CHI | SJS |

### Thu. Nov. 24, 2016

| Game | Visitor | Home |
|---|---|---|
| 300 | CAR | MTL |
| 301 | BOS | OTT |

### Fri. Nov. 25, 2016

| Game | Visitor | Home |
|---|---|---|
| 302 • | NYR | PHI |
| 303 • | PIT | MIN |
| 304 • | CHI | ANA |
| 305 • | NYI | SJS |
| 306 • | BUF | WSH |
| 307 • | WPG | NSH |
| 308 | CGY | BOS |
| 309 | CBJ | TBL |
| 310 | DET | NJD |
| 311 | VAN | DAL |
| 312 | EDM | ARI |

### Sat. Nov. 26, 2016

| Game | Visitor | Home |
|---|---|---|
| 313 | WSH | TOR |
| 314 | CAR | OTT |
| 315 | MTL | DET |
| 316 | CBJ | FLA |
| 317 | NJD | PIT |
| 318 | MIN | STL |
| 319 | VAN | COL |
| 320 | CHI | LAK |
| 321 | ANA | SJS |

### Sun. Nov. 27, 2016

| Game | Visitor | Home |
|---|---|---|
| 322 • | TBL | BOS |
| 323 • | ARI | EDM |
| 324 | FLA | CAR |
| 325 • | NSH | WPG |
| 326 | OTT | NYR |
| 327 | CGY | PHI |

### Mon. Nov. 28, 2016

| Game | Visitor | Home |
|---|---|---|
| 328 | CGY | NYI |
| 329 | DAL | STL |

• *AFTERNOON GAME*

### Tue. Nov. 29, 2016

| Game | Visitor | Home |
|---|---|---|
| 330 | CAR | NYR |
| 331 | BOS | PHI |
| 332 | TBL | CBJ |
| 333 | BUF | OTT |
| 334 | DAL | DET |
| 335 | NJD | WPG |
| 336 | FLA | CHI |
| 337 | NSH | COL |
| 338 | TOR | EDM |
| 339 | MIN | VAN |
| 340 | MTL | ANA |
| 341 | ARI | SJS |

### Wed. Nov. 30, 2016

| Game | Visitor | Home |
|---|---|---|
| 342 | PIT | NYI |
| 343 | TOR | CGY |
| 344 | SJS | LAK |

### Thu. Dec. 1, 2016

| Game | Visitor | Home |
|---|---|---|
| 345 | CAR | BOS |
| 346 | NYR | BUF |
| 347 | DAL | PIT |
| 348 | NYI | WSH |
| 349 | PHI | OTT |
| 350 | FLA | DET |
| 351 | TBL | STL |
| 352 | EDM | WPG |
| 353 | NJD | CHI |
| 354 | CBJ | COL |
| 355 | LAK | ARI |
| 356 | ANA | VAN |

### Fri. Dec. 2, 2016

| Game | Visitor | Home |
|---|---|---|
| 357 | MIN | CGY |
| 358 | MTL | SJS |

### Sat. Dec. 3, 2016

| Game | Visitor | Home |
|---|---|---|
| 359 ● | BOS | BUF |
| 360 ● | CAR | NYR |
| 361 ● | CHI | PHI |
| 362 ● | NJD | NSH |
| 363 | FLA | OTT |
| 364 | WSH | TBL |
| 365 | DET | PIT |
| 366 | WPG | STL |
| 367 ● | TOR | VAN |
| 368 | CBJ | ARI |
| 369 | DAL | COL |
| 370 | ANA | EDM |

### Sun. Dec. 4, 2016

| Game | Visitor | Home |
|---|---|---|
| 371 ● | TBL | CAR |
| 372 | DET | NYI |
| 373 ● | PHI | NSH |
| 374 | WPG | CHI |
| 375 | ANA | CGY |
| 376 | MIN | EDM |
| 377 ● | MTL | LAK |

### Mon. Dec. 5, 2016

| Game | Visitor | Home |
|---|---|---|
| 378 | FLA | BOS |
| 379 | OTT | PIT |
| 380 | BUF | WSH |
| 381 | ARI | CBJ |

### Tue. Dec. 6, 2016

| Game | Visitor | Home |
|---|---|---|
| 382 | EDM | BUF |
| 383 | VAN | NJD |
| 384 | NYR | NYI |
| 385 | FLA | PHI |
| 386 | MTL | STL |
| 387 | COL | NSH |
| 388 | DET | WPG |
| 389 | ARI | CHI |
| 390 | CGY | DAL |

### Wed. Dec. 7, 2016

| Game | Visitor | Home |
|---|---|---|
| 391 | MIN | TOR |
| 392 | BOS | WSH |
| 393 | CAR | ANA |
| 394 | OTT | SJS |

### Thu. Dec. 8, 2016

| Game | Visitor | Home |
|---|---|---|
| 395 | COL | BOS |
| 396 | STL | NYI |
| 397 | EDM | PHI |
| 398 | NJD | MTL |
| 399 | VAN | TBL |
| 400 | PIT | FLA |
| 401 | NYR | WPG |
| 402 | NSH | DAL |
| 403 | CGY | ARI |
| 404 | CAR | LAK |

### Fri. Dec. 9, 2016

| Game | Visitor | Home |
|---|---|---|
| 405 | WSH | BUF |
| 406 | CBJ | DET |
| 407 | STL | NJD |
| 408 | EDM | MIN |
| 409 | NYR | CHI |
| 410 | SJS | ANA |

### Sat. Dec. 10, 2016

| Game | Visitor | Home |
|---|---|---|
| 411 ● | DAL | PHI |
| 412 ● | OTT | LAK |
| 413 | TOR | BOS |
| 414 | COL | MTL |
| 415 | PIT | TBL |
| 416 | VAN | FLA |
| 417 | NYI | CBJ |
| 418 | NSH | ARI |
| 419 | WPG | CGY |
| 420 | CAR | SJS |

### Sun. Dec. 11, 2016

| Game | Visitor | Home |
|---|---|---|
| 421 ● | OTT | ANA |
| 422 ● | PHI | DET |
| 423 ● | VAN | WSH |
| 424 ● | STL | MIN |
| 425 | COL | TOR |
| 426 | NJD | NYR |
| 427 | DAL | CHI |
| 428 | WPG | EDM |

### Mon. Dec. 12, 2016

| Game | Visitor | Home |
|---|---|---|
| 429 | ARI | PIT |
| 430 | BOS | MTL |

### Tue. Dec. 13, 2016

| Game | Visitor | Home |
|---|---|---|
| 431 | LAK | BUF |
| 432 | WSH | NYI |
| 433 | CHI | NYR |
| 434 | VAN | CAR |
| 435 | SJS | TOR |
| 436 | ARI | DET |
| 437 | STL | NSH |
| 438 | FLA | MIN |
| 439 | ANA | DAL |
| 440 | CBJ | EDM |

### Wed. Dec. 14, 2016

| Game | Visitor | Home |
|---|---|---|
| 441 | SJS | OTT |
| 442 | BOS | PIT |
| 443 | TBL | CGY |
| 444 | PHI | COL |

### Thu. Dec. 15, 2016

| Game | Visitor | Home |
|---|---|---|
| 445 | ANA | BOS |
| 446 | CHI | NYI |
| 447 | ARI | TOR |
| 448 | LAK | DET |
| 449 | NJD | STL |
| 450 | MIN | NSH |
| 451 | FLA | WPG |
| 452 | NYR | DAL |

### Fri. Dec. 16, 2016

| Game | Visitor | Home |
|---|---|---|
| 453 | NYI | BUF |
| 454 | LAK | PIT |
| 455 | SJS | MTL |
| 456 | WSH | CAR |
| 457 | FLA | COL |
| 458 | CBJ | CGY |
| 459 | TBL | VAN |

### Sat. Dec. 17, 2016

| Game | Visitor | Home |
|---|---|---|
| 460 ● | PHI | DAL |
| 461 ● | ARI | MIN |
| 462 | PIT | TOR |
| 463 | NJD | OTT |
| 464 | ANA | DET |
| 465 | MTL | WSH |
| 466 | BUF | CAR |
| 467 | CHI | STL |
| 468 | NYR | NSH |
| 469 | TBL | EDM |

### Sun. Dec. 18, 2016

| Game | Visitor | Home |
|---|---|---|
| 470 ● | LAK | BOS |
| 471 ● | COL | WPG |
| 472 ● | CBJ | VAN |
| 473 | OTT | NYI |
| 474 | SJS | CHI |
| 475 | NJD | NYR |

### Mon. Dec. 19, 2016

| Game | Visitor | Home |
|---|---|---|
| 476 | NSH | PHI |
| 477 | DET | CAR |
| 478 | ANA | TOR |
| 479 | EDM | STL |
| 480 | CGY | ARI |

### Tue. Dec. 20, 2016

| Game | Visitor | Home |
|---|---|---|
| 481 | NYI | BOS |
| 482 | NSH | NJD |
| 483 | NYR | PIT |
| 484 | LAK | CBJ |
| 485 | ANA | MTL |
| 486 | DET | TBL |
| 487 | BUF | FLA |
| 488 | COL | MIN |
| 489 | OTT | CHI |
| 490 | STL | DAL |
| 491 | WPG | VAN |
| 492 | CGY | SJS |

### Wed. Dec. 21, 2016

| Game | Visitor | Home |
|---|---|---|
| 493 | WSH | PHI |
| 494 | EDM | ARI |

### Thu. Dec. 22, 2016

| Game | Visitor | Home |
|---|---|---|
| 495 | CAR | BUF |
| 496 | PHI | NJD |
| 497 | PIT | CBJ |
| 498 | MIN | MTL |
| 499 | ANA | OTT |
| 500 | STL | TBL |
| 501 | BOS | FLA |
| 502 | LAK | NSH |
| 503 | TOR | COL |
| 504 | WPG | VAN |

### Fri. Dec. 23, 2016

| Game | Visitor | Home |
|---|---|---|
| 505 | BUF | NYI |
| 506 | MIN | NYR |
| 507 | NJD | PIT |
| 508 | TBL | WSH |
| 509 | MTL | CBJ |
| 510 | DET | FLA |
| 511 | BOS | CAR |
| 512 | COL | CHI |
| 513 | LAK | DAL |
| 514 | VAN | CGY |
| 515 | TOR | ARI |
| 516 | EDM | SJS |

● *AFTERNOON GAME*

# 2016-2017 NHL SCHEDULE

## Tue. Dec. 27, 2016

| Game | Visitor | Home |
|---|---|---|
| 517 | PIT | NJD |
| 518 | WSH | NYI |
| 519 | OTT | NYR |
| 520 | BOS | CBJ |
| 521 | BUF | DET |
| 522 | MIN | NSH |
| 523 | WPG | CHI |
| 524 | CGY | COL |
| 525 | DAL | ARI |
| 526 | SJS | ANA |

## Wed. Dec. 28, 2016

| Game | Visitor | Home |
|---|---|---|
| 527 | TOR | FLA |
| 528 | CAR | PIT |
| 529 | MTL | TBL |
| 530 | PHI | STL |
| 531 | LAK | VAN |

## Thu. Dec. 29, 2016

| Game | Visitor | Home |
|---|---|---|
| 532 | BOS | BUF |
| 533 | NJD | WSH |
| 534 | DET | OTT |
| 535 | TOR | TBL |
| 536 | MTL | FLA |
| 537 | CHI | NSH |
| 538 | NYI | MIN |
| 539 | CBJ | WPG |
| 540 | COL | DAL |
| 541 | ANA | CGY |
| 542 | LAK | EDM |
| 543 | NYR | ARI |

## Fri. Dec. 30, 2016

| Game | Visitor | Home |
|---|---|---|
| 544 | CHI | CAR |
| 545 | NSH | STL |
| 546 | ANA | VAN |
| 547 | PHI | SJS |

## Sat. Dec. 31, 2016

| Game | Visitor | Home |
|---|---|---|
| 548 • | BUF | BOS |
| 549 • | WSH | NJD |
| 550 • | CBJ | MIN |
| 551 | CAR | TBL |
| 552 | MTL | PIT |
| 553 | NYI | WPG |
| 554 | FLA | DAL |
| 555 | NYR | COL |
| 556 | ARI | CGY |
| 557 | VAN | EDM |
| 558 | SJS | LAK |

## Sun. Jan. 1, 2017

| Game | Visitor | Home |
|---|---|---|
| *559 •* | *DET* | *TOR* |
| ***NHL Centennial Classic™** (BMO Field, Toronto, Ont.)* | | |
| 560 | OTT | WSH |
| 561 • | PHI | ANA |

## Mon. Jan. 2, 2017

| Game | Visitor | Home |
|---|---|---|
| *562 •* | *CHI* | *STL* |
| ***2017 Bridgestone NHL Winter Classic®** (Busch Stadium, St. Louis, Mo.)* | | |
| 563 | BOS | NJD |
| 564 | COL | VAN |

## Tue. Jan. 3, 2017

| Game | Visitor | Home |
|---|---|---|
| 565 | BUF | NYR |
| 566 | TOR | WSH |
| 567 | NJD | CAR |
| 568 | EDM | CBJ |
| 569 | WPG | TBL |
| 570 | MTL | NSH |
| 571 | LAK | SJS |

## Wed. Jan. 4, 2017

| Game | Visitor | Home |
|---|---|---|
| 572 | WPG | FLA |
| 573 | NYR | PHI |
| 574 | MTL | DAL |
| 575 | COL | CGY |
| 576 | ARI | VAN |
| 577 | DET | ANA |

## Thu. Jan. 5, 2017

| Game | Visitor | Home |
|---|---|---|
| 578 | EDM | BOS |
| 579 | CBJ | WSH |
| 580 | NSH | TBL |
| 581 | CAR | STL |
| 582 | BUF | CHI |
| 583 | DET | LAK |
| 584 | MIN | SJS |

## Fri. Jan. 6, 2017

| Game | Visitor | Home |
|---|---|---|
| 585 | NSH | FLA |
| 586 | TOR | NJD |
| 587 | CAR | CHI |
| 588 | NYI | COL |
| 589 | CGY | VAN |
| 590 | ARI | ANA |

## Sat. Jan. 7, 2017

| Game | Visitor | Home |
|---|---|---|
| 591 • | WPG | BUF |
| 592 • | TBL | PHI |
| 593 • | MIN | LAK |
| 594 | MTL | TOR |
| 595 | WSH | OTT |
| 596 | BOS | FLA |
| 597 | EDM | NJD |
| 598 | NYR | CBJ |
| 599 | DAL | STL |
| 600 | NYI | ARI |
| 601 | VAN | CGY |
| 602 | DET | SJS |

## Sun. Jan. 8, 2017

| Game | Visitor | Home |
|---|---|---|
| 603 • | TBL | PIT |
| 604 • | BOS | CAR |
| 605 | PHI | CBJ |
| 606 | EDM | OTT |
| 607 | NSH | CHI |
| 608 • | MIN | ANA |

## Mon. Jan. 9, 2017

| Game | Visitor | Home |
|---|---|---|
| 609 | FLA | NJD |
| 610 | WSH | MTL |
| 611 | CGY | WPG |
| 612 | DAL | LAK |

## Tue. Jan. 10, 2017

| Game | Visitor | Home |
|---|---|---|
| 613 | PHI | BUF |
| 614 | CBJ | CAR |
| 615 | BOS | STL |
| 616 | VAN | NSH |
| 617 | DET | CHI |
| 618 | SJS | EDM |
| 619 | DAL | ANA |

## Wed. Jan. 11, 2017

| Game | Visitor | Home |
|---|---|---|
| 620 | FLA | NYI |
| 621 | MTL | WPG |
| 622 | PIT | WSH |
| 623 | SJS | CGY |

## Thu. Jan. 12, 2017

| Game | Visitor | Home |
|---|---|---|
| 624 | VAN | PHI |
| 625 | PIT | OTT |
| 626 | BUF | TBL |
| 627 | BOS | NSH |
| 628 | MTL | MIN |
| 629 | DET | DAL |
| 630 | ANA | COL |
| 631 | NJD | EDM |
| 632 | STL | LAK |

## Fri. Jan. 13, 2017

| Game | Visitor | Home |
|---|---|---|
| 633 | TOR | NYR |
| 634 | CHI | WSH |
| 635 | CBJ | TBL |
| 636 | NYI | FLA |
| 637 | BUF | CAR |
| 638 | NJD | CGY |
| 639 | WPG | ARI |

## Sat. Jan. 14, 2017

| Game | Visitor | Home |
|---|---|---|
| 640 • | PHI | BOS |
| 641 • | NSH | COL |
| 642 | NYR | MTL |
| 643 | TOR | OTT |
| 644 | PIT | DET |
| 645 | CBJ | FLA |
| 646 | NYI | CAR |
| 647 | ANA | ARI |
| 648 | MIN | DAL |
| 649 | CGY | EDM |
| 650 | WPG | LAK |
| 651 | STL | SJS |

## Sun. Jan. 15, 2017

| Game | Visitor | Home |
|---|---|---|
| 652 • | PHI | WSH |
| 653 | MIN | CHI |
| 654 • | NJD | VAN |
| 655 | STL | ANA |

## Mon. Jan. 16, 2017

| Game | Visitor | Home |
|---|---|---|
| 656 • | NYI | BOS |
| 657 • | DAL | BUF |
| 658 • | MTL | DET |
| 659 • | TBL | LAK |
| 660 • | WPG | SJS |
| 661 | WSH | PIT |
| 662 | ARI | EDM |

## Tue. Jan. 17, 2017

| Game | Visitor | Home |
|---|---|---|
| 663 | DAL | NYR |
| 664 | CAR | CBJ |
| 665 | BUF | TOR |
| 666 | OTT | STL |
| 667 | NJD | MIN |
| 668 | CHI | COL |
| 669 | FLA | CGY |
| 670 | NSH | VAN |
| 671 | TBL | ANA |

## Wed. Jan. 18, 2017

| Game | Visitor | Home |
|---|---|---|
| 672 | PIT | MTL |
| 673 | ARI | WPG |
| 674 | BOS | DET |
| 675 | FLA | EDM |
| 676 | SJS | LAK |

## Thu. Jan. 19, 2017

| Game | Visitor | Home |
|---|---|---|
| 677 | DAL | NYI |
| 678 | OTT | CBJ |
| 679 | NYR | TOR |
| 680 | WSH | STL |
| 681 | ARI | MIN |
| 682 | NSH | CGY |
| 683 | COL | ANA |
| 684 | TBL | SJS |

## Fri. Jan. 20, 2017

| Game | Visitor | Home |
|---|---|---|
| 685 | CHI | BOS |
| 686 | DET | BUF |
| 687 | PIT | CAR |
| 688 | MTL | NJD |
| 689 | NSH | EDM |
| 690 | FLA | VAN |

## Sat. Jan. 21, 2017

| Game | Visitor | Home |
|---|---|---|
| 691 • | STL | WPG |
| 692 • | CAR | CBJ |
| 693 | OTT | TOR |
| 694 | BUF | MTL |
| 695 | LAK | NYI |
| 696 | NJD | PHI |
| 697 | WSH | DAL |
| 698 | TBL | ARI |
| 699 | ANA | MIN |
| 700 | EDM | CGY |
| 701 | COL | SJS |

*• AFTERNOON GAME*

### Sun. Jan. 22, 2017

| Game | Visitor | Home |
|---|---|---|
| 702 ● | BOS | PIT |
| 703 ● | NYR | DET |
| 704 ● | CBJ | OTT |
| 705 | PHI | NYI |
| 706 | VAN | CHI |
| 707 | NSH | MIN |

### Mon. Jan. 23, 2017

| Game | Visitor | Home |
|---|---|---|
| 708 | LAK | NYR |
| 709 | CAR | WSH |
| 710 | CGY | TOR |
| 711 | ANA | WPG |
| 712 | SJS | COL |
| 713 | FLA | ARI |

### Tue. Jan. 24, 2017

| Game | Visitor | Home |
|---|---|---|
| 714 | DET | BOS |
| 715 | LAK | NJD |
| 716 | CBJ | NYI |
| 717 | STL | PIT |
| 718 | CGY | MTL |
| 719 | WSH | OTT |
| 720 | BUF | NSH |
| 721 | SJS | WPG |
| 722 | TBL | CHI |
| 723 | MIN | DAL |

### Wed. Jan. 25, 2017

| Game | Visitor | Home |
|---|---|---|
| 724 | TOR | DET |
| 725 | PHI | NYR |
| 726 | VAN | COL |
| 727 | EDM | ANA |

### Thu. Jan. 26, 2017

| Game | Visitor | Home |
|---|---|---|
| 728 | PIT | BOS |
| 729 | WSH | NJD |
| 730 | MTL | NYI |
| 731 | TOR | PHI |
| 732 | LAK | CAR |
| 733 | CGY | OTT |
| 734 | TBL | FLA |
| 735 | CBJ | NSH |
| 736 | STL | MIN |
| 737 | WPG | CHI |
| 738 | BUF | DAL |
| 739 | VAN | ARI |
| 740 | EDM | SJS |

### Sat. Jan. 28, 2017

***NHL All-Star Skills Competition™***
*(STAPLES Center, Los Angeles, Calif.)*

### Sun. Jan. 29, 2017

***NHL All-Star Game***
*(STAPLES Center, Los Angeles, Calif.)*

### Tue. Jan. 31, 2017

| Game | Visitor | Home |
|---|---|---|
| 741 | WSH | NYI |
| 742 | CBJ | NYR |
| 743 | NSH | PIT |
| 744 | PHI | CAR |
| 745 | BUF | MTL |
| 746 | NJD | DET |
| 747 | BOS | TBL |
| 748 | OTT | FLA |
| 749 | WPG | STL |
| 750 | TOR | DAL |
| 751 | MIN | EDM |
| 752 | LAK | ARI |
| 753 | COL | ANA |
| 754 | CHI | SJS |

### Wed. Feb. 1, 2017

| Game | Visitor | Home |
|---|---|---|
| 755 | BOS | WSH |
| 756 | MIN | CGY |
| 757 | COL | LAK |

### Thu. Feb. 2, 2017

| Game | Visitor | Home |
|---|---|---|
| 758 | NYR | BUF |
| 759 | MTL | PHI |
| 760 | OTT | TBL |
| 761 | TOR | STL |
| 762 | EDM | NSH |
| 763 | WPG | DAL |
| 764 | CHI | ARI |
| 765 | SJS | VAN |

### Fri. Feb. 3, 2017

| Game | Visitor | Home |
|---|---|---|
| 766 | CBJ | PIT |
| 767 | NYI | DET |
| 768 | ANA | FLA |
| 769 | CGY | NJD |
| 770 | EDM | CAR |

### Sat. Feb. 4, 2017

| Game | Visitor | Home |
|---|---|---|
| 771 ● | WSH | MTL |
| 772 ● | LAK | PHI |
| 773 ● | WPG | COL |
| 774 | TOR | BOS |
| 775 | OTT | BUF |
| 776 | ANA | TBL |
| 777 | CAR | NYI |
| 778 | NJD | CBJ |
| 779 | PIT | STL |
| 780 | DET | NSH |
| 781 | CHI | DAL |
| 782 | MIN | VAN |
| 783 | ARI | SJS |

### Sun. Feb. 5, 2017

| Game | Visitor | Home |
|---|---|---|
| 784 ● | LAK | WSH |
| 785 ● | EDM | MTL |
| 786 ● | CGY | NYR |

### Mon. Feb. 6, 2017

| Game | Visitor | Home |
|---|---|---|
| 787 | BUF | NJD |
| 788 | TOR | NYI |
| 789 | STL | PHI |

### Tue. Feb. 7, 2017

| Game | Visitor | Home |
|---|---|---|
| 790 | SJS | BUF |
| 791 | ANA | NYR |
| 792 | CGY | PIT |
| 793 | CAR | WSH |
| 794 | DAL | TOR |
| 795 | STL | OTT |
| 796 | CBJ | DET |
| 797 | LAK | TBL |
| 798 | VAN | NSH |
| 799 | MIN | WPG |
| 800 | MTL | COL |

### Wed. Feb. 8, 2017

| Game | Visitor | Home |
|---|---|---|
| 801 | CHI | MIN |

### Thu. Feb. 9, 2017

| Game | Visitor | Home |
|---|---|---|
| 802 | SJS | BOS |
| 803 | ANA | BUF |
| 804 | NSH | NYR |
| 805 | NYI | PHI |
| 806 | DET | WSH |
| 807 | VAN | CBJ |
| 808 | STL | TOR |
| 809 | DAL | OTT |
| 810 | LAK | FLA |
| 811 | PIT | COL |
| 812 | MTL | ARI |

### Fri. Feb. 10, 2017

| Game | Visitor | Home |
|---|---|---|
| 813 | TBL | MIN |
| 814 | CHI | WPG |

### Sat. Feb. 11, 2017

| Game | Visitor | Home |
|---|---|---|
| 815 ● | VAN | BOS |
| 816 ● | NYI | OTT |
| 817 ● | SJS | PHI |
| 818 ● | FLA | NSH |
| 819 ● | CAR | DAL |
| 820 ● | DET | CBJ |
| 821 | BUF | TOR |
| 822 | STL | MTL |
| 823 | COL | NYR |
| 824 | ANA | WSH |
| 825 | TBL | WPG |
| 826 | PIT | ARI |
| 827 | CHI | EDM |

### Sun. Feb. 12, 2017

| Game | Visitor | Home |
|---|---|---|
| 828 ● | SJS | NJD |
| 829 ● | DET | MIN |
| 830 | COL | NYI |
| 831 ● | DAL | NSH |
| 832 | MTL | BOS |
| 833 | VAN | BUF |

### Mon. Feb. 13, 2017

| Game | Visitor | Home |
|---|---|---|
| 834 | NYR | CBJ |
| 835 | ARI | CGY |

### Tue. Feb. 14, 2017

| Game | Visitor | Home |
|---|---|---|
| 836 | COL | NJD |
| 837 | VAN | PIT |
| 838 | NYI | TOR |
| 839 | BUF | OTT |
| 840 | ANA | MIN |
| 841 | DAL | WPG |
| 842 | ARI | EDM |

### Wed. Feb. 15, 2017

| Game | Visitor | Home |
|---|---|---|
| 843 | TOR | CBJ |
| 844 | STL | DET |
| 845 | PHI | CGY |
| 846 | FLA | SJS |

### Thu. Feb. 16, 2017

| Game | Visitor | Home |
|---|---|---|
| 847 | COL | BUF |
| 848 | OTT | NJD |
| 849 | NYR | NYI |
| 850 | WPG | PIT |
| 851 | VAN | STL |
| 852 | DAL | MIN |
| 853 | PHI | EDM |
| 854 | ARI | LAK |

### Fri. Feb. 17, 2017

| Game | Visitor | Home |
|---|---|---|
| 855 | PIT | CBJ |
| 856 | COL | CAR |
| 857 | FLA | ANA |

### Sat. Feb. 18, 2017

| Game | Visitor | Home |
|---|---|---|
| 858 ● | STL | BUF |
| 859 ● | WPG | MTL |
| 860 ● | WSH | DET |
| 861 | OTT | TOR |
| 862 | NYI | NJD |
| 863 | EDM | CHI |
| 864 | TBL | DAL |
| 865 | NSH | MIN |
| 866 | SJS | ARI |
| 867 | CGY | VAN |
| 868 | FLA | LAK |

### Sun. Feb. 19, 2017

| Game | Visitor | Home |
|---|---|---|
| 869 ● | WSH | NYR |
| 870 ● | DET | PIT |
| 871 ● | WPG | OTT |
| 872 | CHI | BUF |
| 873 | NJD | NYI |
| 874 | NSH | CBJ |
| 875 | TOR | CAR |
| 876 | TBL | COL |
| 877 ● | BOS | SJS |
| 878 | LAK | ANA |
| 879 | PHI | VAN |

### Mon. Feb. 20, 2017

| Game | Visitor | Home |
|---|---|---|
| 880 | FLA | STL |
| 881 | ANA | ARI |

● *AFTERNOON GAME*

### Tue. Feb. 21, 2017

| Game | Visitor | Home |
|---|---|---|
| 882 | OTT | NJD |
| 883 | MTL | NYR |
| 884 | PIT | CAR |
| 885 | WPG | TOR |
| 886 | NYI | DET |
| 887 | EDM | TBL |
| 888 | CGY | NSH |
| 889 | CHI | MIN |
| 890 | LAK | COL |

### Wed. Feb. 22, 2017

| Game | Visitor | Home |
|---|---|---|
| 891 | EDM | FLA |
| 892 | WSH | PHI |
| 893 | BOS | ANA |

### Thu. Feb. 23, 2017

| Game | Visitor | Home |
|---|---|---|
| 894 | NYR | TOR |
| 895 | NYI | MTL |
| 896 | CGY | TBL |
| 897 | COL | NSH |
| 898 | ARI | CHI |
| 899 | BOS | LAK |

### Fri. Feb. 24, 2017

| Game | Visitor | Home |
|---|---|---|
| 900 | EDM | WSH |
| 901 | CGY | FLA |
| 902 | OTT | CAR |
| 903 | ARI | DAL |

### Sat. Feb. 25, 2017

| Game | Visitor | Home |
|---|---|---|
| 904 • | ANA | LAK |
| 905 • | NYR | NJD |
| 906 • | WSH | NSH |
| 907 | MTL | TOR |
| *908* | *PHI* | *PIT* |
| *2017 Coors Light NHL Stadium Series™ (Heinz Field, Pittsburgh, Pa.)* | | |
| 909 • | NYI | CBJ |
| 910 | BUF | COL |
| 911 | SJS | VAN |

### Sun. Feb. 26, 2017

| Game | Visitor | Home |
|---|---|---|
| 912 • | BOS | DAL |
| 913 • | CGY | CAR |
| 914 • | CBJ | NYR |
| 915 • | EDM | NSH |
| 916 | OTT | FLA |
| 917 | STL | CHI |
| 918 | BUF | ARI |

### Mon. Feb. 27, 2017

| Game | Visitor | Home |
|---|---|---|
| 919 | MTL | NJD |
| 920 | OTT | TBL |
| 921 | LAK | MIN |

### Tue. Feb. 28, 2017

| Game | Visitor | Home |
|---|---|---|
| 922 | ARI | BOS |
| 923 | NSH | BUF |
| 924 | WSH | NYR |
| 925 | COL | PHI |
| 926 | CBJ | MTL |
| 927 | CAR | FLA |
| 928 | EDM | STL |
| 929 | MIN | WPG |
| 930 | PIT | DAL |
| 931 | LAK | CGY |
| 932 | DET | VAN |
| 933 | TOR | SJS |

### Wed. Mar. 1, 2017

| Game | Visitor | Home |
|---|---|---|
| 934 | CAR | TBL |
| 935 | PIT | CHI |

### Thu. Mar. 2, 2017

| Game | Visitor | Home |
|---|---|---|
| 936 | NYR | BOS |
| 937 | ARI | BUF |
| 938 | FLA | PHI |
| 939 | NJD | WSH |
| 940 | MIN | CBJ |
| 941 | NSH | MTL |
| 942 | COL | OTT |
| 943 | NYI | DAL |
| 944 | TOR | LAK |
| 945 | VAN | SJS |

### Fri. Mar. 3, 2017

| Game | Visitor | Home |
|---|---|---|
| 946 | TBL | PIT |
| 947 | ARI | CAR |
| 948 | STL | WPG |
| 949 | NYI | CHI |
| 950 | DET | CGY |
| 951 | TOR | ANA |

### Sat. Mar. 4, 2017

| Game | Visitor | Home |
|---|---|---|
| 952 | NJD | BOS |
| 953 | TBL | BUF |
| 954 | CBJ | OTT |
| 955 | DAL | FLA |
| 956 | MTL | NYR |
| 957 | PHI | WSH |
| 958 | COL | WPG |
| 959 | CHI | NSH |
| 960 | DET | EDM |
| 961 | VAN | LAK |

### Sun. Mar. 5, 2017

| Game | Visitor | Home |
|---|---|---|
| 962 • | NYI | CGY |
| 963 • | CBJ | NJD |
| 964 • | BUF | PIT |
| 965 • | SJS | MIN |
| 966 | STL | COL |
| 967 • | VAN | ANA |
| 968 | CAR | ARI |

### Mon. Mar. 6, 2017

| Game | Visitor | Home |
|---|---|---|
| 969 | DAL | WSH |
| 970 | BOS | OTT |
| 971 | NYR | TBL |
| 972 | SJS | WPG |

### Tue. Mar. 7, 2017

| Game | Visitor | Home |
|---|---|---|
| 973 | PHI | BUF |
| 974 | NJD | CBJ |
| 975 | DET | TOR |
| 976 | NYR | FLA |
| 977 | STL | MIN |
| 978 | CAR | COL |
| 979 | NYI | EDM |
| 980 | MTL | VAN |
| 981 | NSH | ANA |

### Wed. Mar. 8, 2017

| Game | Visitor | Home |
|---|---|---|
| 982 | DET | BOS |
| 983 | OTT | DAL |
| 984 | PIT | WPG |

### Thu. Mar. 9, 2017

| Game | Visitor | Home |
|---|---|---|
| 985 | NYR | CAR |
| 986 | PHI | TOR |
| 987 | MIN | TBL |
| 988 | ANA | CHI |
| 989 | NJD | COL |
| 990 | MTL | CGY |
| 991 | OTT | ARI |
| 992 | NYI | VAN |
| 993 | NSH | LAK |
| 994 | WSH | SJS |

### Fri. Mar. 10, 2017

| Game | Visitor | Home |
|---|---|---|
| 995 | BUF | CBJ |
| 996 | CHI | DET |
| 997 | MIN | FLA |
| 998 | ANA | STL |
| 999 | PIT | EDM |

### Sat. Mar. 11, 2017

| Game | Visitor | Home |
|---|---|---|
| 1000 • | PHI | BOS |
| 1001 • | NSH | SJS |
| 1002 | CBJ | BUF |
| 1003 | FLA | TBL |
| 1004 | TOR | CAR |
| 1005 | CGY | WPG |
| 1006 • | OTT | COL |
| 1007 | NYI | STL |
| 1008 | NJD | ARI |
| 1009 | PIT | VAN |
| 1010 | WSH | LAK |

### Sun. Mar. 12, 2017

| Game | Visitor | Home |
|---|---|---|
| 1011 • | NYR | DET |
| 1012 | MIN | CHI |
| 1013 • | MTL | EDM |
| 1014 | WSH | ANA |
| 1015 | DAL | SJS |

### Mon. Mar. 13, 2017

| Game | Visitor | Home |
|---|---|---|
| 1016 | CAR | NYI |
| 1017 | TBL | NYR |
| 1018 | CBJ | PHI |
| 1019 | WPG | NSH |
| 1020 | PIT | CGY |
| 1021 | BOS | VAN |
| 1022 | COL | ARI |
| 1023 | STL | LAK |

### Tue. Mar. 14, 2017

| Game | Visitor | Home |
|---|---|---|
| 1024 | WPG | NJD |
| 1025 | MIN | WSH |
| 1026 | NYI | CAR |
| 1027 | CHI | MTL |
| 1028 | TBL | OTT |
| 1029 | TOR | FLA |
| 1030 | DAL | EDM |
| 1031 | ARI | LAK |
| 1032 | BUF | SJS |

### Wed. Mar. 15, 2017

| Game | Visitor | Home |
|---|---|---|
| 1033 | PIT | PHI |
| 1034 | BOS | CGY |
| 1035 | DET | COL |
| 1036 | STL | ANA |

### Thu. Mar. 16, 2017

| Game | Visitor | Home |
|---|---|---|
| 1037 | PHI | NJD |
| 1038 | WPG | NYI |
| 1039 | NSH | WSH |
| 1040 | MIN | CAR |
| 1041 | FLA | CBJ |
| 1042 | CHI | OTT |
| 1043 | TOR | TBL |
| 1044 | BOS | EDM |
| 1045 | DAL | VAN |
| 1046 | DET | ARI |
| 1047 | BUF | LAK |
| 1048 | STL | SJS |

### Fri. Mar. 17, 2017

| Game | Visitor | Home |
|---|---|---|
| 1049 | FLA | NYR |
| 1050 | NJD | PIT |
| 1051 | DAL | CGY |
| 1052 | BUF | ANA |

### Sat. Mar. 18, 2017

| Game | Visitor | Home |
|---|---|---|
| 1053 • | COL | DET |
| 1054 • | CBJ | NYI |
| 1055 | CHI | TOR |
| 1056 | MTL | OTT |
| 1057 | WSH | TBL |
| 1058 | NSH | CAR |
| 1059 | NYR | MIN |
| 1060 | STL | ARI |
| 1061 | VAN | EDM |
| 1062 | ANA | SJS |

• *AFTERNOON GAME*

# 2016-2017 NHL SCHEDULE

### Sun. Mar. 19, 2017

| Game | Visitor | Home |
|---|---|---|
| 1063 ● | CBJ | NJD |
| 1064 ● | FLA | PIT |
| 1065 ● | MIN | WPG |
| 1066 | CAR | PHI |
| 1067 | COL | CHI |
| 1068 | OTT | MTL |
| 1069 | LAK | CGY |

### Mon. Mar. 20, 2017

| Game | Visitor | Home |
|---|---|---|
| 1070 | BOS | TOR |
| 1071 | BUF | DET |
| 1072 | ARI | NSH |
| 1073 | SJS | DAL |
| 1074 | LAK | EDM |

### Tue. Mar. 21, 2017

| Game | Visitor | Home |
|---|---|---|
| 1075 | OTT | BOS |
| 1076 | PIT | BUF |
| 1077 | NYR | NJD |
| 1078 | CGY | WSH |
| 1079 | DET | MTL |
| 1080 | ARI | TBL |
| 1081 | CAR | FLA |
| 1082 | SJS | MIN |
| 1083 | PHI | WPG |
| 1084 | VAN | CHI |
| 1085 | STL | COL |

### Wed. Mar. 22, 2017

| Game | Visitor | Home |
|---|---|---|
| 1086 | TOR | CBJ |
| 1087 | NYI | NYR |
| 1088 | EDM | ANA |

### Thu. Mar. 23, 2017

| Game | Visitor | Home |
|---|---|---|
| 1089 | TBL | BOS |
| 1090 | CBJ | WSH |
| 1091 | NJD | TOR |
| 1092 | CAR | MTL |
| 1093 | PIT | OTT |
| 1094 | ARI | FLA |
| 1095 | VAN | STL |
| 1096 | CGY | NSH |
| 1097 | PHI | MIN |
| 1098 | DAL | CHI |
| 1099 | EDM | COL |
| 1100 | WPG | LAK |

### Fri. Mar. 24, 2017

| Game | Visitor | Home |
|---|---|---|
| 1101 | NYI | PIT |
| 1102 | TBL | DET |
| 1103 | SJS | DAL |
| 1104 | WPG | ANA |

### Sat. Mar. 25, 2017

| Game | Visitor | Home |
|---|---|---|
| 1105 ● | PHI | CBJ |
| 1106 ● | VAN | MIN |
| 1107 | TOR | BUF |
| 1108 | OTT | MTL |
| 1109 | CHI | FLA |
| 1110 | CAR | NJD |
| 1111 | BOS | NYI |
| 1112 | ARI | WSH |
| 1113 | CGY | STL |
| 1114 | SJS | NSH |
| 1115 | COL | EDM |
| 1116 | NYR | LAK |

### Sun. Mar. 26, 2017

| Game | Visitor | Home |
|---|---|---|
| 1117 ● | PHI | PIT |
| 1118 ● | DAL | NJD |
| 1119 | MIN | DET |
| 1120 | VAN | WPG |
| 1121 | NYR | ANA |

### Mon. Mar. 27, 2017

| Game | Visitor | Home |
|---|---|---|
| 1122 | FLA | BUF |
| 1123 | NSH | NYI |
| 1124 | CHI | TBL |
| 1125 | ARI | STL |
| 1126 | COL | CGY |

### Tue. Mar. 28, 2017

| Game | Visitor | Home |
|---|---|---|
| 1127 | NSH | BOS |
| 1128 | OTT | PHI |
| 1129 | DET | CAR |
| 1130 | BUF | CBJ |
| 1131 | FLA | TOR |
| 1132 | DAL | MTL |
| 1133 | WSH | MIN |
| 1134 | LAK | EDM |
| 1135 | ANA | VAN |
| 1136 | NYR | SJS |

### Wed. Mar. 29, 2017

| Game | Visitor | Home |
|---|---|---|
| 1137 | CHI | PIT |
| 1138 | LAK | CGY |
| 1139 | WSH | COL |
| 1140 | STL | ARI |

### Thu. Mar. 30, 2017

| Game | Visitor | Home |
|---|---|---|
| 1141 | DAL | BOS |
| 1142 | NYI | PHI |
| 1143 | CBJ | CAR |
| 1144 | FLA | MTL |
| 1145 | DET | TBL |
| 1146 | TOR | NSH |
| 1147 | OTT | MIN |
| 1148 | ANA | WPG |
| 1149 | SJS | EDM |

### Fri. Mar. 31, 2017

| Game | Visitor | Home |
|---|---|---|
| 1150 | PIT | NYR |
| 1151 | NJD | NYI |
| 1152 | CBJ | CHI |
| 1153 | STL | COL |
| 1154 | SJS | CGY |
| 1155 | LAK | VAN |
| 1156 | WSH | ARI |

### Sat. Apr. 1, 2017

| Game | Visitor | Home |
|---|---|---|
| 1157 ● | FLA | BOS |
| 1158 ● | MIN | NSH |
| 1159 | TOR | DET |
| 1160 | MTL | TBL |
| 1161 | NJD | PHI |
| 1162 | DAL | CAR |
| 1163 | OTT | WPG |
| 1164 | ANA | EDM |

### Sun. Apr. 2, 2017

| Game | Visitor | Home |
|---|---|---|
| 1165 ● | BOS | CHI |
| 1166 ● | NYI | BUF |
| 1167 ● | CAR | PIT |
| 1168 | DAL | TBL |
| 1169 | WSH | CBJ |
| 1170 ● | NSH | STL |
| 1171 ● | COL | MIN |
| 1172 ● | SJS | VAN |
| 1173 | PHI | NYR |
| 1174 | ANA | CGY |
| 1175 | ARI | LAK |

### Mon. Apr. 3, 2017

| Game | Visitor | Home |
|---|---|---|
| 1176 | TOR | BUF |
| 1177 | OTT | DET |
| 1178 | MTL | FLA |

### Tue. Apr. 4, 2017

| Game | Visitor | Home |
|---|---|---|
| 1179 | TBL | BOS |
| 1180 | PHI | NJD |
| 1181 | CBJ | PIT |
| 1182 | WSH | TOR |
| 1183 | DET | OTT |
| 1184 | WPG | STL |
| 1185 | NYI | NSH |
| 1186 | CAR | MIN |
| 1187 | ARI | DAL |
| 1188 | CHI | COL |
| 1189 | CGY | ANA |
| 1190 | EDM | LAK |
| 1191 | VAN | SJS |

### Wed. Apr. 5, 2017

| Game | Visitor | Home |
|---|---|---|
| 1192 | MTL | BUF |
| 1193 | NYR | WSH |

### Thu. Apr. 6, 2017

| Game | Visitor | Home |
|---|---|---|
| 1194 | OTT | BOS |
| 1195 | PIT | NJD |
| 1196 | NYI | CAR |
| 1197 | WPG | CBJ |
| 1198 | TBL | TOR |
| 1199 | STL | FLA |
| 1200 | NSH | DAL |
| 1201 | MIN | COL |
| 1202 | VAN | ARI |
| 1203 | CHI | ANA |
| 1204 | CGY | LAK |
| 1205 | EDM | SJS |

### Fri. Apr. 7, 2017

| Game | Visitor | Home |
|---|---|---|
| 1206 | TBL | MTL |

### Sat. Apr. 8, 2017

| Game | Visitor | Home |
|---|---|---|
| 1207 ● | NYR | OTT |
| 1208 ● | CBJ | PHI |
| 1209 ● | WSH | BOS |
| 1210 | NYI | NJD |
| 1211 | PIT | TOR |
| 1212 | MTL | DET |
| 1213 | BUF | FLA |
| 1214 | STL | CAR |
| 1215 | NSH | WPG |
| 1216 | COL | DAL |
| 1217 | MIN | ARI |
| 1218 | EDM | VAN |
| 1219 | CGY | SJS |
| 1220 ● | CHI | LAK |

### Sun. Apr. 9, 2017

| Game | Visitor | Home |
|---|---|---|
| 1221 ● | NJD | DET |
| 1222 ● | BUF | TBL |
| 1223 ● | OTT | NYI |
| 1224 | CBJ | TOR |
| 1225 ● | COL | STL |
| 1226 | PIT | NYR |
| 1227 | CAR | PHI |
| 1228 | FLA | WSH |
| 1229 ● | LAK | ANA |
| 1230 | VAN | EDM |

● *AFTERNOON GAME*

## *NOTES*